WISDOM
OF
SOULS

About the Authors

©Julie Linz Photography

The authors of this book are members of the Michael Newton Institute's Research Committee. Each is trained and certified in hypnotherapy, past-life regression, and Life Between Lives hypnotherapy and is in active practice. Their previous publication is *Llewellyn's Little Book of Life Between Lives* (2018). For inquiries, please contact: research@newtoninstitute.org.

ANN J. CLARK, Ph.D., RN, Director of Research and member of the board for the Michael Newton Institute, resides in Birmingham, Alabama. She is the owner of Wisdom for Wellness and practices hypnotherapy, past-life and Life Between Lives hypnotherapy. Her research column appears in the Michael Newton Institute's online journal, *Stories of the Afterlife*. She can be contacted at hypnoannclark@gmail.com or visit her website at www .birminghamhypnosis.com.

MARILYN HARGREAVES, BSc, is a multimodal holistic practitioner and owner of Triology Wellness, based in British Columbia, Canada. Her healing approach focuses on the integration of physical, emotional, and spiritual healing by applying her knowledge of the body, mind, and spirit, with the healing properties of herbals, hypnotherapy, and Life Between Lives hypnotherapy. Marilyn is Director of Strategic Planning and member of the board for the Michael Newton Institute. She can be contacted at Marilyn@triology.ca, www.triologywellness.com.

KAREN JOY, BA, DipCM, GDipPsychOrg, a practicing psychologist for decades, is now the principal of Life Between Lives hypnotherapy. She conducts past-life and Life Between Lives sessions at her hypnotherapy studio in Maleny, on the Queensland Sunshine Coast. She has written several books, including *Other Lives, Other Realms: Journeys of Transformation* that is about regressions. Her Facebook, Instagram, and Twitter identity is Karen Joy Author. Sign up for her blog or contact her via her website: LifeBetweenLivesRegression.com.au.

JOANNE SELINSKE, Ph.D., is proprietress of Soul Source, a spiritual center serving Maryland and metropolitan District of Columbia. She is a spiritual counselor. Her hypnotherapy practice focuses on past-life and Life Between Lives hypnotherapy, transpersonal journeys and spirit releasement. She can be contacted at JoanneSelinske@theSoulSource.net.

WISDOM
OF
SOULS

CASE STUDIES OF LIFE BETWEEN LIVES
FROM THE MICHAEL NEWTON INSTITUTE

ANN J. CLARK, PH. D. • KAREN JOY
JOANNE SELINSKE, PH. D. • MARILYN HARGREAVES

LLEWELLYN PUBLICATIONS
WOODBURY, MINNESOTA

FIRST EDITION
Fourth Printing, 2023

Book design by Samantha Penn
Cover design by Shannon McKuhen/Llewellyn Art Department
Editing by Annie Burdick

Llewellyn Publications is a registered trademark of Llewellyn Worldwide Ltd.

Life Between Lives® Hypnotherapy is a registered trademark of the Michael Newton Institute.

Library of Congress Cataloging-in-Publication Data
Names: Clark, Ann J. author. | Michael Newton Institute.
Title: Wisdom of souls : case studies of life between lives from the
    Michael Newtown Institute / Ann J. Clark, Ph. D., Karen Joy, Joanne
    Selinske, Ph. D., Marilyn Hargreaves.
Description: First edition. | Woodbury, Minnesota : Llewellyn Worldwide.
    Ltd, 2019. | Includes bibliographical references and index.
Identifiers: LCCN 2019036192 (print) | LCCN 2019036193 (ebook) | ISBN
    9780738758343 (paperback) | ISBN 9780738759708 (ebook)
Subjects: LCSH: Reincarnation—Case studies. | Spiritualism.
Classification: LCC BF1311.R35 C53 2019 (print) | LCC BF1311.R35 (ebook)
    | DDC 133.901/35—dc23
LC record available at https://lccn.loc.gov/2019036192
LC ebook record available at https://lccn.loc.gov/2019036193

Llewellyn Publications
A Division of Llewellyn Worldwide Ltd.
2143 Wooddale Drive
Woodbury, MN 55125-2989
www.llewellyn.com

Printed in the United States of America

Other Books by the Newton Institute

Destiny of Souls

Journey of Souls

Llewellyn's Little Book of Life Between Lives

Memories of the Afterlife

Stories of the Afterlife

Dedication

It is with great pleasure that we present this book as a tribute to Dr. Michael Newton (1931–2016), developer of Life Between Lives hypnotherapy and founder of the Michael Newton Institute. His work, aided by his lovely wife Peggy, has inspired, healed, and changed the lives of countless numbers of individuals across the globe. His legacy is carried on by the over two hundred members of the Michael Newton Institute, providing Life Between Lives hypnotherapy sessions in forty different countries, in fourteen different languages, all around the world.

CONTENTS

Meet the Contributors ... XIII

Acknowledgments ... XVII

Foreword: A Tribute to Dr. Michael Newton ... XIX

Introduction ... 1

Life Between Lives Hypnotherapy ... 3

The Newton Institute ... 6

What Is Included in This Book ... 7

One: Facing a Health Crisis ... 9

A Message from Your Body ... 10

Cancer, the Dreaded Diagnosis ... 12

Cancer Brings Emotional Healing ... 15

Life after Brain Trauma ... 19

Health Crisis as a Turning Point ... 22

Embracing Vulnerability ... 23

Understanding the Root Cause ... 27

Two: Anxiety and Depression ... 33

Emotional Challenges of the Soul's Plan ... 34

Releasing Depression and Guilt ... 39

Serving Humanity ... 44

Unresolved Past Lives ... 45

Debilitating Anxiety ... 47

Holding Guilt from the Past ... 49

Finding Peace in a Chaotic World ... 51

Three: Healing from Loss ... 53

Lack of Closure ... 55

Healing in the Aftermath of Suicide ... 61

Loving After Loss ... 64

Losing the Love of Your Life ... 68

Four: Navigating Romantic Relationships ... 73

What Is Love? ... 74

The Difference Between Love and Infatuation... 74

Balancing Attachment ... 77

Fulfilling Soul Contracts ... 80

A Pattern of Conflict ... 84

Five: From Self-Sabotage to Strength ... 91

Diminished Self-Worth ... 92

Taking Love for Granted ... 96

Overcoming Rejection ... 99

Overcoming Feelings of Rejection and Jealousy... 104

Protecting a Broken Heart ... 107

Six: Growing Through Family Conflict ... 111

Dealing with Disharmony ... 112

Dysfunctional Families ... 117

Challenging Parents ... 119

Enmeshed Families ... 124

Suicidal Relatives ... 127

Seven: Nurturing Relationships ... 131

Balancing Needs ... 132

Tough Love ... 138

Healing the Unloved ... 139

Forgiveness Heals ... 141

Severed Bonds ... 146

Importance of Self-Love ... 147

A Gift of Unconditional Love ... 149

Eight: Balancing Career and Finances ... 155

Career versus Family ... 156

Choosing Money over Passion ... 159

Money Woes ... 163

Not Living Up to Your Potential ... 164

Always Second ... 167

Gifts from the Past ... 171

Loss of Identity ... 175

Nine: Breaking Free ... 179

Releasing Habits ... 179

Patterns of Belief ... 181

Addictive Echoes from the Past ... 183

Habits That Limit Growth ... 185

Addiction in Families ... 188

Ten: Transformed by a Brush with Death ... 193

Rape at Gunpoint ... 195

Global Tragedy, Personal Awakenings ... 198

Surviving Life-Threatening Events ... 201

Traveling Through the Tunnel of Light ... 204

An Out-of-Body Experience ... .208

A Troubling Accident ... 211

Cosmic Healing ... 213

Revisiting a Mystical Experience from a Coma ... 215

Eleven: Aging and Dying ... 221

Losing Independence ... 222

When Alzheimer's Is Healing ... 226

Dying with Ease and Grace ... 230

Welcome Home ... 234

Conclusion ... 237

Case Contributions from Newton Institute Members ... 239

Bibliography ... 241

Resources ... 243

Index ... 245

MEET THE CONTRIBUTORS

The following Newton Institute Life Between Lives practitioners have, with the permission of their clients, contributed the case studies contained in this book:

Paul Aurand, MHt: New York City, New York; West Palm Beach, Florida, USA
  Email: paul@paulaurand.com
  Website: www.paulaurand.com

Gayle Barklie, CCHT, MFC: Maui, Hawaii, USA
  Email: soulpurposemaui@gmail.com
  Website: www.soulpurposemaui.com

Bryn Blankinship, CMHt, CI: Wilmington, North Carolina, USA
  Email: Bryn@BrynBlankinship.com
  Website: www.BrynBlankinship.com

Rita Borenstein, CHt, DO: Uppsala, Sweden
  Email: lbl@ritaborenstein.se
  Website: www.spiritualregression.se

Eric Christopher, MSMFT, CHt: St. Paul, Minnesota, USA
  Email: eric@ericjchristopher.com
  Website: www.ericjchristopher.com

Ann J. Clark, Ph.D., RN: Birmingham, Alabama, USA
  Email: hypnoannclark@gmail.com
  Website: www.birminghamhypnosis.com

Scott De Tamble, CHt, CMT: Claremont, California, USA
  Email: scott@lightbetweenlives.com
  Website: www.lightbetweenlives.com

Morgan Dhanowa, BSN, RCCH: Victoria, British Columbia, Canada
  Email: morgandhanowa@gmail.com
  Website: www.innervisionhypnotherapy.ca

Patricia Fares O'Malley, Ph.D., NCC, CHt: Wilmington, Illinois, USA
  Email: patiok@sbcglobal.net
  Website: www.pat-omalley.com

Dorothea Fuckert, MD: Waldbrunn, Baden-Wuerttemberg, Germany
  Email: doro.f@gmx.de
  Website: www.fuckert.de

Laura Halls, BA, CHt: Marietta, Georgia, USA
  Email: laurahalls@yahoo.com
  Website: www.hypno-journeys.com

Marilyn Hargreaves, BS: Nanaimo, British Columbia, Canada
  Email: marilyn@triologywellness.ca
  Website: www.triologywellness.com

Billy Hunter, BS, CHt: Fairfield, Iowa, USA
    Email: Billy.B.Hunter@gmail.com
    Website: www.HolisticHealingFairfield.com

Elisabeth Iwona Roepcke, MA, CHt: Bremen, Germany & Poland
    Email: iwonalbl@aol.de
    Website: www.zyciemiedzyzyciami.pl, www.trance-forming.de

Karen Joy, BA, DIP Psych: Maleny, Queensland, Australia
    Email: Karen@lifebetweenlivesregression.com.au
    Website: www.lifebetweenlivesregression.com.au

Hila Kedem-Ferguson, CHt, RMT: Chandler, Arizona, USA
    Email: Hila@door2change.com
    Website: www.Door2Change.com

Sophia Kramer, MHt, RN: Germany & New York City, New York; West
Palm Beach, Florida, USA
    Email: Sophia@SophiaKramer.com
    Website: www.SophiaKramer.com

Lisbeth Lysdal, MSc: Roskilde, Denmark
    Email: lisbeth@lisbethlysdal.dk
    Website: https://lisbethlysdal.dk

Sylvia McLeod, CHt: Cedar Crest, New Mexico, USA
    Email: sylviaclaire10@gmail.com
    Website: www.sylviaclaire.com

Angela Noon, MCHt: East Grinstead, United Kingdom
    Email: hypnonoon@gmail.com
    Website: www.angelanoon.co.uk

Tianna Roser, CHt: Austin, Texas, USA
    Email: tianna@awakeningtransformation.com
    Website: www.awakeningtransformation.com

Joanne Selinske, Ph.D.: Baltimore, Maryland & Metropolitan DC, USA
   Email: JoanneSelinske@theSoulSource.net
   Website: www.theSoulSource.net

Courtney Starkey, MEd, MHt: Herndon, Virginia & Kailua, Hawaii, USA
   Email: courtney@payitforwardhypnosis.com
   Website: www.payitforwardhypnosis.com

Virginia Waldron, CH, CI: Cazenovia, New York, USA
   Email: gatkepr@gmail.com
   Website: www.TheRoseHeartCenter.com

Savarna Wiley, MA, CCHt: Santa Cruz, California, USA
   Email: Savarna.Wiley@icloud.com
   Website: www.HealingJourneysHypnotherapy.com

ACKNOWLEDGMENTS

Writing a book such as this is truly a team effort. Twenty-six Michael Newton Institute members and sixty-two of their clients made contributions, aided by the expert staff of our publisher, Llewellyn Worldwide. We want to give a special thank you to Angela Wix, who shepherded us through the process, and to Annie Burdick, who added the polish to our work. We are especially grateful to our clients who have generously volunteered to share their stories in these pages, so that the wisdom from their Life Between Lives sessions concerning common life problems is made available to us all.

A TRIBUTE TO DR. MICHAEL NEWTON

You will have already seen the Dedication and the beautiful words that echo the thoughts of all of us at the Newton Institute regarding Michael and his legacy for humanity.

It seems fitting that I would write these words on what would have been Michael's eighty-seventh birthday. History records his passing in 2016, though we still feel him around, encouraging and supporting his life's work as we continue what he started.

When Dr. Ann Clark first put forward the idea for *Wisdom of Souls*, it is like a path cleared for the idea to become a full-blown project in a time frame so rarely seen. The pace at which all of this happened showed us that there was an energy behind this book, greater than us.

What this book encapsulates is spiritual wisdom for the challenges we find in human form. This had always been Michael's dream, that we could look at the problems of the world through the higher ideals that the spiritual realm offers us, to bring changed mindsets and spiritual knowing to life on earth. This book echoes what he wanted, and we believe it is a fitting tribute.

In Michael's own words, articulated so beautifully to the members of our Institute in 2011:

> *For spiritual unity to take place we cannot depend on the methods of current religious practices on the one hand, or science on the other to bring answers to the great mystery of life. Our organization is pledged to offer a new way with enlightenment springing from the mind of each, regardless of their prior institutional belief system or lack of it. In the complex world of the twenty-first century, people need the conviction more than ever that a divine universal consciousness exists within a pure spiritual order.*
>
> *They must discover this principle within their own minds for real conviction to take place. Eventually, if enough people come to this realization through our efforts, there will hopefully be a lessening of external conflict in our struggle for survival.*
>
> *The ethical compass of humanity would have a stronger meaning since it would come from personal enlightenment.*

We always saw Michael as a visionary, though we saw him also as humble and humorous. He had a wonderful smile and a booming laugh. He could have a class in hysterics with a funny story and move them to tears moments later. He was all this and more, though there is one powerful role he played more than anything else. He was an ambassador for the spiritual realm of the greatest possible magnitude, and he opened the door for us to commune with our own souls, to access our own immortal wisdom in human form, forged from our deepest and most profound authenticity.

Those of us who knew him will tell you the small things about him. We will tell you that he loved to walk in the mountains so he could be in nature. We will tell you that he had huge crystals the size of a man's head in the garden of his house in California. We will tell you that integrity was everything for him and that he was an old-fashioned "man of his word." We will tell you that he had a favourite pen that he signed books with. We will tell you that with all the correspondence he had received from readers over the years, he answered much of it personally and he kept a small folder at home with some of the letters that had moved him most, so on occasion he could read them and remember the importance of his work.

We will also tell you that after so many decades of marriage to his wonderful wife Peggy, when he spoke of her as his partner in life, his wise counselor and his rock, that his eyes would light up and his voice would fill with love.

Michael Newton is one of the most important spiritual researchers the world has ever known. He has touched the hearts and minds of millions of people who never had the chance to meet him. This book contains the echoes of what he started, and his contribution lives on in us.

We are his ripple effect, and we hope you enjoy *Wisdom of Souls*.

Peter Smith
Director, Michael Newton Legacy
Michael Newton Institute
December 9, 2018

INTRODUCTION

How do we learn and grow from difficulties in our lives instead of just suffering through them? Life can be hard, presenting us with a host of problems and unpleasant occurrences. However, if we remember that we are souls who have come to earth for specific reasons, we can see these challenges in a different light.

As souls, our true home is in the spirit world, a space of universal harmony, love, compassion, forgiveness, and peace. We can experience these things on earth as well, but in contrast, on earth there is also disharmony, conflict, strong emotions, injustice, and pain. Earth is a place where we have free will and the ability to create our own circumstances.

We incarnate on earth in a human body to learn and evolve spiritually, but a portion of our soul energy always remains in the spirit world. Through the self-improvement process of reincarnation, we can return to earth repeatedly to learn additional lessons on a journey to eventual enlightenment as souls.

Reincarnation means the soul returns to earth in a new body after death. It's as if we are playing a different role in a new play. After our death in this new life, we return home to the spirit world to reflect on the life just lived, integrate the learning achieved, and in time, plan our next life on earth.

We can think of coming to live on earth as going away to school. Each of our lives are planned by us with supportive guidance from wise and kind beings who love us and want to help us. We do this while we are still at home in the spiritual realm, just as we would plan a class schedule. But the memory of what we wanted to learn, how we planned to do it, and why we planned to do so fades quickly once we have incarnated. We then come to identify strongly with our human body and believe our current life situation is all there is.

When we incarnate on earth, we bring with us all the experiences of our past lives and our spiritual experiences between lives. Any unresolved fear, sense of guilt, or physical affliction from a past life can be carried into a future life. Our souls retain all former karmic influences, and these forces impact our feelings and behaviors in our new lives. Karma is not meant to be punitive, but rather to balance the sum of our deeds in past lives to help us evolve spiritually. We can even carry past physical injuries into a new life as an unexplained pain, scar, or physical deformity.

As we live our lives on earth as incarnated souls, the experiences we planned for learning purposes unfold. The experiences may not occur exactly as planned. On earth, we have free will. We may not stick to the plan, and other incarnated souls whom we have recruited to play supporting roles in our lives might not either. Our memory of arranging events to help us evolve fades and we now see these occurrences as challenges, difficulties, or road blocks. The issues these experiences create can seem unfair and very troublesome.

We don't come to earth alone. Each of us has kind, loving guidance from our spirit guides, angels, departed loved ones, and wise elders in the spirit world. We are also able to connect with our higher self, the portion of our soul energy that is always connected to our immortal self. Yet we may be unaware of all this potential assistance because we have amnesia. We agreed to forget so that we could fully engage in life on earth.

Life Between Lives Hypnotherapy

So, how do we access this hidden wisdom? While there are multiple methods to accomplish this, Life Between Lives hypnotherapy provides particularly insightful personal guidance for the individuals who experience it. This is because, during a Life Between Lives session, you are guided into a deep hypnotic trance, in which you experience yourself as an immortal soul, visiting the spirit world. You learn about your plan for your current incarnated life on earth, meet your spirit guide and teachers, reunite with your soul family and, possibly, with your departed loved ones.

Although you are in an altered state, you are fully aware. You can ask questions, as you have access to the wisdom of the spiritual realm. You might ask:

- What is behind the emotional or physical suffering I'm experiencing?
- How can I break the patterns in my life that don't serve me?
- What are these difficult relationships trying to teach me?
- What happens after we die?

Answers will come to you during the session and, upon later reflection, you may become aware of even more helpful information. A Life Between Lives session generally lasts four to six hours and is a profound, life-changing experience.

Insights gained through a Life Between Lives session have a far-reaching effect on your life, allowing you to gain new perspectives on issues that may have been plaguing you for multiple lifetimes. This fresh perspective allows you to become "unstuck" and experience substantial spiritual growth.

Before scheduling a Life Between Lives session, you must experience a past-life regression. A past-life regression uses hypnotherapy to take you back in time to previous incarnations by accessing memories and experiences that are usually not available to you. By reexperiencing past incarnations, you can determine ways that your past is influencing your current life. Previous lives can leave imprints of emotional or physical wounds that can be healed during a regression. Experiencing past lives can also remind you of useful skills, special talents, knowledge, and character strengths that you possess. And a past-life regression can reveal information about soul contracts you have made with other souls, which can assist you in better understanding relationships in your current life.

The Life Between Lives process begins with preparation by you and the practitioner. The practitioner will get to know you and evaluate your readiness for the experience. You will also be asked to make a list of questions to which you would like to receive answers.

The Life Between Lives session will begin with a long, slow hypnotic induction that guides you to the brain wave pattern necessary to access the superconscious mind where soul memories are stored. Your physical body becomes so relaxed that it is almost suspended in time. Initially you will recall some pleasant childhood memories, as you experience yourself becoming younger and younger until you reach the womb of your mother. There you will have an opportunity to review your thoughts about the life to come and assess your mother's feelings about your birth. At this point you are beginning to awaken to your soul identity.

As you travel back in time, you will visit a past life that is relevant to what you are seeking from the Life Between Lives experience. After discovering who you were, characteristics of your personality, and the circumstances and significant events of that life, you will be guided to the last day of that life. Then you will move through your death in that past life to allow you as a soul to transition naturally back to the spirit world. You will have an awareness of being dead and will likely see your body from above before leaving the earth realm.

As the practitioner guides you to move on, you will experience a sense of timelessness and a sense of gently being pulled or moving upward or into a tunnel. You may see a white light, or experience vivid colors, sounds, or visions. You will probably encounter and be able to communicate telepathically with beings of light. Often you are met by your primary spirit guide. These experiences are accompanied by feelings of unconditional love, peace, and joy.

It's typical after passing through the gateway into the spiritual realm that you will spend time with your guide, receiving an orientation to the spiritual realm and discussing the life that you just lived. You will meet with your soul group and learn who in your current life is part of this group. This will be a joyous homecoming.

Your soul invests a variable amount of energy into each incarnation, and some of your soul energy remains in the spirit world. This means you can connect with members of your group even if they are incarnated.

Your guide may answer some of your questions and address some of the issues on your mind. You can also obtain further information by visiting the "library," where you can review your life book. The life book is a record of all your soul's incarnations. You can review experiences and challenges in past lives and perhaps even see small glimpses of the future. Further information about your current life and how you are progressing will be available during a visit to the council of wise elders. While you are with the council, you may also receive answers to some of the questions you prepared.

If you have not already received the answers you were seeking, you may visit the place of life selection. Here you can learn about your purpose and plans you made for your current lifetime. You can review your choices about where you will incarnate, the body you select, who you will be, and what other souls you will incarnate with—parents, siblings, mates, and others who are significant in your life.

Other experiences you may have during a Life Between Lives session include visiting learning centers and classrooms, as well as areas of rest and healing in the spirit world. You might also learn about activities and specializations you are engaged in during your life in the spirit world. Perhaps you will join in recreation or even travel with your soul group. You may be able to reunite with lost loved ones. Possibly you will reunite with a soul who has hurt you, presenting you with an opportunity for healing. Often you are given assistance with forming a closer connection with your higher self and communicating with your guides.

Reports reveal that individuals who experience a Life Between Lives session receive many benefits and often encounter profound healing. Some things you may experience include the following:

- elimination of your fear of death
- a new perspective on your life's challenges
- new insights into your current relationships
- a changed view of the nature of reality

- transformation of your beliefs and values
- healing of your interpersonal wounds

These results are often life-changing. When we strive to understand and cope more successfully with difficult situations in our lives, we not only accelerate our spiritual growth, but can make our life on earth easier and more joyful.

The Newton Institute

The method used in the Life Between Lives sessions in this book was developed by Dr. Michael Newton through his thousands of regressions during twenty-five years in practice. During this time, Dr. Newton mapped out the spiritual realm and developed a method to allow clients to access it. In 2000, Dr. Newton began training other therapists to conduct these sessions and formed a small society to support the work. As the work expanded, this early organization became the Newton Institute in 2005. The organization now includes over 200 members worldwide. As of 2018, it is estimated that over 50,000 Life Between Lives sessions have been conducted by members in forty different countries, in fourteen different languages.

If you are unfamiliar with life between lives, you may wish to read *Llewellyn's Little Book of Life Between Lives* (2018), by the authors of this book. This is a concise, updated description of the process, with new case studies. You may also wish to refer to an earlier Newton Institute book, edited by Dr. Newton, with case studies from Newton Institute members, *Memories of the Afterlife* (2010). Dr. Newton's other three books were *Journey of Souls* (1994), *Destiny of Souls* (2001), and *Life Between Lives Hypnotherapy* (2004). You may also be interested in subscribing to the Newton Institute's online journal, *Stories of the Afterlife*, to explore new cases and learn more about research into the afterlife.

Life Between Lives is a term originated by Dr. Newton and copyrighted by the Newton Institute. A Newton Institute member is a well-trained, certified Life Between Lives practitioner who follows a strict code of ethics. You can locate a Life Between Lives practitioner by checking the listing at http://www.newtoninstitute.org.

What Is Included in This Book

Although the advice given during a Life Between Lives session is personal, it commonly involves situations that we all experience in our lives. Thus, the insights and wisdom received during a session can often help many of us through life challenges. This book presents a compilation of wise advice received by clients of Newton Institute practitioners, all of whom lovingly agreed to share their experiences to assist others facing similar life challenges. You might find that some of the cases and experiences of others resonate with you and allow you to view your own situation differently.

In chapter one, you will meet individuals who have serious health problems. Caring for and maintaining the health of a human body is an experience that is unique to an earth incarnation. Health problems provide multiple opportunities for growth. The cases included do not provide medical advice, but rather guidance to help us advance spiritually. Another unique aspect of life on earth is coping with conflict, fear, and strong emotions. Souls acclimated to the unconditional love, forgiveness, and harmony of the spirit world may find adjusting to earth life difficult. In chapter two, cases of depression and anxiety are covered.

Healing from loss is presented in chapter three. Surviving the loss of a loved one is one of life's hardest ordeals. For those who view death as the end, despair and hopelessness can set in. Here you will find wise advice for mourning.

On earth, the relationships we have with others offer many opportunities for evolving spiritually. We can give and receive love. Romantic relationships can bring happiness, but also can be very vexing. Chapters four and five present cases involving difficulties with romantic relationships.

Cases involving family conflict are covered in chapter six. Such conflicts can be very painful and affect us for long periods of time. Wisdom on nurturing relationships is included in the cases in chapter seven. Through relationships, we learn to help others and to forgive. Relationships bring us joy and fulfillment and can also offer us some of our most valuable lessons.

When, as souls, we incarnate on earth, we are faced with the responsibility of finding a way to support ourselves and our families. Facing work difficulties or a lack of money can produce powerful learning. Advice given on work, money, and balancing career and financial responsibilities with family responsibilities is included the cases in chapter eight.

In chapter nine, cases involving harmful habits and addictions are presented. Addictive behaviors have become a major issue in our time. While the results of this behavior can be quite destructive, we learn that wisdom and spiritual assistance is available to help us move beyond the addiction and evolve spiritually.

Experiencing a situation in which you come very close to death can trigger powerful transformation and healing. In chapter ten, cases of violent encounters and some examples of near-death experiences are explored. Situations in which individuals are coping with aging and impending death are covered in chapter eleven. Youth is highly valued in many parts of the world, and large numbers of us are not adequately prepared for the challenges that growing older will bring. This time in our lives offers us an opportunity to reflect and integrate the experiences of our life, consolidating our learning. The cases presented are not meant to comprehensively cover the issues addressed, but rather to provide examples of healing spiritual guidance.

Every life adds to our collective store of soul wisdom. Between incarnations, our guides and the wise beings that we encounter help us make sense of life's greatest challenges. They show us how to navigate our relationships with friends, family, and lovers, how to overcome illness, financial problems, and addictions. Most importantly, they draw aside the veil and reveal the most powerful secret of all: that death is not the end, but simply another step in the great dance of the soul. Thanks to the generosity of our clients and the talent of our practitioners, we share this emerging wisdom with you. On every page, you will find the courage and the insights you need to guide you on your soul's journey.

One

FACING A
HEALTH CRISIS

Learning that you have a serious illness or that an injury has caused permanent damage can strike fear in your heart. Suddenly trivial matters don't seem so important, and fears about what this crisis may mean to you and your loved ones emerge. The problem can be non-life threatening, or it can be catastrophic. In either case, it signals a change and provides an optimal time for taking stock of your life. Health problems serve as a wake-up call, causing us to slow down, giving us the opportunity to examine our lives.

The health crisis may only slow you down temporarily, but things may never be the same again. If it results in a permanent condition or disability, you may be required to reinvent the way you live your life. Or, it may foretell your likely or imminent death.

Most serious health problems are planned by us while we are still at home in the spirit world, to help us learn specific lessons. We can choose to have major life events, such as a serious illness or injury, occur at certain points in life to provide specific experiences. Minor illnesses or injuries do not fit this situation.

Cases included in this chapter are from individuals who sought a Life Between Lives session to learn more about their health problems and what spiritual meaning these occurrences might have. The wise advice they received is applicable to many health issues.

A Message from Your Body

Valerie, a sixty-seven-year-old divorced woman, was close to retiring from her successful career two years ago, when she had a serious accident. While carrying several packages in from her car, she fell coming up her back steps and shattered one of her shoulders. This moved her retirement timetable up a bit, but that was manageable. What was harder for her to accept was that the first surgery was not successful. She had to undergo a second surgery for a full shoulder replacement.

A protracted period of healing followed, which was a major disruption to the way she thought she might be spending her early retirement days. It was even more difficult because she had been so independent and self-sufficient. She found that while her shoulder healed, not being able to do many things for herself was very frustrating. She was able to return to her usual activities in due time, as her shoulder healed well. However, that was not the end of the story.

During her recovery, another problem, the gastric reflux she had occasionally been experiencing, became worse. She had difficulty eating and lost weight. Eventually she was able to manage this condition with medication and diet, but the problem was not totally resolved. On top of this, she had been putting cataract surgery off until after her retirement, and her rapidly failing vision was making reading, one of her pleasures, difficult and tiring.

She went ahead with the cataract surgery. The surgery went well, but she developed an unusual complication afterward that temporarily affected her vision. She was unable to drive or engage in her usual routine for several weeks until her vision cleared. She found this very exasperating and was beginning to question why she kept having so many health problems.

But it was not until she fell again, this time fracturing her hip, that she really became depressed and worried. She had by now experienced nearly two years of one health problem after another, and this was taking a toll on her. Her latest injury was painful and very debilitating. She harbored a fear that she might never be able to walk normally again. She wondered what her body was trying to tell her and why she kept repeatedly finding herself unable to engage in her usual activities without assistance. Her feisty sense of self-reliance was waning.

She scheduled a Life Between Lives session hoping to gain some insight regarding her health issues. During the session, Valerie discovers her soul's reason for her many health challenges. Once in contact with her soul as her higher self, she shares the following insights.

> *My health problems have slowed me down so that I can look at areas in my life that need changing. I know that I am judgmental and am not always compassionate toward others. I'm proud of being independent and self-sufficient and expect others to be as well. But these health issues have given me a chance to see things from a different perspective. I know now how hard it is not being able to do things for yourself. How depressing that is!*

The vulnerability brought about by the repeated health and functional difficulties that Valerie had experienced over the past two years allowed her to accept compassion and nonjudgmental support from others. She acknowledges how vital the empathy and kindness are to her well-being. She realizes that she doesn't always have to be so self-sufficient, that she can accept help from others. This, in turn, helps her to feel closer and more empathetic toward others and ready to help them in the future when she can. She says:

> *I needed help and my family and friends were so caring and supportive. It made such a difference. This has given me a new perspective.*

Valerie relates, at the end of her session, how grateful she is for all the help she has received. She also reports that she feels her health problems will get better now, as she knows how her attitude toward others has changed. And she is so right. She completed rehabilitation for her hip and can walk well now. A follow-up finds her getting ready to leave on a trip to visit her grandchildren.

Things are going well. But then Valerie slips and falls while at a resort with friends and breaks her elbow. She has surgery to repair it and starts rehabilitation again. However, it is a very different experience this time. She asks for the help she needs, and with assistance for a short period of time, can continue to socialize regularly. Her attitude is very positive, and she returns to her usual activities very quickly. Sometimes there is a little post-test to allow us to put what we have learned into practice.

Cancer, the Dreaded Diagnosis

Molly, a sixty-four-year-old widow, has a large family living nearby. She's a wonderful cook and hostess, frequently entertaining her many relatives. She's very nurturing and involved with her family, babysitting often and caring for her aging mother. She's very active, always doing something for her family.

She is in shock when she is diagnosed with ovarian cancer after seeking medical assistance for some vague symptoms. She decides to have the surgery to remove the cancer but is unsure about whether to follow a course of chemotherapy treatment afterward. While preparing for her Life Between Lives session, one other complaint she voices is having difficulty in getting along with her mother. She describes how her mother calls her frequently, wanting attention, when she is in the middle of an important activity. This is very exasperating to her, and she resents it at times.

When she is guided to a past life, she finds herself as a middle-aged woman with a husband and several children. She lives in a warm climate in a semi-rural area in about 1934. Her name is Rose, and she is a small woman with light brown skin and dark hair.

> *I feel frustrated trying to take care of everybody and do everything for my family. I just can't keep up. Somebody is always needing something and there is too much work to do. I just don't have time to play with the little girls or even talk much to the older children. I feel stressed and irritable. I never have any time for myself.*

The practitioner asks if anyone helps her.

> *No, it's MY responsibility to take care of things!! But I don't keep up! I don't take care of my family the way I want to. Mary and Helen [her young daughters] are with me now, playing on the floor, but I'm too busy to pay any attention to them and I don't feel well.*

The practitioner asks if Molly recognizes them as anyone from her current life.

> *Oh my gosh, it's my mother and my aunt!*

Then Rose appeared to slump.

> *I'm so tired and I don't feel very well, but I must keep going. I'm getting sick, but I can't let anyone know. My girls are still so little. They need me. My family needs me.*

The next scene finds Rose on her deathbed, unable to keep up any longer. The girls are still quite young, and she feels badly about leaving them. She regrets that she never seems to have any time to spend with them. She also wonders if this would be happening if she had taken better care of herself. Molly then breaks through excitedly.

> *Rose is my grandmother! I was my grandmother!!*

Molly had never met her grandmother, as she died before Molly was born. However, she knew that her grandmother died of ovarian cancer. Molly also knew that her mother and grandmother did not get along very well. Molly's mother had told her that her grandmother was always busy with the family or too tired or sick to ever pay any attention to her.

Later in the session, the subject of chemotherapy is raised.

> *The guides are telling me that chemotherapy will not make any difference. What would make a difference is a change in attitude. This life is a chance for me to do things differently*

from when I was my grandmother. I am keeping up well now, but just like my grandmother, all my energy goes toward taking care of my family. I am not putting any energy into taking care of myself. I don't usually tell them when I am tired or not feeling well, I just try to be there for them. I don't even think about what I need. But what I do need is to think about myself more and take care of myself instead of being so involved in caretaking. I need to share more about how I'm feeling and what I need. It's all about balance.

While specific medical advice is not given, as Molly has hoped, she is alerted to the imbalance in her life and her lack of attention to self-care. Molly's overinvolvement in caretaking not only inhibits her self-care, but also her ability to develop closer relationships with her family. Rather than engaging in the give-and-take of a healthy relationship, Molly is doing most of the giving. As a result, she often feels too depleted to truly enjoy being with her family. As in Valerie's case previously discussed, health problems can serve as a "wake-up call," encouraging us to examine our lives to achieve better balance and personal growth.

Later in the session, Molly's relationship with her mother is addressed by the guides.

My mother and I have switched roles from our past life when she was my daughter. She is now my mother in my current life. We did not have a good relationship when I was her mother. Now, in my current life, I have another chance to develop a closer relationship with her. She is still seeking the attention she didn't get as a child. This time I have a chance to build a more balanced relationship with her. I can give her more of the attention she craves, but I shouldn't be doing all the giving. I need to let her know how I feel and what I need sometimes.

Molly is struck by how she is repeating the pattern of neglecting her own self-care and keeping very occupied with family care in her current lifetime. While she truly enjoys taking care of her family, she can clearly see that her life is unbalanced. It is not lost on her that she has developed the same disease she had in her previous life as her grandmother. She admits how tired and frustrated she is sometimes because of all the things she is doing for her family. Molly leaves the session determined to put an emphasis on her own self-care and lessen the amount of caretaking she is doing. She also vows to work on creating a better relationship with her mother.

A later follow-up finds Molly doing very well, despite having decided not to take chemotherapy. She has been doing some traveling with friends and taking more time for herself. She is doing less caretaking and creating more balance in her life. She also reports spending more time with her mother and an improvement in that relationship.

Just as we were finishing this book, Molly contacted the practitioner to report that her mother died during a short hospital stay. She wanted to disclose that while her mother was generally oriented and recognized all the other family members, when asked who Molly was, she repeatedly said, "That's my mother."

Cancer Brings Emotional Healing

Bill, a sixty-seven-year-old naturopathic doctor, plans to work for as long as he is physically able, as he loves his work. He has a happy marriage and a good relationship with his three adult children. About six months before he comes in for his session, he begins having digestive symptoms, which initially he treats with natural remedies. However, he experiences no relief, and so goes to see a gastroenterologist for a diagnosis.

After a series of tests, he is diagnosed with liver cancer. His inclination is to continue to use natural methods to treat the cancer, but his family talks him into accepting medical treatment. He is having a difficult time with the treatment and is experiencing no improvement. His symptoms are becoming worse and there is now significant metastasis. He comes in for a session to gain clarity about his situation. While it seems that his condition is getting worse, he feels that he is having this illness so that he will be better equipped to help others in the future. He has even been thinking about writing a book about his experiences.

Early in his session, Bill's guides tell him that he is always caring for others, but now he is being cared for. He is also informed that he has done well with his current life and has now completed all he had planned. Bill protests that there are several things from the past in this life that he feels are incomplete and that he still has things he wants to do, such as share what he has learned about coping with a serious illness. He asks to examine a feeling of deep loneliness that he has experienced during different points in his life. The guides take him back to his earliest memory of this feeling in his current life.

> *I am about four or five and I am playing in our front yard with my friend Gail. She gets mad at me and yanks a hunk of hair off my head. It really hurts. Now she won't play with me. I'm crying because I feel so lonely. My parents don't pay much attention to me.*

Next Bill finds himself at nineteen, just three weeks after he marries his first wife.

> *She's a nurse in the military and she is being deployed. I feel so lonely now that she's gone. She won't be home for two years. She doesn't write to me much, but I understand that maybe she just doesn't have the chance.*
>
> *When she comes home, it's like she is a different person and things are terrible. I guess today you would call it post-traumatic stress syndrome. It's like I don't even know her. There is no caring. We just can't communicate and then she just leaves without a word. I am miserable and can't imagine ever being happy again.*

Bill claims that the years after his wife leaves are hard. He feels alone and abandoned. But just two years later, he meets and marries his current wife and has been happily married to her for the last forty-four years.

However, when he is in his mid-fifties, he experiences another lonely period. His wife's very successful sales career is requiring her to travel extensively for about a year. It is like a flashback to earlier times.

> *My wife is traveling all the time and I am left here alone at home by myself. I'm lonely and I feel abandoned. Even though*

my wife calls frequently and comes home as often as she can,
I am back to feeling like I did during my first marriage. I'm
afraid she'll be different when she comes home to stay. I guess
that's how I felt when I was five too. It's a feeling of being all
alone and not safe, even though I know better. It's like nobody
will be there for me when I need them.

The practitioner suggests that Bill ask for assistance with these feelings of abandonment. The guides take him to a place of healing where he experiences the following vision.

I'm a blob and I'm in this big bubble and there are lots of other
bubbles around. I'm feeling very happy and bouncing around.
We're all safe in the bubbles because nothing can get in. This
is a different dimension and bubbles are for protection. Others
can't hurt me because they can't penetrate the bubble. I feel joy-
ful and I am completely safe. Now I see a bright light. It's more
white than yellow, but it seems like the sun spread all over the
horizon. It's very warm and protective and comforting.

Bill takes several minutes to absorb this feeling.

Now I get it! I am completely safe and nothing can hurt me.

Both Bill and the practitioner sense an advanced presence in the room. Bill describes this as an overwhelming feeling of peace and well-being and a knowing that all is well. Bill spends several more minutes to assimilate with this profound experience.

Now the practitioner asks Bill to imagine communicating with his cancer. Bill responds as a soul through his higher self.

The cancer has come to allow my life to take a new direc-
tion. I can experience support from my wife now and know
that she is here for me. I am not abandoned. It has slowed my
life down so that I can help others in a new way. I can teach
them new ways to look at things, how to live naturally. I can

teach my wife not to fear passing and to have healthy attitudes about illness and dying.

Bill then asks the guides if using his natural methods will work best for him now and if he will be able to write a book about his experiences.

They are telling me that it does not matter if I use natural methods or not. I can write a book if I want to, but I am already gaining the learning. They are telling me that I am healing, but healing takes many forms. Some will be healed of illness, but there is also mental and emotional healing. The cancer is offering me emotional healing and understanding of my feelings of abandonment. As I struggle to continue, I see that I am never alone. I feel all the love and support. I am gaining wisdom. The words I speak to others will be what they need to hear.

Bill reports that he feels a profound sense of peace at the end of his session. He shares that he feels safe and guided and that the "presence" he has experienced remains with him, giving him comfort. He makes the following comment.

I know now death is nothing to be feared and I am okay no matter what happens.

Things do not improve and about a month after his session, he goes into home hospice care. He remains consciously aware and makes his transition three weeks later, surrounded by his family.

Although Bill dies, he is healed in many ways. He is given an opportunity to review his life during the session. He completely loses his fear of death, receiving a sense of peace so comforting that he can calmly remain present with his family until the end.

The guidance given is not meant to provide medical advice, but rather to promote soul healing. Recognizing and learning from the lessons behind a health crisis can bring peace, whether physical healing occurs or not. It is our attitude toward the health issues we are presented with and our willingness to look deeper and learn from them that is the key.

Life after Brain Trauma

Susan, a fifty-one-year-old married technical assistant with one adult son, comes in for a session to gain a new perspective on her current health situation. Over a decade ago, she contracted herpes encephalitis, which resulted in some permanent brain damage. She claims that this changed everything and forced her to find a new way of living. Now, she can no longer think in the same way she was able to before the illness. She explains that this creates many restrictions and limits the things she is still able to do. Her family and friends don't seem to know what she is going through.

Susan admits that she constantly struggles to get back to who she was before the brain injury, and all she could do back then. Nothing less than getting all her old abilities back is acceptable to her. She refuses to accept her limitations and has been continually grappling to overcome her disability. We begin her case with her time in the womb, as she is beginning her current life as Susan. It is here that she awakens to her soul self.

> *My head is in the wrong position; my head is up, and my feet are down. I should be upside down. Mother is angry and a little scared because I'm in the wrong position. But if I turn my head down, I won't be able to fit inside the body. The body is perfect, but everything is wrong. The body is so tiny, and I am so large. I have trouble fitting in such a small body. My brain will break!*

The practitioner asks why she has chosen a brain that will break.

> *Otherwise I will not learn.*

Next, we move on to a past life, where she is a young girl in slavery, named Cara. She is intelligent and curious and wants to know how things work. She asks too many questions and bothers people in the village. They throw her off a cliff and she dies instantly from a head injury.

Just after leaving the body in the past life, her guide accompanies her through the gateway into the spirit world. Susan's soul self gives the following report.

> *I feel welcome, I see light, everything is light. I am on my way to peace. There's a large golden disc that opens in the middle and I enter. I am coming home. I just move around very fast and check that everything is in order, that this is real, that I am here.*

She is welcomed by her soul family and taken into their circle of light. Her guide tells her that she has done well enough but there is a plan that she needs to remember. He tells her he sends her into lives to help people because she needs to learn to embrace and to love.

> *I feel I am nothingness and it makes me happy. I can do any-thing in this emptiness. It is healing. I want to stay here for a while.*

Susan takes some time to absorb these feelings. Then she says that it feels like someone is holding on to her and it is incredibly hot.

> *We are in a cave with a view over water. I am sitting on a stump and my other guide is sitting in my lap. He says I need to learn to be alone and find my own way. That's what I needed to learn in that life as Cara and that is like what I need to learn now. I need to find my strength. He says that I am on the right track and that I know what to do, but that I don't see it that way in my life as Susan. Susan believes others know better. I just need to open my eyes and see.*

Next Susan moves on to a meeting with her council of wise beings.

> *They tell me I need to move on and gain a higher perspective. They tell me that I am blocking my own development. I need to stop waiting for others to understand; they don't need to*

understand. I have the strength to take the path alone. No one can show me how. That is what I have to learn.

Susan asks for clearer guidance and is taken to the library by her guide.

I'm flying over meadows and see all my past lives down under me. The hardest lives are those when I cannot show myself and be in touch with my soul self. Often, I don't make that spiritual connection because I am worried that others will not understand. I see that in my life as Susan I have been too focused on others and have a deep need to impress and be the best and the fastest. Seeing this, it feels like I can let all old beliefs go.

Susan takes the message about finding her own way to heart. Since the session, she has been building her new life on her own and is still discovering new resources and abilities. At a later follow-up, she relates the following information.

I have a deeper understanding that the old Susan is not coming back. I can live my life and not constantly think about how it used to be. I can let things happen. I no longer have the urge to prove to myself and others that I can do things even if I have brain damage.

I trust my ability to learn new work assignments—new challenges. I do them at my own speed and experience that I can do it. I'm accepting my limitations in a different way. I don't have to compete.

I gained an understanding that some things are more important. I have that choice. Now I follow my own path regardless of what others think I should do. I am me and I stand by my choices. Before my session and even before the brain damage, I was not able to do that. Before the injury, I did not love my life. I was always focused on doing the right thing. Now I enjoy life.

After the session, I do not feel the same pain. I do not push myself and I feel good about it. My use of painkillers is only half what it was before the session.

We see that Susan's acceptance of a limiting condition planned before her birth is bringing her a sense of peace and new joy in her daily life. She is learning to adapt to her limitations and live life her way, instead of listening to what others think she should be doing. An important lesson she has learned from experiencing a permanent disability is that it is not important to impress others or to try to make them understand her situation. Others are not on her path, and she alone can achieve the learning and personal growth that can come from her disability. After her session, Susan reports a deep calm and a sense that she has been set free.

Health Crisis as a Turning Point

Lynn is a sixty-eight-year-old married woman who is in an abusive marriage. She is also suffering from a rare blood disease and is chronically ill. Living with the stress of an angry, demanding husband, her health condition worsens. Her husband refuses to pay for the expensive medication she needs to keep her health condition stable.

Finally, her sister, who is very concerned about her, convinces her to leave her husband. With this encouragement, she moves some distance to be with her sister and aging mother. Her sister helps her receive the medical and welfare assistance she needs. The Life Between Lives session is a gift from her family to help her adjust to her new situation. Lynn has many questions about her rare blood disease during the session. She receives many answers when visiting with her council of wise beings during the session.

They are telling me that having this rare blood disease was not planned for this life. The disease came to help me learn, because I was not getting it. I have a pattern of staying in negative situations too long and not protecting myself. The disease came when I was working as a laboratory assistant in a very negative place. The people I worked with were very hard to get along with and I got yelled at a lot. That was a time when

I cried almost every day. But I believed that we needed the money and that I couldn't leave my job. It was harmful to me to be there like that.

The practitioner asks her to explain this further.

I see that once I became ill, I had to leave that job, and that really upset my husband. He thought I was "faking." I became so weak and tired that I couldn't do everything he had been demanding of me and I could no longer keep him from getting so angry. He just got meaner and meaner and I just got sicker and sicker. But I didn't have the energy to leave. The disease came to help me learn to protect myself. To seek positive situations and learn to love and care for myself.

Lynn reports many insights from the session. She recalls other times in her life when she has stayed in negative situations until her health suffered, most recently her abusive marriage. And she had also done the same thing in her first marriage. She vows to protect herself by seeking relationships and situations that are positive and uplifting from now on. She intends to take better care of herself and shield herself from stressful situations. With the assistance of her sister, she goes into remission and begins enjoying life again.

It is interesting to note that health problems may not be preplanned, but if we are not learning the lessons we planned, an illness or injury may be a contingency plan to help us find our way. This development can provide an opportunity for us to "wake up" and get back on track.

Lynn and Molly learn from their health challenges to take better care of themselves. Health issues slow us down. By taking the time to examine our lives at this point, rather than struggling to bring things back to normal as quickly as possible or passively letting things get worse, we can uncover the guidance the illness is offering to us.

Embracing Vulnerability

Alexa, a fifty-five-year-old divorced woman, has systemic lupus and her health has been up and down for years. The last four years have been especially difficult, as she has been too ill to work steadily and has been without a home. During this time, she has moved several times, staying with friends and family all over the country. She works as she can, freelancing as a writer for various companies and magazines. As complications from her illness flare up, she is in and out of hospitals. Several months ago, she became critically ill and almost died.

When her illness was at the most critical point, she was visited by her guide, who asked her what she wanted to do. Alexa was told that she could go back home to the spirit world or she could stay. If she decides to stay, she will write the book that needs to be written. She is not told what the book is about, or that it will be a commercial success, only that it is important to share it.

> *My guide tells me that they have no judgment if I choose to go home. My soul contracts are essentially complete. They understand that I am tired and in pain. It is a tough choice because my pain levels are running so high, and I am physically exhausted. At first, I want to just pass on and leave the work to someone else. After a bit though, I realize that staying will allow for more growth.*

Once Alexa makes the decision to stay, her heart, kidneys, and lungs all improve, and her pain levels begin going down. She loves the city she is in, and as her health improves, she seeks out new work opportunities. She finds a potential business relationship, but it is stressful and falls through when she won't accept the unreasonable terms. Feeling the need for more stability in her living situation, Alexa decides to come back to her hometown.

She feels that she is at a crossroads in her life now, after walking away from a work contract that was not right for her and a city she loved because her unstable living situation had begun to feel unhealthy emotionally. After enduring years of childhood and marital abuse, she has learned the lesson of honoring herself and is adamant that she won't go backward. Alexa wants to move forward now, especially considering the information she has received from her guide. But she continues to grapple with several health issues that keep her from fully thriving in her new life, including lupus, high blood pressure, kidney problems, nerve issues, and back pain. She is dismayed that after making such bold, positive changes in her life, she still feels so restrained, because of her health problems. She wonders if these issues can be healed.

Alexa also continues to harbor some fear about her health due to her close call with death and her continued health issues. She learns during her Life Between Lives session that she has chosen difficult situations so that she can experience vulnerability and fully understand it. During the session, Alexa is given healing energy and an adjustment to the amount of soul energy she carries in her physical body. One of the decisions made by souls as they are planning each incarnation is how much soul energy they will bring into the life they are about to live in order to accomplish the learning they have planned. Dr. Newton originally believed that the amount of energy brought into an incarnation was static. However, we have since encountered sessions with special circumstances when this might not be the case. An example is a situation in which more rapid spiritual growth than expected occurs or when there is a miscalculation about the amount of energy needed to accomplish the goals set for a life.

Alexa is ambitious and didn't bring as much soul energy into her body in this life as she could have. The powerful spiritual energy flooding her body is felt by both Alexa and the practitioner. Alexa is flooded with healing and joy.

She is told by her guide that through the difficult situations she has previously experienced, she has learned the lesson of vulnerability. Now she can let go of the fear connected to these past difficulties, which is still hurting her. With the healing energy she is receiving, Alexa can release the fear. The key message repeated over and over by the guides in the session is to focus on joy. Joy creates flow. Embracing joy is the path to healing for her and for all of us. Alexa, as her higher self, explains this further.

> It is so easy to forget who we are when we're here [on earth]. These bodies are dampening. While they allow us to live in this dimension, they also dampen the energy. Sometimes it becomes warped as it tries to seep through. Think of energy coming through a sieve. It is fragmented because of the nature of the travel it must traverse. These bodies can create dampening, and if we bring too much energy it blows the circuits. If we do not get enough energy, and it is easy to do one way or the

other, it is difficult to communicate. If we get too much energy, then it's difficult for us to be grounded in the reality that we must experience.

Some of us have a habit that when we are young [souls] we want to take everything; we want to take all our energy. When we are older, we don't want to take as much; however, we may underestimate the need. We feel confident and therefore we think we can go without it, but no. The energy level can be adjusted. We are constantly being assisted even as we assist.

Alexa learns that she has planned for this lifetime and others to be difficult to enable her to feel vulnerable. She wants to experience vulnerability so she can teach about vulnerability. She has succeeded in learning that lesson. Thus, the health problems, unstable living situations, and abuse that allowed her to feel vulnerable are no longer required and will no longer be present. The guides explain this further.

She will teach many people. She has a difficult time staying in this physical form. The body breaks down and the mind breaks down more, wanting to go home, not understanding that it is purposeless to come here without completing the task. Although nothing is wasted. She will begin to thrive. Most of the learning has been achieved and the difficult conditions are no longer necessary.

Focus on the joy. Focus on the wonder. Enjoy life and don't be afraid. This is the most healing thing she can do. She loves the outdoors. She started exercising again. This is good. Walking is very good. Yoga would be excellent. She needs the flexibility.

This problem with her physical being will work itself out in time. The reason the nerves hurt is blockages that are difficult to explain. They will be healed. She needs to let go of the fear. Most is gone. It is leaving, but she must focus on joy and on gratitude. Then she will find that everything flows.

Let the love flow through. She has been afraid to love or to allow herself to be loved. This has caused her much physical pain. Her soul requires a high amount of love because it is her nature. When she keeps herself from this, for the block in this case is her own, it causes physical pain. This is a signal that she is not loving herself and allowing the joy to come through. She must focus on joy. On creating joy for others as well, which she does. This will be the path to healing.

We see in this case that the difficult situations that occurred in Alexa's life were planned by her to help her learn the lesson of vulnerability. While she learned this lesson and overcame enough fear to go after a new life situation, some fear remained. This kept her from fully loving and caring for herself. Letting go of the residual fear and embracing joy and gratitude was the final test. The healing energy and insights from her session will allow her to thrive.

Alexa's case shows us that an important part of self-care is loving ourselves. We are encouraged to embrace joy and bring it to others.

Understanding the Root Cause

Meghan, a thirty-nine-year-old lawyer, comes in for a Life Between Lives session to gain some insight regarding her recurrent stomach problems and inability to eat most foods. She reports a history of chronic stomach and digestive problems for the past twenty years, which medical care has been unable to alleviate. While her current marriage is stable, with two children, nine and twelve years of age, she has endured much abuse in a past relationship.

She reports that she didn't have any stomach problems until she was in high school and loved food and cooking. The first episode she recalls is when she was sixteen and diagnosed with gastritis. She doesn't recall what might have triggered that first episode, but does remember being very lonely in high school.

A year later she met a soldier in the war in Croatia who seemed kind and gentle, and she fell in love. They started dating and were together for five years. For the first six months, it was nice. After that he became very rude to her and soon the relationship became abusive. The stomach problems reoccurred, and she became weak. When she tried to leave, he threatened her. He asked her, "Do you know how many people I have killed? Do you think I can't do it again?"

When summer came, he wouldn't go to the beach with her because he says her legs were too fat. He wanted her to go on a weight loss diet. She started to hate him and couldn't stand it when he touched her. But he kept touching her and she spent hours in the shower afterward trying to wash herself clean. But she didn't feel clean and started to hate herself.

Once he almost killed her, and the next day she developed horrible spasms in her stomach. Her parents took her to the hospital, where she remained for the next two months. They ran multiple tests and finally diagnosed her with irritable bowel syndrome.

When she returned home, her boyfriend reappeared, and the abuse started again. Her stomach pain became worse and she lost more weight. She became unable to digest food and later developed a fever and abdominal distention. She was hospitalized again in very serious condition, unable to eat anything. The doctors couldn't figure out what was wrong with her. However, one of them suggested she try homeopathy. She reported that this saved her life. But, while the pain and problems with digestion got better, she continued to eat only a very limited, bland diet. The abusive boyfriend was gone by this time, and she went on with her life. But in all the subsequent years, she is living with a fear of food.

During the regression to childhood, Meghan remembers her sister's birthday party and how her father blocked the children from coming in to play. He finally left to go to his card game, but she feels ashamed of her father's behavior in front of the other children. And her stomach hurt. The practitioner guides Meghan to comfort the child she is then and let her know that her father's bad behavior is not her fault. She is directed to let go of the feelings of shame she feels then and other times.

When regressed to the womb, Meghan feels cold and unwelcome. She reports that her mother feels tired and heavy and that there are no feelings of love. The practitioner guides her to send love and warmth to her young self, to tell her that she is loved and wanted, and to welcome her to the world. Things feel much better to her after doing that, but Meghan reports that she still feels alone. Then, the practitioner asks her what she has come here to learn.

I came to share love even when I am alone. I don't stay in the womb. I go to the light. I don't feel alone there. I'm there with many. They are joking, and they are a little naughty and funny. I see two of them sitting off to the side and they are sad. They are telling me that I shouldn't go there. I shouldn't go into that body because it will be hard. I tell them not to worry, as I am sure. I have made a deal with my mother. My sister is there. She takes me somewhere to show me about the deal I made.

Next Meghan moves on to a past life.

Now I see a woman in a dress. She's in the garden in front of the house. I stay on the side and I am hiding from her. She's doing something with a towel. I feel pain. I don't like her. I want to just stay hidden, but I am so angry. I did something to her. She doesn't know that I'm angry. I want to stay hidden, but I see stones and I hit her with the stones. I'm a man and I am just so angry. I killed her with the stones. She was evil. Now it hurts even more, and I fall to my knees crying.

In the next scene, he is taken to be hanged.

I feel so weak and I feel pain in my entire body. I see a group of men and I am in the middle. Two of them held me under my arms and they pull me off the floor, because I can't stand on my feet. I feel so weak, without any strength in my body. I'm not afraid of hanging. I know what they will do. I leave the body a moment before the hanging. I leave the body slowly, like I need a few minutes. I move up. I feel released.

The practitioner asks why the man hated the woman so much and why he thought that she was evil.

She killed my baby. She shook the baby too much. She didn't feel guilty. I don't feel guilty for killing her. I want her to feel guilty.

Now I am with the others and they are washing me and singing. They are washing away all the guilt and shame I brought into that body. I feel clean and easy now. I am back home, and I feel happy. I am now gold and I shine. Then I go to a special room. There are three elders and one is higher than the other two. I'm not afraid of them, but I have respect for them. I know I didn't do my best in this life. I'm all alone with them and the others wait outside the door. They don't say anything, they're just watching me. I feel their energy.

They are not happy. I did not learn. They send me to another room with books. I am learning patience. I am afraid. When I entered, a "book of light" came to me, but I was afraid to look at it. There are others here, but I don't speak with them. I don't recognize anybody.

The practitioner guides Meghan to ask for assistance. The guides give her the following information.

I am learning to forgive, to not judge, and to be good to the people who are not good. I tell them that I am not Mother Teresa and that is why I am here. Strange. They want me to be good to people who are not good to me, to not judge and to forgive. I must be openhearted to those kinds of people. Loving with an open heart is my essence.

They are healing me. One stays behind me and one stays in front. I feel heat and see light coming into me. My appearance is changing. I look like them now. The one who is staying behind me is the higher one, but I see him as if he were in front of me. He is so powerful.

The practitioner guides Meghan to ask about her stomach.

It is guilt. I've been carrying that anger and guilt for a long time. I need to love and forgive myself. I have the tools to heal myself. I came to earth this time to make my mother feel guilty. But I need to forgive her for shaking that baby. I need to forgive the man I was then who killed her. I also need to forgive the father who wouldn't let the kids in for my sister's birthday.

Meghan reports that after her session, she wants to eat foods that she has been avoiding for twenty years. She is now eating meat and pasta and feels no pain. She is slowly adding in other foods that she hasn't been able to eat for years, giving her digestive system time to adjust.

Meghan agreed to help her mother experience guilt in this lifetime so that her mother can grow. However, the guilt and anger she herself continues to carry over from that previous life is the reason behind her stomach problems in this life. Letting go of guilt and forgiving herself and her parents in this lifetime results in significant healing.

———————

We see from the cases in this chapter that health problems are planned by us to help us evolve spiritually. They can alert us to areas in our lives where we need to make changes in order to continue to grow, and they can remind us of the importance of loving and caring for ourselves.

Health issues can provide us with the opportunity to heal emotional wounds and to let go of fear, anger, or guilt. They can slow us down and provide us with an opportunity to examine our lives to release limiting attitudes or to achieve more balance in our lives. While we may not always heal physically from a health crisis, we can heal emotionally and be transformed.

Life Between Lives sessions are an excellent way to uncover the hidden gifts brought by health challenges. The sessions do not provide medical advice, but rather healing guidance to advance the soul.

Two

ANXIETY AND DEPRESSION

E arth school provides the perfect environment to experience a wide range of emotions, from happiness and elation on one end of the spectrum to sadness and despair on the other. This is a major consideration in the soul's decision to incarnate here rather than in a less emotion-packed world. An earth incarnation provides the richness of experiencing emotions over merely thinking about them.

Souls are immersed in peace, joy, and love when they are at home in the spiritual realm. The pain resulting from decisions made and directions taken in prior lifetimes on earth does not exist in this realm. Within this context, you make decisions about your plan for the coming incarnation. Having released the suffering or trauma of a previous life, you may have an inflated sense of what you are ready to handle or merely not have a clear grasp of the unintended consequences of the goals you are setting for your upcoming life.

With such lofty goals, you may wonder, *what could possibly go wrong?* Once you incarnate on earth you begin to implement the plan you crafted for the lifetime. But even as your plan begins to unfold, circumstances change, and things turn out to not be as you intended. You, and those close to you, exert free will, potentially altering the direction of your life. Challenges arise and setbacks occur, many of which exert an emotional toll. As your life unfolds, two of the more common emotional byproducts are anxiety and depression.

Emotional Challenges of the Soul's Plan

With Dan we see the emotional toll that some people endure to achieve their soul's plan for this lifetime. He is a forty-year-old bachelor. Dan is independent, self-reliant, and self-sufficient. Others view him as dependable, responsible, and the go-to person for help and assistance. By all outward appearances, he appears to have a charmed life. Few know the emotional torment that he has coped with throughout his life.

Dan is the oldest of four brothers. His early childhood was happy, but from the age of ten he became preoccupied with a feeling that he was going to die. Two years later he began having trouble sleeping and developed the first symptoms of obsessive-compulsive disorder (OCD).

A self-described loner throughout high school, when he reached college he came out of his shell and was very outgoing and popular. Despite enjoying many female friendships, he had little interest in romantic or sexual involvements. In his earliest dating relationships, Dan experienced crippling sexual performance anxiety that dampened his interest in developing intimate relationships. The serious emotional damage this caused persists to this day, although his relationships have improved over the years. He admits that while he has been successful winning over women for romantic relationships, he has had only fleeting interest in any of them. Almost all his relationships have been ended by him. Over the years he has experienced bouts of anxiety and depression.

During his twenties, Dan's OCD, anxiety, and depression worsen. The medications he takes over the next few years provide minimal relief and problematic side effects.

At forty, Dan currently enjoys great success in his career on the faculty of an Ivy League university, but experiences great anxiety when faced with important decisions in many aspects of his life. Dan has been dating Angelina for the last eighteen months. Sensing she is a member of his soul family, he feels he is destined to marry her. But he is conflicted, feeling ambivalent about this decision. He wants to understand why he is suffering this dilemma. In addition, he is hoping to uncover the reason for his depression and anxiety. He poses the following questions about his depression.

If this is my lifetime to have the experience of depression and get it out of the way, then so be it. I'll take one for the team this time, if I don't have to ever experience it again. Or, is my depression challenging me to maintain hope; a form of suffering that must be experienced to be understood and is part of my soul's long-term growth? Perhaps these emotional challenges are a gift to provide guidance on the right path and when I have deviated from it.

Dan's intuition was spot-on. There is a higher purpose to be served through his decades-long struggle with depression and anxiety. His own words "I'll take one for the team" reflected an inner knowing. Through his spirit guide, he learns that he has included these challenges in his soul's plan. But why? His guide gives the following information.

Dan is preparing to be a spirit guide! A role that is available for all souls to choose, if they have the capacity, plus the interest and motivation to pursue this path.

With his guide's counsel, Dan had included intense learning in his life plan that would prepare him to work with a wide range of souls, coping with a broad range of challenges. His guide offers further information.

He doesn't want to specialize. He wants to learn about everything.

As to the specific purpose served, his struggles with depression and anxiety provide Dan with opportunities to feel, and to experience the emotional aspects of life. This experience will serve him well when he becomes a guide. Dan's guide elaborates.

> *Dan needs to learn how to feel, as well as to learn how he can gain understanding through feeling. A big part of overcoming his depression is learning to feel through that experience. He needs to become comfortable with negative as well as positive feelings. The experience of feelings contains many different varieties and, for Dan, it's important that he experience as many as possible.*

Dan's guide challenges him to dive deep into his feelings, whether positive or negative, to learn everything the feeling can teach him. Dan's earlier lives have emphasized skill development, enhancement, achievement, and leadership.

> *Dan needs to express more, stop thinking, stop overanalyzing. He needs to jump in and relate more on a feeling level. For Dan, relationships provide that opportunity. The sexual performance issues that he has struggled with for years are recurring chances for him to learn to be humble, to be vulnerable, to trust, and to love.*

His guide confirms that Angelina is a part of Dan's soul group and like him, she is similarly advanced and motivated. Although Dan's life plan includes marriage, he has a choice. He can refuse to marry, marry Angelina, or marry someone else. It doesn't matter who he marries, whether she is a soul mate or not, if his wife agrees to help him accomplish what he has planned. Regardless of which choice he makes, he will face the same life lessons.

> *Angelina will provide more challenges but also more rewards. Others would be different with different challenges and different rewards. Each presents an opportunity to learn. Ultimately, there is no right decision. The different routes offer joy at different times, but neither route has much short-term peace. The different routes will eventually bring some joy*

along with everything else that comes with it. The path with Angelina is one that brings the most development. The other possibilities also bring development, but in different ways.

There are always more opportunities. If you want to try them, there's always going to be more. You never only have once chance to learn. You may have one chance with a particular person or opportunity, but you don't have only one chance with the lesson.

Dan discovers from his guide that his decades-long struggle with depression and anxiety is related to his desire to more quickly become a guide. With that goal set, he has thrust himself into a life filled with significant challenges and opportunities to resolve intense emotions. Dan's life path offers constant opportunities for "feeling calisthenics," not surprising given his serious nature, zeal, and spiritual ambition.

His guide chides Dan that his life has been devoid of joy.

I have been trying to tell him that he needs to prioritize joy and fun! Dan believes that joy and fun are less virtuous. But in fact, they are virtuous opportunities for learning. There is a balance that needs to be achieved for those who are goal oriented. Goofing off can have a real value. It's more valuable than most people realize.

There is a pathway for life to be easier, less challenging. In fact, it's not just a path, it's an inevitability. The goal is not to find the quickest way there, but to find the best way, the most complete way. Dan's plan calls for certain things to be learned, which has caused him to suffer. There is a path that leads out of the pain and suffering, which he will inevitably reach. Connection to divinity is a way to heal every ailment of life, and that includes escaping suffering and experiencing joy.

Going forward, Dan would benefit if he could enjoy living life as fully as possible and reflect on moments of happiness that occur that he doesn't seem to process. People's lives are generally led to the full extent. It's how they process and reflect that differentiates their experience.

The life he planned is a good one. It includes joy and suffering. Both are required for fulfilling the goals. These are experiences that many have had before. They are not unique. They can be overcome and looked back on with pride in the accomplishments.

Dan's council echoed a similar theme.

You were not intended to suffer. Life has challenges, but you should not get stuck in the misery. Maintain hope and appreciation for the opportunity of life, even when it is challenging. The forks in the road don't have to be as difficult as you make them. Trust that there will never be a fork in the road that is unbearable. Know that you will end up in the same place regardless.

One of the more poignant matters that Dan sought understanding of is what he labels his apathy and general disinterest in life, and whether this is the cause of his depression.

Dan has barely valued his lives other than as a means to an end. Through many of them he has held an understanding of what needs be done and then accomplished it, but he hasn't always experienced the richness of what we've created. Some lives have been more prone to this than others—this one being an extreme example.

So, for Dan, his apathy and disinterest are related to, but not equal to, his depression. Nor is depression a result of early life trauma. We shouldn't be disinterested in our lives. They are important. This is the same lesson we've given him before. He is not so much a slow learner as he is stubborn. His apathy and disinterest are a challenge to be outgrown.

The guide counsels us all not to assume that life challenges are reminders that we have detoured from our life plan.

> *Many well-intentioned people think that way. It's not true that feelings of discontent mean you are on the wrong path or that you are being punished. You may have built them into your life plan so that you can accomplish your life goals.*

In a follow-up session a month after his Life Between Lives session, Dan reported that his most recent eight-month depression has lifted. With the insight gleaned from his Life Between Lives session, he has stopped worrying about his relationship with Angelina. He is allowing himself to focus on how he feels about her and how he feels about what life would be like if they married. With an ease that was absent during earlier sessions, he said that he knows whatever decision he makes will be alright. He has found peace in the knowledge that he is following his soul's plan for this lifetime.

Releasing Depression and Guilt

Mette is a single mother, raising a fifteen-year-old daughter, Anna. Six years ago, she separated from her husband Bjorg, who died soon after due to his drug addiction. No stranger to the death of a beloved, she had earlier lost a baby boy, and as a young girl, her mother. Shortly after her husband's death, Mette was severely injured in a motorcycle accident in which she almost died. The life that she once enjoyed began to crumble around her.

Mette seeks a Life Between Lives session with hopes of overcoming suicidal thoughts, debilitating depression, and the tremendous guilt that she has regarding her husband's death.

Family finances grow strained as Mette is unable to continue work as an accountant. She is increasingly worried about her daughter's well-being. Her daughter is showing signs of depression and struggling in school. As external circumstances strain, Mette and Anna's relationship frays, with discussions often spiraling downward into emotional arguments. Sadly, Mette has come to believe that she is no longer a good mother. All of this contributes to her increasing emotional frailty.

Motivated by a belief that it will be good to find a new father for Anna, Mette begins to date. Perhaps because of her own ambivalent or confused motivation, she dates quite a few men without any success. Despite her intelligence, education, and natural beauty, the men she meets never call her back or abruptly end dates with her.

In despair, Mette cries out at the outset of her session:

> How can I get myself back to being alive? It is so hard for me to live. It would feel easier to be on the other side. If it was not for Anna, I would not want to continue living. And I can't find a new father for her. Why can't I find a new man? I don't want to lose another man! I can't go through losing someone again.

Mette is calmed by the welcoming sight of her grandmother, who was her primary caregiver after her mother's death. Her grandmother, who is in training to become Mette's guide, escorts her to a beautiful spa-like room where she begins to breathe, relax, and restore. Soon after, Mette's grandmother takes her to a place of learning where Mette encounters her soul group, of which her grandmother is a member. She cries softly.

> I see and feel my group, my people; these are my friends who I care about. I feel very disconnected from them. I have not followed through. This is my cluster group; they are waiting for my return. It's like I need some energy from my group. I need courage from them. It is a problem for me to do this alone in the physical.
>
> I need to listen more. To connect with them. I am noticing my daughter's and my husband's energy here. It is not like in the physical, but I do know it's their energy. It is the energy that I deeply know. That I know on so many levels. It is a kind of calm excitement. We know that we are connected. It's all these energies, all these soul friends, who are helping me while I am in the physical. [cries] I feel so loved.

A circle of eleven or twelve souls envelope Mette.

They tell me they all worked with me in the past. They all know I am on this journey. Now they are giving me a mental boost. They show me I have different choices, different tracks to choose from. I get it! I kind of jumped off the track. My mind clouded my soul. I really separated myself from my connection to my group and from my connection to the spirit world. I allowed this to happen. I did not listen anymore, and I numbed my feelings.

To ensure that Mette understands, the practitioner probes further. Mette as her soul self responds.

It is part of my lesson. The physical Mette, me, must experience the separation. To feel this desperation. To feel so disconnected and hopeless was my choice, because I needed to experience all this to wake up.

Mette understands that she disconnected herself from her group and from the spirit realm. She now understands that being disconnected clouds her thinking and causes her depression. And she is willing to accept the responsibility for waking up.

Bjorg is coming toward me now. He explains to me that he slowly killed himself. He was not able to free himself. But he chose this! He is very loving. I need to stop beating myself up over it. This is the lesson I need to learn if I want to progress forward and keep up with my soul group. I am stuck in the guilt. We had so many lives as lovers. So many happy ones. This one was planned to be different.

I didn't keep up with my soul group. They all evolved faster than me. I chose this experience to evolve, so I could keep up with my group.

After a long pause, Mette cringes as she continues to elaborate.

I am a bit of a hesitant soul. I don't want to rush.

Mette is next brought by her grandmother to meet with the council of elders, in a place of nonjudgment and unconditional love. She is initially uncomfortable in their presence.

> *I have mixed feelings. Happy but also ashamed. They're look-*
> *ing very friendly and are kind of humorous. It is for my sake*
> *so that I am not scared. They appear more human than they*
> *are, so that I recognize them.*

Mette's Life Between Lives practitioner begins to ask the questions that Mette hoped to have answered in the session. The first was whether it is possible to change something that she incorporated in her soul's plan for the upcoming lifetime. And if so, are there limits to the changes that can be made?

> *Yes, partially. Some things we can change, some things we*
> *can't. I cannot change things that involve others. Other spirits.*
> *It feels like my daughter Anna and I have decided something*
> *together! Something we are supposed to do. And that I cannot*
> *change! I do not know what it is, but it is not changeable. It*
> *will become clear at some point in the future. I can change the*
> *path, but what I need to learn will be in every path I take.*

No matter which path Mette chooses, what she needs to learn will show up anyway. Mette is further told that she is doing better than expected on the path she chose that has brought her so much sorrow. The path that is so filled with loss enables her to advance more rapidly. It has the added advantage of providing Anna with circumstances that her soul wants to experience.

The elders bring Mette to the place of life selection where the details about her upcoming life are being planned. She can hear the discussion that takes place regarding the roles that members of her soul family will assume in her life as Mette.

> *Oh, Anna is in this too! I am told there is a lesson she needs to*
> *learn embedded in my soul plan! I am helping her! We are all*
> *in this together. The three of us are together.*

Mette learns that because of Bjorg's deep feelings for Anna, he was torn about leaving according to his soul's plan. He so enjoyed being her father that he wanted to stay, to be there for her if possible. He could have gone even earlier but remained as long as he could.

Mette is relieved and pleased to learn that her future holds the promise of finding another partner. She also receives other guidance from the elders.

> *I need to stop being loyal. I need to separate the spirit world from this world. It is good that I am loyal, but when it comes to love, I need to understand that that loyalty doesn't get me anywhere. That's why he is not here yet. I need to open myself for physical love. And I need to find a man because I want a man! Anna has a father. I can't replace her father. Stop searching for that, they tell me. And we all love, we are all love. That's what connects us, love. Love is all there is. We all love each other here. And we love everyone and everything. On earth it is sometimes not easy to love everyone. But we need to remember that everyone is connected by love, only by love. I need to trust that I can find love with another man in the physical form.*

In parting words, Mette is applauded by the elders for her parenting. In a high compliment, they acknowledge that her loving care is helping Anna to grow spiritually. They also encourage her to not be so serious all the time and to loosen up a bit. She should not be afraid. They are always available for her to call on them.

Mette's session enabled her to gradually rebuild her life. The insight she gained helped her to overcome her debilitating depression and guilt. She returned to work after finding a more satisfying and less stressful job. Her relationship with Anna improved significantly, and their arguments all but disappeared. As a bonus, Anna's grades improved, which is helping her to stay active and more positive. Mette abandoned her search for a new father for Anna, and with renewed enthusiasm begins looking for a new love for herself.

Mette's experience illustrates how, once you gain an understanding about your soul's intention, you can be free from the burden of the false belief that you have failed.

Serving Humanity

During the life-planning process, souls enter into mutual agreements that will serve each other during the upcoming life. With Theresa, we see this dynamic in action when we are also introduced to another element of the soul planning process: the decision to serve humanity through one's own emotional struggles and spiritual growth.

Theresa is a fifty-five-year-old healer, married with two children, who are young adults. She schedules her Life Between Lives session hoping to understand the depression she has suffered since her teens. She also worries about her children, both of whom also suffer from depression.

Theresa has never made her own healing a priority. She does not share her feelings with others because she doesn't want to burden them. When she encounters matters beyond her control, she asks the archangel Michael for assistance. Although at times she can trust that everything in the universe is happening exactly as it should, she cannot sustain it. There are other times when she is not able to stop worrying about her life and children.

In her session, Theresa gains information that will help her with this in the future.

> *It's hard when it's our kids; we want to protect them. But we forget sometimes that they are souls here in their own right. They are here for their own lessons. I can't protect them regardless of how painful it is to watch. I must not lose sight of the big picture. I must trust the universe.*

Through her connection with her guides, Theresa is reminded that they are always present and willing to work with her. This reminder provides relief. As her session continues, Theresa's guides offer insight into the purpose served by her depression.

> *The guides are telling me that having depression means I have unresolved issues. The depression is like a beacon in the body*

and the mind, reminding me that the issues have not yet been released. I can release them, but I will have to make changes in my relationships with my husband and my children. There will be opportunities to do this and they will help.

The guides now encourage Theresa to connect with the souls of her husband and children and ask if they support making these changes. It seems Theresa needs this confirmation to change herself. She hates burdening other people with her problems. She admits that she doesn't focus on her own healing. The guides don't tell her specifically what to do, but it is obvious she needs to focus on her herself. Their approach left room for the unfolding of other potentialities for Theresa and her family.

During the post-session discussion, Theresa reveals yet another gift bestowed by her guides. They communicated that the energetic frequency of the depression that she has struggled with for so long matches the pattern of an energy that plagues the earth at this time. Theresa, as well as her children, agreed to incorporate depression into their life plans to serve others who are similarly burdened by it. As they work to heal their depression, they will be contributing to the healing of others, including ancestral lines and the earth's energy.

At a later point, reflecting on the value of the Life Between Lives session, Theresa tells her practitioner the following.

The information I received from the guides has helped me to shift my perspective and provided a sense of relief. Instead of looking at depression as an unfortunate legacy for my children, I know now that healing myself will help me to heal others down the ancestral line. Understanding this gives it more of a purpose and is a reminder that I must continue to work on this.

Unresolved Past Lives

The origin of the emotional challenges that many grapple with in life can be found in unresolved matters from prior lives. Ken, a thirty-nine-year-old carpenter, has had a lifelong battle with depression that he feels unable to shake. He hopes to learn more about why this feeling is so persistent in his life. He is happily married and has no children. He and his wife have many friends and lead an active social life. He can think of no reason why he has always felt depressed.

As he moves to the origin of these feelings of depression, Ken finds himself in a past life, as a male named Arthur, in his early twenties. He lives somewhere in Europe during the Middle Ages. Dressed in rags and worn-out boots, Arthur is in the woods outside of the small village where he lives.

> *I hear noises. I think they are coming again. The Vikings—a raiding party came before and destroyed our village. They killed many of the men and took the women as captives. I was just a child. They are coming again. I run back to the village to get prepared. We must stop them before they get to the village.*

Arthur describes the village as small, and there are only four other men to protect the village besides himself. He goes to the blacksmith to get a sword and a horse. The five men ride out to intercept the Vikings. His mother and sister, along with the other adults, elderly people, and children, are left in the village, unable to defend themselves.

Arthur describes the scene that unfolds.

> *There are about ten of them coming at us fast. I kill one of them. There is a big fight, but we are outnumbered.*

Arthur is struck in the shoulder with a sword and knocked off his horse. The blacksmith alone is left to hold them off because the others have been killed or injured. Ultimately, he too is struck down and the raiders head for the village. The Vikings torch the village, killing many and taking some women as captives. Arthur manages to get himself back to the village. Bleeding heavily, he only lives long enough to round up the children and send them off to find another village.

Ken sees, as he returns to his earlier life, that Arthur wrongly concluded that the death and destruction inflicted by the Vikings was his fault. At the time, he took responsibility for not warning the villagers in time. Without early warning, the villagers were not able to hide to escape the Vikings.

With the higher perspective of his afterlife experience, Ken can release the emotions that he has carried from Arthur's life. The weight of his depression has lifted. Ken now sees clearly that there was nothing Arthur could have done at the time to save the village and its inhabitants.

Souls face many challenges as they navigate the complexities of earth. Whether the outcome is positive or negative, there are often emotional by-products to the experiences. For younger souls, navigating the complexities of the earth may be more challenging given their limited experiences.

Debilitating Anxiety

Christine is a forty-year-old woman. She has coped with anxiety disorder and attention deficit disorder (ADD) from a very young age. Her conditions necessitate taking prescribed medications for both.

In addition to finding relief for her anxiety and ADD, Christine hopes to understand her lack of a sense of home. She describes feeling unsettled and displaced all her life. Even as a child she longed to "be home." As an adult she understands that what she has felt all along is a sense of detachment. She yearns to overcome it.

Christine is a stay-at-home mom and says that she often feels overwhelmed having to take care of her two small boys, ages three and five. She is particularly stressed about how her youngest son cries frequently at night. Her husband has become less and less tolerant of her hyperactivity and nervousness. He feels that both are having a negative impact on their life. So much so that he thinks that their marriage is about to fall apart.

Christine, one of six girls, was born just before the seventh child, her brother. Once in trance she is guided back through childhood memories to the womb, before regressing into a past life. Christine is guided to explore her first impressions of incarnating on earth as a soul joining with the baby forming in her mother's womb. Her mother's anxiety is so great that Christine's soul chooses to travel outside of the womb as she develops. Christine observes her mother's tremendous sadness caused by learning that she is not about to deliver a boy.

> I don't spend much time in there! It's so uncomfortable. I go outside of the body. I look and observe. I wonder what to do.

It is so uncomfortable and crazy making in there. I don't like it. I just don't like it! But there is lots to do! I look around to see where I am going, what to expect, who is with me. Earth is beautiful. There are so many things here that are different and special. It is an opportunity to be there. But my mom, she is so stressed. It is hurting me to feel all that. I do not want to get back into the body, but I know that I must.

I had an agreement with my brother! We made a deal that we would go together and that I would be born first. I think I talked him into going, and then I had to follow through. So, if I were to be a boy, my mom would not have had any more kids! Since we both wanted to come, I had to come as a girl, and he would come after me as a boy.

It is difficult for me to focus with this brain. It is difficult to deal with the energies down here. The brain is good for me though. It helps me to be here. It helps me to not be too serious. If I lighten up and accept this, it helps me. It's not about being too serious. I'm here to learn to accept people. I'm here to enjoy people and to bring love to them.

After exploring in the womb, Christine moves into a past life during the time of the Holocaust. She is horrified at how she and others are treated in the concentration camp. She is sobbing.

I don't understand people. I want to get away from this. I really don't understand people!

Leaving behind the horrors of the camp, Christine arrives in the afterlife following her death at the hands of a guard. She is overcome with joy.

I am HOME! This is home! It is so bright and peaceful here! We are trying to grow spiritually. Every being here is in the most loving state. We are all explorers. There are no predators. It is so peaceful here!

Probing for more details, the facilitator asks Christine what she is sensing and feeling. She explains that the other members of her soul group have all left, including her brother, who is a part of her group. She discovers that this is only her third life on earth.

> It is like a joke to come to earth. It is like watching a movie. But certain things you can't learn here [at home], like anger, jealousy, hatred, or pain. I want to experience that. That's why I came to earth. Earth is cut off from love. Humanity stays in the dark. The existence without love is not real! Every human must commit to love. Only love. Earth has the agreement to serve people to learn this. She lets people grow up.

Christine immediately feels better after the session. She has gained an understanding of who she is and the circumstances that set the stage for her anxiety and ADD. Returning home is restorative and deeply healing. Recognizing the contract with her brother helps her to accept life in a deeper way.

Over time, she begins to see life from a more lighthearted perspective. Her anxiety becomes far less debilitating. Her lessened anxiety positively affects her family life, as well as her own well-being. She now brings love and compassion to her family and the people around her. She reports doing very well and that life is good.

Holding Guilt from the Past

We gain further understanding of the things carried forward from past lives from Carol, a young mother in her mid-twenties. Carol is seeking relief from anxiety, depression, anger, and an overwhelming sense that she is a bad mother. She is particularly stressed about her son constantly crying at night.

Carol regresses to a life as a decorated male military officer during a time of war. In this role, he gave orders that resulted in the death of many soldiers. In his official capacity, he visits the families of some of the men under his command, after they have died in battle. He believes he is responsible for the grief and struggle that he caused in these fatherless homes. The guilt weighs heavily on him.

Speaking as the military officer, Carol's own words begin to fill in the picture of her current emotional challenges. Carol has carried forward into this current life the energy of the commanding officer's unresolved emotions.

> *As I grow old, I become mean and grumpy because I ruined so many people's lives under my orders. I am bitter because I had no choice. I don't talk about it. I think a lot about Jesus, and I hope I go to heaven. I didn't treat my wife well until I started to die.*

Carol views the officer's death and sees that his soul stays around until after his funeral. He realizes that it is only after death that he is finally able to take in the love that people had for him.

> *People are proud of those medals, but I had to do a lot of bad stuff to get them. I wanted to let them love me in that life, but I thought if they knew what I did, they wouldn't have loved me. I can take in that love now and it feels so good. I can be at peace. Time to go. If I come back, I want to make a happy home.*

Upon reaching the afterlife, the military officer takes the opportunity to apologize to the souls of the families who were impacted by his orders. Within the realm of unconditional love and acceptance, he is reminded that apologies are unnecessary, because everyone was blindly role-playing on earth.

Through this reexperience, Carol remembers that human struggles are opportunities for soul growth, and that everything ultimately turns out fine in the end. She is gifted with wisdom that will enable her to unburden the weight of her depression, anxiety, anger, and doubt.

Through the practitioner's facilitation, Carol releases the energy of guilt, anger, and fear. Once released, she can connect deeply to the power and intensity of pure love and physically experience its brightness and warmth. Steeped in the higher vibration of pure love, Carol has some realizations.

I need to be with my son from a place of love, not fear. It's okay to have feelings and feel frustrated at times; it doesn't mean I'm a bad mother. I know I'm a good mother.

Carol's release of long-held false beliefs and attendant emotions paved the way for her to connect to her immortal identity. She experiences the freedom, peace, and clarity of her soul self. She can release old, conditioned, fear-based beliefs. Carol's experience reminds us of our own ability to release residue from earlier lives and to break their hold on us.

Six weeks after her session, Carol shares the following.

The session was a big help to me. I felt better right away regarding my son and his crying at night. As the weeks went by, I slowly started feeling less anxious on deeper levels.

Finding Peace in a Chaotic World

We are living in a time when global events play out in real time on our television and computer screens, exposing all of us to the pain of natural disasters and man-made catastrophes. In addition to those immediately affected, others may be indirectly impacted. Developing a way to cope when tragedy strikes around the world has become important for one's emotional health and spiritual development.

But lest we forget the big picture, Gerald provides a powerful reminder.

Gerald is a thirty-four-year-old analyst with the federal government. In addition to his desire to understand the neglect and abuse he suffered as a child, he is seeking insight about managing emotions during times of great global anxiety.

Through Gerald's session, we are reminded that all life experience offers the soul an opportunity to advance. There is benefit for yourself and others when you do not overreact and manage to keep your emotions in check. Gerald's guide offers a perspective that can resonate for us all.

There is tragedy on earth, but there is much that can be done to mitigate it. It is not limiting you. You can still do what you need to do. Everyone can. That is why we all incarnated where we did. It allows us to do what we need to do: to grow, heal, balance the past, and serve. Sometimes people need to go through miserable times to accomplish their soul's plan. Once we are done learning, we can return to our natural state of happiness.

It is essential to have steady points of positive energy on the planet to counterbalance negative energy, and to enable us to return to our natural state of happiness. Your natural state is secure, loving, and joyful. Continue working to retain the positive energy and preserve it for the others to have when they are ready.

Those who choose to incarnate on earth do so because it offers rich emotional experience. Our choice to return is a choice to dive fully into both the ups and downs of life. We are mindful of the potential setbacks, but our longing for spiritual growth propels us forward. Time and again we endure, and time and again we prevail.

Not losing site of the context of our earthly adventure can ease suffering. At the same time, when we can rise out of and above the tumult, we are not only growing spiritually, we are helping others not to succumb to the negativity. Upon our return to the spiritual realm, the experiences we have had deepen our capacity to revel in the peace, joy, and unconditional love that pervades our eternal home.

Three

HEALING FROM LOSS

Coping with the loss of a loved one is a universal experience, whether loss comes through death or separation. Awareness that some of our loved ones will likely die before us does not shield us from the pain of our loss, or the grief that typically results. Nor does knowing that many loving relationships are not permanent. Regardless of the circumstances of the loss, the experience is dreaded by most of us.

The cycle of life, birth, and death almost guarantees that each of us will face the loss of a loved one, relative, or friend and the grief that follows. Tragic and unexpected deaths are painful and difficult to cope with. So too is the loss that results from separation, divorce, abandonment, and other circumstances that permanently end a loving or nurturing relationship. If you have had to cope with the loss of a loved one, you may be familiar with the range of emotions that people experience.

The recent loss of a loved one may have set you on the path that has led you to read this book. Perhaps a friend gave you this book to help ease your grief. Or like those who search for understanding in a Life Between

Lives session, you may be seeking higher wisdom about a loss that you have endured.

When you are grieving the loss of a loved one, you are affirming your capacity for love and your ability to connect with the essence of another. No human experience is more essential to happiness and well-being than loving another. And no human experience is more important to your soul's growth. Loss offers the soul a richer environment to learn, to heal, to balance, or to serve. Love is so valuable and coveted that people who have failed to connect and to love also experience profound grief. Understandably, the death of a loved one or the end of a loving relationship is an intensely emotional time.

Responses to the loss of a loved one may include denial, anger, bargaining, depression, and, if the grieving process is completed effectively, acceptance. The path through these emotions is not linear, although acceptance usually signals the end of the grieving process. No two people will experience loss in the exact same way. Loss of a loved one is personal. And each of us copes with it in our own way.

You or someone you know may have initially reacted to the death of a loved one by saying, "I just can't believe she died." This is not a literal disbelief, but an indication that the grieving process is not complete, and the loss has not been emotionally integrated. The person is not yet ready to move on beyond the loss. Someone else may react angrily: "I will never forgive him for leaving me behind." You may know someone who responded to the imminent loss of a loved one by bargaining with God: "Please spare them, I will do anything you ask," or in the case of a parent facing the death of a child, "Please God, she is too young to die, please take me instead."

If you have lost a loved one, you may be intimately aware of the overwhelming sadness that seems like it will never lift. The profound grief renders you at least temporarily unable to consider how you will live on without your loved one. You withdraw, pulling back from the people and activities that filled a typical day. For some, this depression is so all-encompassing that they lose their own desire to continue living or begin to question the point of life. This is a question that often inspires someone to schedule a Life Between Lives session.

As you move toward acceptance of the loss, the emotional numbness begins to wear off. You reach the point when you realize that life must go on without your loved one, that you must finally accept that she or he will not return. What it takes to reach the point of acceptance is highly individual. Grief recovery entails discovering and completing what is unfinished for us in the relationship. Time alone does not heal; it is what you do within time that will help you heal the pain caused by loss.

Lack of Closure

With seventy-three-year-old Mayumi, we see the role that understanding and growing acceptance plays in coping with the loss of loved ones. She is an accomplished and well-known writer, herself on a spiritual path. Her popular metaphysical books have been translated into many languages. Through them she has induced readers around the world to look beyond their everyday, physical world. The death of two sons, Mathew and Tom, twelve years apart, left Mayumi emotionally devastated. Both situations were deeply wounding. The cause of their deaths and the fact that she had no opportunity to say goodbye intensified her grief. Mayumi has two other children—another son, Chris, and a daughter, Liz—but that fact did little to mitigate her sense of loss.

Recognizing the deep emotional scars left by the loss of her sons, Mayumi scheduled a Life Between Lives session. She hoped to gain an understanding of the higher purposes served by the untimely death of two of her sons.

During the Life Between Lives process, the practitioner first conducts a past-life regression in which Mayumi learns of her own early death at forty-two in a prior life. Mayumi identifies herself as Leonora Brewer Cuddahy. Born into high society, she lives within the constraints and social mores of her social class. She is stifled. She describes being surrounded constantly by servants who leave her feeling as if she cannot freely live her own life. She is trapped in an emotionally unsatisfying relationship with her husband, who is having an affair with another woman. His coldness and detachment are a constant contributor to her misery.

She sees herself at home standing in front of the fireplace in the front room of her Chicago apartment. She is alone, having just returned from a doctor's appointment in which she received news that she has cancer. When asked by the practitioner how she feels knowing that her cancer is terminal, she gives the following answer.

I'm relieved to know that I can get out of here. On the one hand I'm facing the reality of it, that I'm going to die, but the feeling that I'm going to get out of here is bigger than the other feeling. I don't know how long it will take me or if it will be horrible. But I'm happy. I'm happy to know that it's actually coming to an end. I have four children and a husband and I'm still happy it's coming to an end. I'm okay with that, and even then, for me, death is not an issue at all. And everybody else, I know they're all going to be freaked out and do some things about it, but not me. I don't care.

Her husband's behavior and treatment of her has been so horrible that it has left Mayumi believing that escaping the situation is the best outcome that can be expected.

I do have a feeling about my cancer. I do feel that I created it on some level, which again is okay, but the most important thing is the conclusion I come to on that day. If I just surrender and let everything be the way it's going to be, then it won't be so bad. Whereas, if I fight it, if I try to do something to fight it, it will be a terrible experience. So, I just decide. I don't care what anybody else has to say about it. I decide that I'm not going to fight this. And so, it's not so bad. It's a mess for everyone else. One of the reasons I want to get out of here is that the atmosphere in the house is just awful, and it's because of my husband. He's so bad that it's worth dying to just get out of here. I do feel a little bit of a tug because of the kids, but it's just so bad that I've got to get out of here.

Mayumi's reflections suggest a realistic acceptance of the actuality of her imminent death, while hinting that she is suppressing true feelings about the sadness of leaving her children behind. Perhaps indicating the maturity of her soul, she explains further.

The interesting thing is, now I know that what I know in this lifetime as Leonora, and what I know in my current lifetime as

Mayumi are connected. That's interesting. At this point in my
life as Leonora, when I would have really started to transform
myself and grow and develop as a person, but in that environ-
ment with my husband, it was going to just be a trap. So, since
it was going to be a trap, why not get out of it? Even with the
children, I still conclude that it's better to get out, and the rea-
son is because I needed to transform. I could feel the midlife
crisis thing, but there was no way I was going to be able to do
it, except for basically to blow the place up. There's no way I
was going to be able to do that.

Mayumi gleans insight into Leonora's emotional detachment when she describes being prevented from deep connection with her children. Given the family's social status, the children are sent to boarding schools, and even when they are home, they are in the care of their governess.

I wanted to spend a lot of time with them, but it wasn't
allowed, so with each of the children it became more and
more sad. And they also wanted to spend time with me, but it
wasn't allowed.

Mayumi's desire for a deeper connection with her children is palpable. Her life has lacked this deeply satisfying connection with her children. Denied it, she sees no reason to carry on. Lacking it, she does not have the will to live.

Mayumi describes the last day of her life as Leonora. She is pleased and grateful that the nurse caring for her honors her wishes and brings the children to visit Leonora one by one. With amazement, Mayumi explains that normally, given their time away at school, the children would not even know what had happened to her.

But because of the nurse's compassion, she can visit with each one, one more time, and say goodbye. This, she adds, is the problem she must come to terms with. In the current lifetime, she was not able to say goodbye to either of her boys.

During her Life Between Lives session, we learn that Mayumi has included in her soul's plan for this lifetime the opportunity for a deeply loving and satisfying relationship with her two sons. She considers her life enriched by the years they shared. This joy is matched with the incredible pain of their deaths. Not being able to say goodbye has prolonged her suffering and delayed her acceptance.

Early in her session, Mayumi encounters her spiritual guide.

> *He's got a big job, boy oh boy, an immense job. He is the one that is monitoring all these situations where people are ready to pass on, and he is making sure that the things that really need to happen regarding these situations do happen.*

Mayumi wants to know why she has lost two children, whom she dearly loved. The guide first focuses her attention on her son Mathew, and she is surprised to learn that at an intuitive level he knew that he would die.

Mayumi's difficulty accepting Mathew's death is exacerbated by the uncertainty around his death. The coroner could not conclude whether he died of a heart attack in a boat or whether he just fell out of the boat and drowned. This uncertainty would evaporate as her guide offered important details about Mathew's death that would help her find closure.

Mayumi learns from him that three weeks before he died, Mathew went to the emergency room for what presented as a severe digestive disturbance, noteworthy given his high pain tolerance developed as a mountain climber. The emergency room staff examined Mathew but sent him home without doing an electrocardiogram (EKG). The possibility that Mathew's death could have been prevented had an EKG been done made accepting his death more difficult. With her guide's help, she now sees that Mathew died of a heart attack.

As the session continues, Mayumi is reminded by her guide about a conversation that she had with Mathew a month before he died, an exchange made even more significant given its history. Despite Mayumi's prolific writing and publications, Mathew had never read any of Mayumi's work, telling her some years before that if he read her books, he would never be able to function on a logical level to complete his Ph.D. During this last conversation with Mathew, he shared that he had just finished reading her most successful metaphysical publication. Mayumi now came to see that Mathew's validation of her works and writings were his way of saying goodbye.

"Mom, you really do know what you're doing. I got it, and you do know what you're talking about."

Knowing how Mathew died provided Mayumi with solace. She hoped it would free her to move through her grief and reach acceptance about his death. Would she be so fortunate in her effort to come to terms with the death of her second son, Tom, at forty-one, twelve years earlier? Would her guide once again be able to lead her successfully to understanding and acceptance?

Despite being healthy, Tom's transition to independence had been difficult. He needed family support to find housing and employment. Despite his age, the family only learned that he was diagnosed with Asperger's syndrome right before he died. Despite Mayumi's repeated efforts from the time he was born, and over the next four decades, she was not able to fully connect with him. Her determination to make eye contact with him was based on her understanding that doing so was essential to engaging with and connecting to him emotionally.

Four months before he died, Tom looked at Mayumi with his beautiful, sapphire eyes for the very first time. With the gentle and loving assurance common to all spiritual helpers, her guide confirmed that this had been Tom's way of saying goodbye.

Mayumi and her family were horrified about the circumstances surrounding Tom's death. The pain of their loss was intensified by the many questions that remained unanswered. He was found hung in a tree, and it was believed by some that he had committed suicide. Because they were so distraught after hearing of his death, no one in the family went to identify the body. This added to their lingering uncertainty and disbelief.

Mayumi's guide shows her what happened.

Tom didn't hang himself. He was killed by three people who thought that he might have had some money in his back-pack. Tom just let the three kill him. Despite being strong and tough enough to have defended himself, Tom chose not to. He wanted to die. Tom didn't believe he was getting anywhere in life while struggling with his limitations.

This insight enables Mayumi to acknowledge that, in his own way, Tom basically did commit suicide, even though he didn't die at his own hand. The impact of the information Mayumi gleans about the loss of both of her sons is immediate and profound. While still hypnotized, she muses.

I'm in touch with them both, and as much as I'd like them to still be here with us, I now don't feel out of touch. I know that Tommy is still guarding us to some degree. I feel him in ways I did when he was alive and it's very comforting. Both Mathew and Tommy had simply finished what they came here to do.

With this understanding, Mayumi acknowledges an attitude shift with her surviving son and daughter, Chris and Liz. She now feels able to give them her full attention.

The first thing I did when Mathew and Tommy died was feel grateful for the time I had with them. It doesn't feel that way with Chris and Liz. It doesn't feel like I need to be grateful for the time I have left with them. Perhaps it is because intuitively I know that we will have many more years together. And that I feel like I'll be able to say goodbye to them.

Like for many others, the Life Between Lives experience continued to offer Mayumi insight and comfort well beyond the session's end. She shares her relief in a letter sent to her practitioner.

Good news! I think our work with Tom has freed him in some way. Suddenly he is coming to my husband and our daughter in dreams. Good work, his spirit is more untethered.

I am so pleased I was able to see that both the boys had said goodbye to me a few weeks before their deaths because their souls knew they were soon going. Recovering this memory of my last time with them is very healing, and knowing

more about the circumstances of their deaths makes it easier
to live with the pain.

Healing in the Aftermath of Suicide

In extreme cases, some people suffer for years or even decades before their grief is resolved. Such instances offer clues to possible unresolved emotional issues that prevent a person from reaching acceptance after the death of their loved one. The case of Evelyn is illustrative.

Evelyn, fifty-eight, comes for a Life Between Lives session seeking relief for chronic depression that she has suffered for more than forty years after the suicide of her sixteen-year-old twin brother, Sven. Unable to save Sven from their mother's abuse or from committing suicide, Evelyn fell into a profound depression. Their years of suffering childhood abuse played a major role in the strong emotional bond that prevents Evelyn from full acceptance of the loss. Despite her years of depression, Evelyn and her husband raised four children who, like their parents, have successful professional careers.

Over the four decades, Evelyn has reached a place of understanding and compassion about her mother's mistreatment of her brother and herself. What remains are her feelings about Sven. She has visions of his soul being stuck in a desperate, lost state. These visions trigger feelings of deep guilt.

During her session, Evelyn is released from death after an unspectacular past life. While crossing over into the afterlife, she experiences only darkness at first, almost blackness. Gradually, her surroundings begin to lighten.

Evelyn senses safety and warmth before her guide approaches. He tells her he has been with her forever and infuses her with strength and love.

He answers the questions Evelyn prepared for her session. She discovers her life purpose is giving and receiving as much love as possible, and that she is already fulfilling this purpose well. She learns that the pain she has experienced in this life has been for a purpose. In her past lives, Evelyn tended to be proud and stubborn. Her soul planned a life to overcome these tendencies, along with her propensity to see herself apart from others. Her guide congratulates her on dissolving her pride and developing humility and advises that she can heal further.

You can become joyful and happy in your life if you stop tak-
ing on problems, work, and responsibility for others; focus on
friendliness, benevolence, approval, acknowledgment. Your chil-
dren can take over their own responsibilities as adults.

The focus within the Life Between Lives session shifts to the questions Evelyn has regarding Sven's suicide. When her guide affirms that the possibility of suicide was understood before Sven and she incarnated, Evelyn collapses into heartbroken crying. For her, this idea is intolerable, and she angrily starts defying her guide.

Evelyn angrily shouts the following.

He was pried from me abruptly without any forewarning.
Why? Our soul connection was ruptured! I want him back!

Within minutes, Evelyn senses Sven holding her in his arms. Begging, she cries out to him.

Stay with me now, don't leave me! We are united again.
Together we are whole and now I am going to swallow him, so
he will stay with me. We are now joined in a beautiful round
circle. He shall stay with me.
*   He says it was too terrible down here. He couldn't stand it*
any longer. I was not the cause and I was not involved. I have
nothing to do with his suicide.

Evelyn is bereft upon learning that Sven has incarnated again in another location on earth, far from her. He is fine, married with two daughters.

Evelyn is angered by the practitioner's suggestion that she ask Sven to visit with her from time to time.

No, I won't ask that. He shall stay with me. He shall stay,
please stay! He asks me now why he is so important for me.
What a stupid question!

Cowering together under their mother's lash, Evelyn formed a tight bond with Sven. When he died, she was shocked and isolated, harboring a simmering anger. Unresolved, it has prevented her from reaching acceptance despite the long passage of time. Even now, hearing from him, she cannot accept that he had his way of coping with their mother's mistreatment and that in choosing to kill himself he was exercising his free will.

> *He doesn't want to stay. He wants to go his own way. We only had each other. Wasn't I important to him?*

Sven tells Evelyn that she will have to wait until they are reunited on the spiritual plane to reconnect with him on a regular basis.

> *He says that it's not possible for him to stay, but that he is leaving a tiny bit of himself with me. He asks why I cry so much for him. You dimwit! You know that. Dimwit! How can one be so dumb? He knows how much I miss him! He denies this and doesn't want me to miss him so much.*

Evelyn is not willing to immediately relinquish her need for Sven and let him pursue his own desires, which is evident as she tries to assert her wishes over his. It seems she retains some remnants of stubbornness. Having an abusive mother who was unable to express love and kindness bound her to Sven emotionally. Her soul set up the difficult circumstances of her childhood to test her. At this stage, she is still using Sven to fill her childhood need for love.

In her interaction with her practitioner, Evelyn reflects on the shock of losing him so abruptly. Understandably, she was furious at the time. Evelyn sees how the anger and guilt that she let fester for four decades has contributed to her depression. She now sees that he had become a substitute for the parental love she did not receive. Losing him, losing his love, left her with a void that no one else could fill, and with unresolved emotions that eventually brought her to her Life Between Lives session. Resolving these emotions is key to Evelyn's acceptance.

Evelyn acknowledges that if she truly loves Sven, she will let him be free, and that he must do what is best for himself. She is ready to shift from neediness and anger to love and acceptance and to be in touch with her true self, a loving and compassionate woman.

> *He deserves all his happiness. I am happy that he has such a good life with a loving family and that he is moving forward with his development. Now I can let him go.*

The session closes with her guide helping Evelyn immerse into the light, which he tells her is her soul's ultimate purpose.

Evelyn expresses both gratitude and joy in a note to her practitioner a few days after the session.

> *The session has helped me incredibly. I can only say that there has been a huge release. I can hardly describe this change. Finally, I am journeying through life with light baggage. I am serene and cheerful, and life is easy. I owe that to you and to your wonderful work.*

As the months pass following the Life Between Lives session, Evelyn's reflections underscore the growing value of her experience.

> *I now have a completely different sense of life and feel so much better than before. I am often in touch with my guide, receiving signals from him and experiencing our communication as playful. I am getting to know and to love myself as a very special person. Each day, I am finding new aspects of myself, and accepting myself lovingly as the person I am.*

Loving After Loss

As difficult and paradoxical as it may seem, losing a loved one creates opportunities for spiritual growth for the soul to accomplish goals set for a lifetime. The death of Barbara's grandparents in a car accident and her mother later that same year when Barbara was only ten years old shaped her beliefs and expectations regarding the risk of having an open heart. She scheduled her Life Between Lives session with the hope of better understanding her current situation, including her intense feelings of loneliness and emotional detachment despite her marriage to Richard. When asked about her marriage, Barbara said she had one foot out the door.

As Barbara dies in her past life and enters the afterlife, she is met by her guide, who places his hand over her heart. She is stunned by the intense burning in and around her heart as he places his hand over it. His energetic healing is accompanied by an explanation of why she experienced so much loss early in her life.

> *I chose to have my heart broken early in life. I wanted to understand unconditional love more deeply. A broken heart can open the heart. For hearts to truly be open, there must be compassion. Hearts must be broken on the earth plane.*
>
> *My mother and grandparents agreed to play these important roles in my life. My grandmother had such a pure heart. She was so loving. She was a role model for loving unconditionally. Losing them broke my heart. This great loss set the stage for me to grow to understand love and compassion.*

Barbara tearfully shares what she is learning from her guide.

> *He is pointing out that there was a risk with this strategy. It was risky because there is a lot of fear that came with it. In fact, there was the possibility that I would become so fearful that I might not get the deep lesson I was wanting.*
>
> *He says that I am aware that the fear can block me and that I also have an awareness of the fear that was blocking me. I fear more loss. I fear life. After all that loss, I wanted to keep closed.*

Although the message is painful, through her guide's healing and sharing, Barbara has come to understand the tough lesson that she embedded in her life plan.

> *The fear causes you to want to close yourself off, but you must be open. It's a tough lesson. But understanding this will help*

you cope with loss in the future without shutting yourself off from the joy of an open heart.

Intensifying the healing that has already taken place, Barbara's mother joins her, and she is overwhelmed with emotion.

My mother is so beautiful now! She wants me to look after my brothers. She is concerned that they are not connected. They are not connected with their spiritual souls in the way I am. She is reminding me that although I might get caught up in the busyness of life, she would like me to look out for them. She thinks I am doing fine. She is telling me that it was hard to leave us all, but that it was important.

Prompted by her practitioner's questions about the impact of her mother's death on other family members, Barbara conveys what she has come to understand through the session.

Each of us has our own lessons. I feel like my twin brother is with me right now. He is showing me his family. His two boys are also twins; they are identical. My brother's lesson is about family, but it is different than mine. It is something about not having a family and having a family. He is a loner. He likes to be alone a lot. Despite this, he planned to be my twin so that he would not be alone in our family. His life plan includes what seems to be different aspects; being married, having a family, yet being a loner. I don't really understand what I am being shown. The guide is indicating that the details about my brother's plan are very private. It is not really for me to understand.

In a somewhat whimsical segue, her guide now appears dressed as a warrior to escort Barbara into an ancient Greek temple. Somewhat bewildered, she relays her experience as she enters the temple on her own.

There are all these rooms. This is crazy! I just keep going and going through the rooms. People keep pointing. I keep meeting different beings. One being after another, and each points in another direction. They just lead me to another room, and there is another being that points me to another room, and then another one points to another room! I finally go up to the roof. There is someone resembling a Native American chief there. He is the one I am supposed to meet.

Barbara begins to cry as she elaborates.

It took forever to reach him because of my tendency to always doubt myself. I am always telling myself "that's not it, that's not it, that's not it." Self-doubt has held me back.

As they walk together on the beach, the chief sheds light on Barbara's sense that there is something missing in her marriage and on her indecision about how to resolve this feeling. She finds it uncomfortable to confront these truths but understands that the chief's admonishments are offered with unconditional love and acceptance.

He says that my focus is off. One of my setbacks is that I focus on what I am lacking more than what I have. The amount of loss I have experienced can have that effect. He is telling me that I am not as lonely as I think I am, that I have a rich life and a rich relationship. I am just seeing it through a sort of filter.

The chief is emphasizing that it is my choice. Every day I make that choice. Each day I decide how I want to see it. He is telling me that I need to look carefully at what is there. He's repeating this to underscore his point. I need to focus on what is there, rather than what I wish was there. I might be surprised when I do! The chief is reminding me that my soul's plan included everything I would need.

To anchor the insight Barbara has gained, her practitioner closes with a reminder for her to allow the chief's words, his wisdom, and his love into the depths of her being, encouraging her to let it redirect her focus and clear up some of her misunderstandings.

If she can overcome her fear of loss, Barbara will find that both her loving relationships and her life are enriched. The wisdom and love that she has experienced in her Life Between Lives session will serve as a guiding light as she works to integrate these lessons into the future choices she makes.

Losing the Love of Your Life

Go-Gi introduces us to another soul plan that includes loss of a loved one. She is a beautiful twenty-eight-year-old who immigrated to another country as a child. Her close-knit family eased the suffering of a debilitating health condition that limited her ability to walk and even move at various points earlier in life.

A self-described deep thinker who is very private, she found Jeffrey, someone she wanted to share everything with. With him by her side, Go-Gi felt she could meet any challenge in life. But their plans for a future together were shattered when Jeffrey died unexpectedly. Go-Gi became so depressed. Losing Jeffrey left Go-Gi with no interest in life. Devastated by the loss of the love of her life, she contemplated suicide. She scheduled her Life Between Lives session with the hope of understanding why her time with Jeffrey was cut short.

Upon entering the afterlife, she encounters her spirit guide who has worked with her over many lifetimes. Go-Gi discovers that she is meant to learn how to give without expecting anything in return.

> *The love that you and Jeffrey shared was deep and beautiful.*
> *Your souls experience that love even more intensely, way more*
> *than you were able to in human form.*

Like many others who have lost a beloved loved one, Go-Gi hopes to connect with Jeffrey. She learns that with time and patience this could be possible.

> *I can find him through things that I do selflessly for others,*
> *remembering and completing what we have started together.*
> *I can do what he did and help people and be there for anybody*
> *that I can be of help to. From this flows a connecting cord.*

I can feel it now. I can learn how to live without his physical presence.

Go-Gi learns that the brevity of her relationship with Jeffrey was built into her soul plan.

We did plan it, but it was not to cause suffering. I volunteered to go through it, to be with him. The lessons and experiences were primarily for him. My lessons were indirect.

I helped him to get his life together. I helped him better himself and complete something important with one member of his family. Jeffrey's turnaround strengthened his connection to his family. They had more respect for him than ever before, and that was what was important. In the end, it was natural for me to suffer, given my deep love for him. But it was a sacrifice I willingly made because of our deep and abiding love.

As the exchange continues, her guide acknowledges with a note of admiration that coping with Jeffrey's death was a lot harder than Go-Gi imagined when she agreed to assume this vital role in Jeffrey's soul plan. Expressing both optimism and encouragement, he adds that something on the horizon will help Go-Gi get through it.

While these insights cannot bring Jeffrey back, the joy that she taps into during her Life Between Lives session helps Go-Gi regain emotional balance and calm. Even lacking clarity about what the future holds, Go-Gi finds peace connecting to the depth of her love for Jeffrey, a bond that she now understands transcends time and lifetimes. Realizing that her soul has crafted a plan for this lifetime gives her the resolve to move forward in life, open to undefined potentialities and possibilities. She offers the following understanding.

When we are on earth, we are not meant to suffer pointlessly. We don't just suffer forever and then it all comes to an end. Good things happen again. Jeffrey and I will be back together again, but there are important things that first need to be accomplished. I need to remain focused on that and complete

what I came to accomplish in this lifetime. When I am ready
and complete, I can see him again.

Many people respond to the loss of loved ones through coping mechanisms that seem effective, but that ultimately do not serve them well. For example, isolation, overworking, or compulsive spending can be comforting and distracting at first, but do not help us move through our grief. Overcoming grief, for many, includes remembering the simple pleasures and joys of everyday life and seeing the possibilities and promise for joy and happiness that lie ahead. While the loved one is never forgotten, for most people, the searing pain of loss subsides over time and is replaced by the comforting memories of the shared love. For some, the power of a Life Between Lives session helps ease the loss, enabling them to find hope for a more promising future.

The death of a loved one, or the end of a loving relationship, is an intensely emotional time. It is a period of upheaval that is highly personal, and which progresses you through a range of emotions. As you proceed, you may experience temporary relief. But, because the path is not linear, you may find yourself in a spiral of emotions. Feeling good one day and unable to function or control your emotions on the next.

How you cope reflects both your prior experience with loss and the beliefs that you hold. There is no countdown clock on this process. It too is highly personal. You will know you have finished grieving when you have fully accepted the reality of your loss, when you resume your usual day-to-day routines, and when you begin to plan for a future that no longer includes your loved one.

Those who believe that "love never dies" retain a connection to the lost loved one that offers comfort, while someone who believes that the death or separation represents an abandonment is more likely to struggle. Belief shapes your expectation, which in turn influences your reaction.

Mayumi, Evelyn, Barbara, and Go-Gi held different beliefs about their loss, and each coped in their own way. What they all share is the decision to schedule a Life Between Lives session to heal and to bring closure. Perhaps a personal loss has led you to this book or other books from the Michael Newton Institute. Perhaps, like them, you are seeking to put your loss of a loved one into a broader context. Through each of their stories, we have felt the searing pain that accompanies the loss of a loved one.

For both Mayumi and Evelyn, long-festering grief was eased through the wisdom gleaned during Life Between Lives sessions. Both found closure and acceptance in the insight and understanding the sessions provided. Each in their own way and at their own pace eventually moved through the natural phases of grief. Each reached acceptance aided by the higher wisdom they received about the devastating loss they had endured.

In her Life Between Lives session, the lessons Barbara gleaned allowed her to make sense of the losses that she experienced as a young child and to shed light on coping mechanisms that had outlived their usefulness. The experience empowered her to reshape her beliefs and begin to make new choices. With Go-Gi, loss led her to realize that she had agreed to endure the pain of loss to play an important role in her beloved's soul plan.

Through their losses, all four affirmed their capacity for love and connection with their heart. Each of them experienced love in a way that enriched their lives even though the loss of love robbed them of some of life's joy.

Through their sessions, each of them learned that loving another affords the soul the opportunity to accomplish its purpose, whether it be to learn, to heal, to balance, or to serve. They were able to open their hearts and to take down the barriers that they had erected to protect themselves from further pain. And each of them came to understand the importance of love for their soul's growth and understanding.

Four

NAVIGATING ROMANTIC RELATIONSHIPS

For some people, walking into a new relationship is like walking into a minefield. We don't know what is ahead, so some of us wear armor to protect ourselves.

Our heart can sing with joy when we are together, but when we are alone the fears can crowd in. Does our lover feel the way we do? Could we be dumped? Will our love last?

If we get through our initial fears and stay together, another danger is familiarity and tedium. The highs of a relationship can dwindle down into apathy caused by petty arguments, unmet needs, and misunderstandings.

Some arguments are explosive and damage our trust in each other. Recurring trivial arguments take their toll, while we become more entrenched in reacting to our partner in the same ineffective way. We can become resentful and miss opportunities to appreciate our partner.

We all want to successfully navigate any tumultuous emotions of our romantic relationships. In this chapter, we explore cases that illustrate the pitfalls of mistaking infatuation for love, being too attached or too detached, confronting soul contracts, and dealing with frequent conflict.

We discover how these traps can be resolved. We learn how we grow by understanding our history, our fears, our self-judgments, and our purpose, and by connecting with our eternal self. Learning how to navigate our romantic relationships is important to the growth of our soul.

What Is Love?

Defining love can be difficult. There are so many mixed messages about love in our world, no wonder many people are confused. When we feel great desire and passion, we are likely to assume we are in love. This love is thrilling and exciting and we feel we cannot do without our new lover. But our happiness comes with a downside. Fear. We don't want to lose our newfound happiness. We want reassurance that our lover will not let us down or desert us. Intense feelings place a great strain on a relationship, especially if we think this is "the one."

But are such intense feelings really love anyway? Research tells us that this honeymoon period only lasts up to a year or two at best. What comes after is the real test.

Many young people believe desire and passion is the beginning of a long-term relationship, but older people can become confused too, especially if they are newly single and back on the dating scene.

The Difference Between Love and Infatuation

Sharon, age sixty-nine, enjoyed a long and happy marriage before her husband died from a prolonged illness. There were no children of the marriage, and after a few years of widowhood, she felt lonely. She started dating, hoping to again share her life with someone.

These new relationships were exciting to begin with, but further interaction with the people she dated didn't go so well, and the relationships ended. The emotional ups and downs soon became draining. While she is now dating someone new, she is concerned that this relationship too might take the same course and end in disappointment.

She really wants a stable, lasting relationship with a suitable person that can give her a sense of contentment. She comes for a session seeking guidance on how to achieve that.

During the session, Sharon is taken back to a past life in eighteenth-century England.

> *I'm a male and it's daytime. I'm walking in the countryside and it looks like something out of a Thomas Hardy novel. My name is Jonathan and I'm sixteen. I'm feeling on top of the world. Tonight, I will be taking my special girl to the May dance. She's beautiful with blonde hair and blue eyes. We're in love. She's fifteen and we've been talking about getting married. Her parents don't think I'm good enough for her and my parents think we are too young. My father tells me I would have no way to support a wife at this time. But we will find a way.*

In the next scene, Jonathan walks his girl to the May dance. He is so happy he can hardly contain his joy.

> *We dance the first dance. Everyone is looking at her because she is so beautiful. But before I know it, she is surrounded by other boys and I can't even get close. She keeps dancing with various guys, and I don't get another chance. Well, we'll make up for it when I walk her home.*

Unfortunately, it doesn't work out the way Jonathan expects. Without even giving him a second thought, his special girl lets another boy walk her home. In addition to being shocked and deeply disappointed, his heart is broken.

Jonathan continues to live at home with his parents. He gives up his interest in girls, instead working hard on the farm, helping his father. When he turns twenty-two, his father gives him some land of his own.

Over the next few years, he successfully farms his plot of land until he is in a good financial position. He could now afford to get married, but he is wary and still doesn't trust women much. But he is not lonely, having relatives in the district who keep him company.

I go with a friend to visit a cousin in a village, not far from where we live. That's where I meet Mary. She's very pretty and serious, and I find myself drawn to her. It's not like it was before. I'm not so deliriously happy, but it still feels good.

Jonathan ends up marrying Mary and they have three children, two boys and a girl. Together they work hard, making a good living. Their life with each other is harmonious and filled with contentment.

In old age, Jonathan dies peacefully, rejoining the soul that he shares with Sharon.

Sharon reflects on the lessons from Jonathan's life. In his teens, he suffered the extreme highs and lows of a relationship. Feeling deeply let down by his first love, he shied away from women. But over time he matured and found a more substantial love in Mary.

Sharon is given advice from her guides, relevant to anyone hoping for a long-lasting relationship of love and contentment.

The message is that happiness is fleeting, but contentment lasts. Happiness is ephemeral and can come and go. Understanding is more important than happiness and makes for a better life. So, seek contentment in life. Find a mate who understands you and is willing to work with you to make a good life.

Life doesn't always work out as you plan at first, but if you are patient and do your own work, you can find contentment. Lay the groundwork. Happiness is like a drug; it is addictive because it feels so good in an intense and fervent way.

Sharon asks her guides how to temper the drug of happiness into the permanence of contentment.

Be aware of the fleetingness of happiness. It is like watching fireflies on a summer's night. They glow brightly for a while and then die. In contrast, contentment is like starlight, always beautiful but also permanent. Do the work. Lay the groundwork. It is not easy, but it is worth it.

Sharon realizes the man she is currently dating has the potential to be a suitable match. Together, they can develop a comfortable relationship with each other. She recalls how the early happiness and excitement of her marriage matured into the peaceful pleasure she had with her husband. The years following the death of her husband were difficult, but now she sees the possibility of a contented life once again.

Two years later, the practitioner catches up with her and discovers that Sharon did marry the person she had been dating. Even though she has the usual ups and downs that life entails, Sharon reports feeling contented with her marriage and her life.

Passion is celebrated in our culture, but passion is rarely an enduring love. As Sharon discovers, high emotion can turn into a contented, loving relationship, but it can also fizzle out if we don't make the necessary adjustments to our expectations. Sharon is a good example of someone who did this and did it well. She worked out what she really wanted with her feet firmly on the ground. She utilized the experience of her past life and her first marriage to create the contented relationship she desired.

Balancing Attachment

Some people are so attached to those they love that they cannot live without them. Others can be out of balance in the opposite direction, being so absorbed in their own needs and projects that they are neglectful of their partner's needs. How do we balance our love for others with our love for ourselves? The next case gives us examples of these two extremes, showing us the importance of eventually getting this balance right.

Oliver, forty-two, has been with his partner, Glenda, for over a decade. During his session he is taken to a past life where he is Martha, a widow and pioneer. Her only child is a teenage son who shares the same soul as Oliver's current life partner, Glenda.

Martha is part of a tribe who recently left the oppression of their homeland. They travel, eventually finding a place to settle. The elders choose Martha's son to go and make peace with their neighbors. Her son returns, thinking he has done well after taking part in some rituals with the neighbors. But he is mistaken. He has been poisoned and soon becomes ill and dies.

Martha is distraught. She blames herself for encouraging him to go.

I had a big vision for my son, seeing him as a leader of our community one day. Not only am I losing him, but we are all losing him and the potential he had. I am having a lot of trouble forgiving myself for not foreseeing what could happen.

Losing my son is an inconsolable grief. I have nothing left. I cannot find a way of seeing anything good, just hopelessness. Every day is a prison of suffering and I am waiting to die. I was angry but now I am resigned. Despair fills every fiber of my being and I am not interested in eating or drinking.

The community decides to move on and Martha leaves with them, lying in a wagon, gravely ill.

During the night while everyone is sleeping, I drift off to sleep. I get a sense of looking down and seeing everyone—like a bird looking below. Even through the dark, I can see clearly.

Suddenly, I am not thirsty. I think I am dreaming that I can fly. Now I want to fly higher. And there is some hope in the dream because, as a bird, I can go anywhere. I am enjoying it. I don't realize it's not a dream. Somehow, in this dream, a weight is dropping. The embrace of that hurt, regret, and guilt is loosening. I have been experiencing all that hurt, but it is not all I am. Now I am floating so high I cannot make out where I came from. But I feel less worried. I am letting go. Now I am getting the feeling of reassurance that everything will be okay. I am surprised because I cannot understand any reason for this positive feeling, but I am feeling it. I am above the horrible feelings. I am aware of joy again. It is a sense of love. Wow!

Martha doesn't yet realize it, but she is already in her life between lives, having passed over in a most gentle way.

I think it is a dream. My son appears, and he is reaching out to hug me. I feel his love. I have an overwhelming sense of forgiveness. He is okay. Another part of me thinks he is dead, but

I feel the most loving moment ever with him. So much love. I so needed it. Amazing! He tells me there is nothing to worry about, that everything is okay.

I am now getting the idea that I am not alive anymore. I have remembered how sick I was when I fell asleep and he confirms that I have died.

He thanks me for being his mom. Ah! Wow! I am now seeing his life through his eyes, and how much he loved me, no matter what I said or did. He is proud of me and everything was perfect from his point of view. I just got to feel it from his heart. [sobbing]

He is telling me I have done well. I wouldn't have accepted that until this moment now, seeing it from his perspective. We did well and can rejoice in the life we had. I am honoring the love I had for my son, not the results. My intention was loving.

We need the challenges to prove we are being true to ourselves. Even when my son didn't like what I did—for example, restricting him—he can see that my intention was love. He gets to see this from my perspective. No action can devalue how magnificent we truly are.

Oliver remembers a recent interaction between Glenda and him.

Glenda has been sick for a while because of something I did. She visited friends in another state. While she was away, instead of doing the dishes and organizing the place, I ignored it. She specifically asked if she could come back to an empty sink, but there was a double stack of dishes in the sink when she returned. I was focused on other priorities that I value, such as property and research.

Oliver recalls his life when he was young. His mother remarried when he was four. His stepfather didn't accept him, so he lived with his grandmother, a loving and caring woman. She did everything around the house, so he developed a pattern of ignoring chores. After Glenda returned from her trip, she washed all the dishes.

It was a big job. It smelled. I felt bad because I had forgotten to do them. A few days after that, she became unwell. She got so weak she couldn't stand up. She was in some sort of septic shock and ended up in intensive care. She had golden staph in her bloodstream and they looked for a source. Her thumb on her left hand was red, and part of her thumb had to be amputated.

Although no one knows the exact cause of Glenda's life-threatening condition, Oliver feels guilty. After the session, he reflects on his life as Martha and how much love was between Martha and her son. In that life, Martha was so attached to her son she could not go on without him. In his current life, Oliver was not attached enough, instead focusing on his own needs. He had forgotten how important Glenda was to him.

Up until the point of her illness, I had taken Glenda for granted.

Oliver understands that it is pointless to take on guilt for results that are unforeseeable. He did not cause the amputation of Glenda's thumb. But he did let her down by not doing the dishes, especially when she made a specific request.

We never know when disaster will strike, and Oliver is fortunate that the outcome of Glenda's illness was not worse. He resolves to be more mindful and not take his loved ones for granted in future.

Oliver is on a journey of refinement. He is learning how to refine the balance between his needs and the needs of others. His past life and his current life are useful guides, helping him to balance these competing needs.

Fulfilling Soul Contracts

Some people stay married even when the relationship is far from ideal. Friends and relatives often wonder why. Although many of us will leave these challenging relationships, there is a reason why some couples stay together. Something deeper is going on here, as the following case demonstrates.

Gracie comes for a Life Between Lives session to receive guidance about her marriage to Ian. She feels she has limited time on earth and she doesn't want to waste it. She feels she has much to do and that her husband is holding her back. One source of conflict is the impact of Ian's business on their relationship. Although Gracie loves her husband, she is considering leaving the marriage. She feels sad as she grapples with this decision.

> *I seek understanding of my purpose in this life. I feel at a mid-life crossroads. I have been in service to others for much of my adult life, to my children, my husband, and a family business. I am not sure what it is I am supposed to do as the REAL ME. I am craving creative expression and a more authentic emotional life.*

During the regression, Gracie learns her soul name is Kasha and her soul purpose is to help others remember their true eternal self. Her first step in her life as Gracie is to remember who she is. Her guide says this can be difficult for Kasha, when incarnated, as she can easily forget. This happens because she often has low energy in her lives. The guide explains why.

> *One of the difficulties for Kasha is that she incarnates more than once at the same time. Not all souls do this, but it is not uncommon. Splitting her energy is part of her path and her growth. It means she does not always have a lot of energy as a physical body and that means she can be distracted from her spiritual path.*
>
> *Kasha has developed some human blocks that also contribute to this low energy. She is an old soul and old souls are loving and caring. Knowing others suffer is hard for these old souls because their last lessons are to let others be. This means "being" rather than "doing." This is a lesson that Kasha has been trying to complete for several lives. She forgets that souls only suffer because it is their path, and part of their lessons. Souls only feel hurt, believing it is awful, if they are resisting their path or their lessons.*
>
> *Kasha seeks opportunities to be loved for doing. Generally, her actions are positive, but this does not help her achieve her last lesson, which is understanding that we are loved just for*

being. This is hard to accept. In her life as Gracie, she has a strong will and sense of physical existence.

A need to serve indicates a lack of confidence of the soul itself, which doesn't realize that just "being" is enough to be loved. Such souls tend to define themselves by the help they give to others.

Also, she left a lot of her energy with her soul companions when she incarnated in these last few lives, which leaves her with less incarnated energy. She has a sense of dislocation, which will persist until she remembers and finds a way to connect to her higher self.

As Gracie, she is never going to be a highly energetic human, but she could have more energy than she has now by seeking alternative healing.

After receiving this information, Kasha is ready to move on. She visits her soul group and sees the soul of Ian. She is told they have had many incarnations together. The guide explains the importance of their relationship.

In this lifetime as Gracie and Ian, there is a soul agreement. They agreed to help each other remember and wake up. Gracie has awakened enough to realize she has a path she is supposed to follow, and that Ian is supposed to come with her. But she didn't know it was an agreement. Ian is remembering now, but of course he has free will.

The business is an extension of the human persona that Ian has created. His soul is a large energy and he tends to take up a lot of space in life, feeling quite passionate about things. In this incarnation, he has a sense of wanting to make things better on earth. That is what the business represents for him. During this awakening, he is having difficulty recognizing that his achievements at the business level are done. If he is to fulfill his agreement with Gracie, he needs to step away from letting the business dominate his attention. Ian is stuck right now, which is part of his path. He needs to work through his own stuff. That is his responsibility.

Gracie has a sense of time passing in her life, thinking, perhaps, there are other ways she could serve, learn, and progress as a soul. She is allowing herself to feel held back, and so she is struggling with what to do.

Fear is playing a role for both. Gracie has some fear about confidently following her internal compass. Ian has some fear about giving up the persona he has developed in this incarnation. They both are a bit off track, but not irrevocably. They can find their way back and fulfill their agreement.

Gracie has questions about why her relationship with Ian is somewhat non-sexual on her part. Sexual energy with Ian in this life is not the point of their relationship, as it would detract energy away from their intended purpose and agreement. Fulfilling their purpose means that some other aspects of being human are just less important.

The practitioner asks Kasha's guide about the business itself, as it is part of the conflict between Ian and Gracie.

This is difficult for Kasha as Gracie. She will need to sort it out for herself. I suggest she remember and follow the soul agreement she made, as well as charting her own path. Souls who have an agreement still have their own path as well as their path together. Gracie and Ian have already completed a certain amount of their agreement. They do not know what is to come and they are not to know that yet. They need to struggle through what they are trying to learn.

Gracie needs to remember her own path and perhaps be less focused on what she thinks Ian should do in his life. Pulling back might help Ian find his way.

Throughout the session, Kasha's guide emphasizes the importance of the agreement between Gracie and Ian, even though they do not yet know the complete agreement apart from it having something to do with waking each other up to knowing their true selves. Kasha is told she is on her last earth lesson, which is learning how to *be* rather than *do*. While the guide acknowledges her difficulty of letting go of her do-good behavior, he lets her know that helping others by "doing" is no longer her purpose. In this vein, Gracie is also counseled to pull back from focusing on what she wants Ian to do and focus on herself.

At the end of her session, Gracie is a little reluctant to return to her human state after enjoying the security of being in her life between lives.

> *This sense of infinite space and energy that I am a part of is what I want to take back to earth with me. The vastness and connection to All That Is. That remembrance will help me fulfill my purpose.*

Kasha, as Gracie, has free will. She could still leave her husband if she wanted, and yet her guidance clearly suggests she stay. She has habits to break, namely her drive to be actively of service to others and her negative focus on her husband's slower pace. He has habits to break too, including his identity and much of his time being caught up in his business. For each of them, fulfilling their purpose involves finding a genuine peace within themselves and with each other.

A soul agreement is sacred. Souls always want to fulfill their agreements but, when they are in a physical body, they can easily put their contracts aside and become caught up in their usual ways of behaving.

Waking up to knowing our true self is a noble purpose. Many people have this purpose. When we know who we truly are, we need do nothing except follow our inner guidance. Our service to others is not driven by any need. We have no needs when we feel complete. Our service to others comes from our heart and is organic and natural, fueled only by unconditional love.

A Pattern of Conflict

Iris, twenty-eight, is a lively blonde. Iris describes her marriage as "on the brink." Iris and her husband, Gabriel, live with their beautiful three-year-old daughter. Both wish to save their marriage, and yet they cannot seem to stop fighting.

Gabriel often criticizes Iris, and Iris feels blamed and guilty. She becomes angry and defensive, snapping at her husband. Gabriel then passively retreats. His withdrawal creates panic in Iris, and she expresses her fear by losing her temper. Soon after spiraling into this argumentative pattern, they both feel bruised, and they shut down emotionally to each other.

Before the Life Between Lives session, the practitioner had already conducted several past-life regressions with Iris who goes easily into trance. Before reaching her life between lives, Iris experiences a significant past life in which she and Gabriel are brothers living in Germany. Iris is Emil, an eighteen-year-old young man and Gabriel is Gerhard, his older brother of twenty-two. In this scene, they are celebrating Gerhard's engagement to a beautiful, young blonde woman.

The brothers are standing in a lush garden in front of a house in countryside Bavaria. It is summertime and they are surrounded by ripe raspberries, roses, and other vibrant flowers. Laughter wafts from the house as the brothers quietly sense the significance of this day. Their parents died nearly a decade ago in an accident. Since then, Gerhard has looked after his younger brother, Emil.

Gerhard is like a father to me. We are very close.

The practitioner moves Iris to another scene, discovering Emil and Gerhard are now soldiers in World War II. They are beside each other in a trench, shooting at the enemy.

Suddenly, Gerhard recoils and collapses. Emil continues shooting until he realizes Gerhard is still. Emil drops his gun and throws himself on top of his brother's body, trying to protect him from enemy fire. But it is too late. The wound in Gerhard's chest is bleeding heavily. Emil cannot accept that the wound is mortal. All the sounds of the battle recede as Emil lovingly holds his brother in his arms. There is nothing else he can do. While still being held by Emil, Gerhard dies.

Iris is shaking uncontrollably.

Gerhard is Gabriel! Oh my God! I am so upset! This is such a surprise! Oh my God, this is terrible!

Iris is sobbing.

> *It all went so fast! I can't believe this. Why did they kill him*
> *and not me? Why did I survive? They should have shot me!*

The practitioner pauses, giving Iris, as Emil, plenty of time to take in the disturbing realization that Gerhard is gone. Gradually Iris calms down.

The practitioner moves Iris to the end of Emil's short life and discovers Emil never came to terms with the loss of his brother.

> *I die thinking of Gerhard. I miss him so much. I still feel so*
> *guilty that he was killed and I didn't save him.*

Rising over his body, Emil pledges to make up for his brother's death.

> *I promise myself to be stronger next time and help Gerhard*
> *stay.*

Emil's soul moves quickly up into the realms of Spirit.

> *There are no limits, I am moving up as fast as I can. I am fly-*
> *ing through darkness and space. Now I start to see many stars,*
> *many lights. Oh! These are clumps of souls. I feel such joy! I*
> *am home.*

Tears of joy are streaming down Iris's face.

> *I feel drawn toward a huge bright light.*

The light is her guide, who appears as a long, tall female being. The guide shows her scenes from the past life and Iris, as Emil, again feels the grief and guilt.

> *I can see various scenes. I see that life passing by and am feel-*
> *ing so bad about Gerhard.*

My guide tells me it was not my fault my brother died or my task to save him. She says I must understand that. Iris sighs and the practitioner feels a shift in Iris's expression and body. The practitioner asks where her guide is now taking her.

I am going to a circle of friends.

About twenty souls greet her, but one is particularly relevant to the past life and her current life.

> *It is Gabriel. He tells me that I need to learn to trust. I must learn to trust life and to trust him. And I need to face my anger! When I am feeling guilty, I become angry and out of control. Gabriel says I must trust that he is here with me and he will be staying here this lifetime. He is not leaving. My anger comes from my guilt, the guilt I felt in the life we lived as brothers. The guilt drives a deep wedge between us in our current life.*

This is a moment of profound understanding for Iris. She looks deeply moved. After a pause, her guide now takes Iris to her council of elders.

> *We are flowing through space before walking down a long path, shimmering and sparkling gold. I feel humbled.*

She arrives at a place like a Roman temple. Entering, she is in a large bright hall with twelve elders sitting in a semicircle. Iris is very emotional.

> *I have been here many times before. They all are wearing deep purple robes with medallions. The most advanced being is the male in the middle. He is leading all the communication.*
>
> *He says they are making me aware of my anger. I have experienced anger in many other lives. This lifetime I have the chance to do it differently. He explains the similarities of my lifetime as Emil to other lives I've lived before. This life is the life to clear it up.*

Iris is crying softly.

> *I am so amazed about being here. I am so relieved to understand my lesson. I can see how our past lives lead up to our present life experiences. I now have hope that our marriage can work out.*

The council gives her encouragement, suggesting she can find solutions and inner peace within her marriage. Understanding the reason for her anger and reactivity gives her choices. They encourage her to face her anger and to develop more trust. Anger has been her main emotional response in many lifetimes. Iris returns to the present, bringing new hope and understanding with her.

Shortly after her session, Iris reports there have been changes in her marriage and in herself. She is taking steps to change her behavior, enrolling in various classes for self-development.

Gabriel and Iris understand their differences from a new perspective. They learn to be more compassionate with each other and stop fighting. As Iris releases her guilt, her anger subsides.

Nine years later, Iris and Gabriel's marriage is full of trust and harmony. Their daughter has grown into a smart and talented teenager. Iris reports that she still has a vivid memory of her Life Between Lives session, which she describes as one of the most profound experiences of her life.

As Emil died, he made a vow to prevent his brother from ever leaving again. Emil made the vow when he was in a highly emotional state. The emotion was profound guilt and loss. A vow charged with that much emotional energy will always reverberate into future lives until it is released and rescinded.

To Emil, this vow meant keeping any incarnation of Gerhard's soul nearby and never parting. In his next incarnation, as Iris, the effect of the vow did not play out well. Iris wanted to keep Gabriel around so desperately that she felt threatened by any argument between them. With her history of anger, going back many lifetimes, her volatile reactions were driving them apart.

How many people are struggling in their current lives and relationships because of highly charged vows that have outlived their usefulness? Michael

Newton Institute practitioners find many people are carrying these energies and rejoice when they can facilitate their release.

One of the most rewarding experiences we can have on the planet is a loving, enduring couple relationship. Many people strive to find this, but few manage to create it. As we have seen in this chapter, there are many pitfalls to overcome.

Effort is needed to create a loving relationship, but some of us are hampered by baggage we are not even aware of. We find ourselves reacting in ways that are not conducive to a healthy relationship. Some of us fail to balance our needs with the needs of others, being selfless or selfish. We fail to listen to our hearts, so we judge ourselves and others harshly. We don't know, or we forget, that our purpose on the planet is to learn to let go of judgment and control so we can be loving and accepting.

By facing our old habits and releasing them, we can build true intimacy with our partner. When we are convinced that nothing in the physical world lasts, we become patient and treasure our beloved.

We still need to be brave navigating our relationships, but this is easier when the past is put to rest. The guides emphasize the importance of honesty. Being honest about our emotions is challenging. We fear our partner will take advantage of us if we share our vulnerabilities. The truth is that of course we don't really want to be with someone who would use our sincerity against us. By being open and honest, we are allowing ourselves to be known. When we both know and accept the truth of our partner, we can build intimacy.

Five

FROM SELF-SABOTAGE TO STRENGTH

Self-sabotage is counterproductive, and yet all of us do it at some point in our relationships. Although there is a reason for this behavior, we are not always clear on exactly what we are doing or why. We need to dig deeply into our history and motivations to uncover our reasons.

While we desire a loving, happy relationship, we also fear it. We have been hurt or disappointed in the past. We have been rejected or felt the loss of a loved one. Our sabotaging behavior is trying to protect us from feeling this pain again.

Until we understand the deeper reasons for our confusing behavior, we are likely to continue it, needing to feel close to our partner sometimes and at other times, pulling away. What we really want is love, but this is not what we are consistently expressing. Withdrawing isn't love. Being angry isn't love. Putting up with inappropriate behavior isn't love either.

Although our behavior is supposed to protect us, this doesn't work. We end up getting hurt anyway. In a way, we have been dishonest, with ourselves and our partners.

Self-fulfilled people are consistent in their relationships. They know what they want, and if there are problems in the relationship they want to explore, understand, and correct the issues.

How do we stop sabotaging our relationships? We need to address our diminished self-worth. Our first case explores this problem.

Diminished Self-Worth

Anna, thirty-six, comes to her Life Between Lives session feeling devastated after a series of abusive relationships. Her previous partner, Fred, was abusive too, so she left. Now she is in a new relationship with a man called Max. Feeling anxious and doubtful, she wonders if she can trust any man again. Her deepest hope is to be a mother in a loving family.

She comes to a session wanting to know why she has had so many unhappy relationships and how she can fulfill her dream of creating a close and happy family. During the session, Anna's guide answers her questions about her relationship with her ex-partner, Fred.

> *Together they had agreed on their relationship before they incarnated. The souls of Anna and Fred have shared many incarnations and played many different roles. Anna's relationship with Fred in her current life has a specific purpose. She is to develop strength from the pain she experiences in the relationship. Anna has now learned what was needed. They had a past life together with an impact on her current life.*

In this earlier life in the sixteenth century, Anna was a man named Karl, while Fred was Karl's crippled sister. Karl had cared for his sister throughout her life. This information clears up something that had puzzled Anna. She now understands why she has felt so much care for Fred in her current life.

The practitioner asks Anna's guide for information about the abusive relationships in Anna's current life and what Anna is meant to learn.

Mainly she is to learn strength. As a human being, she needs to experience the loss of her partners to develop strength. It is the only way her soul can bring her into full awareness of her whole soul self.

The guide agrees that Anna carries a deep separation anxiety that influences her tendency to self-sabotage. Because she is afraid of losing her partners, she tolerates their destructive treatment. Her fear of loss is greater than her current self-worth. The guide says that most of Anna's undercurrent of fear and anxiety has now been dissolved. He addresses her inability to feel deep love for her new partner, Max.

It's a protective shield against old painful experiences. Handle it with understanding and compassion for yourself. You also need patience at certain moments. The protective shield will dissolve over time. Base your communications on love. Express your feelings, your needs, thoughts, and impulses clearly and honestly. Be authentic and reflect his responses. When appropriate, dispute with him and set your boundaries. As you begin doing this, he will learn as well.

Anna discovers that she has not yet fully learned her lessons from the abusive relationships. She still needs to discover her true self-worth. Her guide gives her more information.

Your purpose is using your intuition to help others. Give your intuition more attention and influence in your daily life. Intuition and feeling constitute your inner perception and are great gifts. Other objectives are learning to trust yourself. You can do this through meditation and being in contact with me, your guide. In your daily life, you can receive my guidance whenever you want. You are aware of the signs in your body that tell you when you and I are connected.

Anna reports feeling goose bumps all over her body. This is one of her signs.

The practitioner asks Anna to gaze into a special mirror that will reflect her soul, suggesting she can remember and reexperience her whole soul self. Anna does this for some time before describing what she sees.

I am a bright, golden, oval-shaped being, radiating warmth, cordiality, joy, lightness, playfulness, purity, trust, compassion, and love.

Anna is deeply touched as she acknowledges the beauty, power, and wisdom of her soul, knowing she can recall her true self any moment of her life. Anna is now taken to a reunion with her soul family. She recognizes people from her present life.

Fred, my ex-partner, is there. He takes my hand, indicating that he regrets his destructive behavior and apologizes for it.

Max is there but a bit at the back. Others are there too. We have so much warmth, sympathy, familiarity, and liveliness together.

Anna is immersed in this love for some time before a shadow of sadness crosses her face.

It is sadness about the past. I am at odds with myself.

Anna is feeling guilty because of her past life as Karl. She feels Karl didn't care enough for his sister. She also feels guilty for sabotaging her relationships in her current life. The guide explains how to release her guilt.

She can release the guilt by recognizing that she just couldn't do better and accepting that, as a human being, she is not perfect.

The guide explains that perfectionism is a kind of pride. This is arrogance, which means trying to be like a God, all powerful and perfect. The opposite of conceit is humility. Natural pride is a sense of joy that is shared with others, while perfectionism is driven by deep feelings of inadequacy. The guide instructs Anna to let go of all her perfectionism, guilt feelings and self-condemnation. Anna says she senses a change as her guide imbues her with the energy of this new way of being. After a pause, Anna declares that all is well with her ex-partner Fred. Then she reports what is happening with her new partner, Max.

Max is stepping forward toward me and I see him also as a brilliant light, radiating calm, strength, honesty and confidence. It feels like he stands totally behind me. I feel now like I am entering a peaceful love which I couldn't feel before. This is totally new for me, especially the calmness. Before, I always thought a love relationship had to be thrilling.

Soon after, Anna thanks her guide and says goodbye, promising she will be in touch. She comes out of the trance sensing a change has taken place. Nine months after the session, Anna gives the practitioner an update on her progress.

I often think of my session with you. What I experienced helped me tremendously with my self-confidence. I closed the issue with my ex-partner completely. My empathy and sensitivity intensified, and I am in close contact now with my guardian angel and all spirit helpers. Again and again, I delight that I can see my guide and I am so thrilled whenever I think of my soul group. They give me security.

This year my grandma died. I miss her, but I know now that she belongs to my soul group and that I will see her again. I helped her a little during her passing. The session showed me how to say farewell to earth, how to leave the body and go home. I could tell her my experience, reducing her fear of dying and assuring her that all will be well. The session helped me greatly in the relationship with my new partner, Max. I am still seeing his radiant soul coming forward, showing me that I don't need to fear him, and that I can trust him to not disappoint me. I am more deeply involved with him as we have now moved in together.

Two years later, Anna shares some good news.

I want to let you know that six months ago I delivered our daughter and I feel proud of the little one, as she is so special. In the beginning it was not always easy, but each day I learned with her and she is the love of my life. We are indeed a beautiful small family. I think often of my session. Back then I couldn't have imagined how wonderfully everything would develop.

Anna has put her guilt to rest. Unworthiness was the source of her self-sabotaging behavior. She has stayed in relationships that a person with healthy self-worth would have left. Perhaps they wouldn't even have started such a relationship in the first place.

Before she came for her Life Between Lives session, Anna knew she was in trouble. She was anxious and beginning to see the signs of the same old patterns starting again. She carried so much fear and guilt, she didn't know how to be relaxed and trusting in a relationship. Anna was taken to the source of her problems to release the past and gain a new healthy perspective that built her self-worth on the inside.

Low self-worth increases our fear of rejection. Feeling unworthy, we look for evidence of our self-worth from others. Instead of looking within, we look for validation externally. The guides often advise us, "Look within!"

Taking Love for Granted

Sometimes we sabotage our relationships by taking our loved ones for granted. This is always a risk within a relationship. The old saying "familiarity breeds contempt" is relevant here. Whatever or whomever we have present around us all the time we often devalue. Keeping a sense of death nearby can enhance our appreciation of life. This sounds morose, but there is wisdom in these words. Being aware of the impermanent nature of life and our relationships is wise.

The case of Roger demonstrates how fear can inhibit our expression of love. Because of our fears, we can miss opportunities and take the presence of our loved one for granted.

Roger, a thirty-six-year-old gay man, has just returned to his hometown after working for several years in another city. He quickly finds a new job and a pleasant place to live, but he still feels unsettled. His family of origin, who live in the area, have accepted his homosexuality but the small town and the church are judgmental. The problem becomes acute when Roger meets Jerry, a new boyfriend he likes a lot. He feels guilty about having a controversial relationship, and this constrains him from pursuing it. He is not sure this narrow-minded town is the best place to be. He comes in for a Life Between Lives session to gain insight into his dilemma.

While exploring his doubts, Roger finds himself back in ancient Italy. He is a man of about thirty, named Christian, who is a guard in the army based in Rome.

> *My responsibility is to patrol the surrounding villages. I usually go by myself, as things are generally peaceful. The worst trouble I have faced is breaking up a squabble amongst villagers. I live in a two-room stone structure with the other single guards. We play games and do drills. I was recruited when I was seventeen years old and have been a guard ever since. I would like to get married and have a family. In one of the villages, there is this girl who I have noticed. She is very beautiful.*

Christian does not pursue a relationship with this girl. Instead, he stays in the army, living with the other single guards. At forty he retires.

> *After leaving the army, I move into the hills outside of Rome where I live by myself. I feel guilty because I am attracted to other men. That is why I need to get away from Rome. Occasionally I see some of my old army friends, but I am lonely.*
>
> *Sometimes I go to the tavern in the village. One day, I meet this guy and we start talking about horses. His name is James. He invites me to see his horses. We become friends and then we become more than friends. Relationships between men are not against the law, but they do make you an outcast from society. That is why it takes some time before we become lovers. We move in together and we are happy.*

At this point, Roger realizes that James in Christian's life shares the same soul as Jerry, his new boyfriend in his current life.

Christian explains that after many happy years of being with James, he comes home from the market one day and finds that James is dead. There are no signs of foul play and James had not been ill, not to Christian's knowledge anyway. Christian is shocked. He grieves deeply for this loss. He continues to live in James's house and look after the horses, but he is lonely. Finally, he goes back to the tavern hoping to make some new friends. He does make a few casual friends, but he never finds another lover. He lives alone until he dies quietly, after a brief illness, at about age sixty.

> *Now I know that true love exists, because I had it with James. I also learned that you can't replace love with other activities, you must rely on yourself. I could have found another relationship if I had really tried.*
>
> *I realize I should have let James know a lot sooner how I felt about him, because I let too much time go by. My guilt about being attracted to other men kept me from expressing my feelings.*

The practitioner asks Roger what he has learned about his current life challenges in the light of Christian's life.

> *I can see that you need to love and hold on to the people you care about the most because you are not guaranteed future time together. Once you love someone and they become a big part of your life, you are lonely when they are gone. Then you need to be around others, to talk to others and to be open to another love. Christian's love for James kept him from looking for anyone else. I need to love Jerry and hold on to him. I've been feeling too guilty to let him know how I feel, but love is important enough to go after.*

Roger left the session determined to pursue a relationship with Jerry regardless of what others might think. At last contact, Roger and Jerry were spending a lot of time together, allowing their relationship to develop.

Roger, in his life as Christian, had taken James for granted by ignoring opportunities to express his love. He was inhibited by guilt about the nature of the relationship. After James died, his guilt took a different turn. Now he feels guilty for not expressing his love to James. This prevents him from taking opportunities to develop a new relationship.

Roger receives useful knowledge from his regression. He can see how the fear of humiliation is holding him back from expressing love. Many people sabotage their relationships because of fear. We gain power when we understand our fears and the sad consequences of letting fear rule us. With this knowledge, we are motivated to address our sabotaging behavior and move forward. We then have an opportunity to fulfill our dreams of a loving relationship.

Overcoming Rejection

We don't realize how frequently the patterns of behavior we exhibit are habits that have been with us in several lifetimes. Humans are habitual, and repetitive thoughts and actions create patterns. It simply means that when we are faced with the same circumstances, we react in familiar ways. This is a bit like tunnel vision. With certain problems, we have the same attitude and solution that we held in the past.

To break a pattern, we need to know we are caught in its grip. Once we get an inkling that we are repeating a pattern, we have an opportunity to be present and observe our behavior, seeking ways to stop any sabotaging pattern that affects our relationships.

Tina, thirty-six, is the single mother of two teenage children. She works as a social educator in a school and is a part-time psychic. She comes to her Life Between Lives session wanting to know why her relationships with men have been so disappointing.

Her biological father left her mother for another woman before she was born. During the summer vacations with him, he spent more time flirting with women and socializing with adults than getting to know her, his daughter. Her husband also left her for another woman.

During her session. Tina relives a past life as a dark-skinned man in North America in the 1950s. He is a tall, handsome professional dancer named Michael, aged twenty-three.

I do not get the respect I deserve. I am in love with a woman of a different race. [deep sigh] We must hide. She and I work together but we are not allowed to be seen together even privately. [crying loudly] I need to use a separate door and cannot live in the same place when we travel.

Michael has a very loving family consisting of a widowed mother and siblings. The practitioner asks about the woman he loves.

She came to sing with our band. [cries deeply] She lost our child! It's an impossible romantic relationship. We have different skin color.

Michael's life is short. He feels broken and tired of life, drowning his sorrows in alcohol. Eventually he ends it all with an overdose. Tina meets her guide, who explains why Michael faced the challenge of an interracial relationship.

Having a close loving relationship to someone can hurt you the most. If you manage to cope with close romantic relationships, you will cope with a lot of other difficulties. It is a way to learn. Tina is learning that a romantic relationship is worth waiting for and fighting for. She needs to wait. The general theme in her incarnations is loss, dejection, and sorrow. When love ends, it hurts. It is about learning to cope with strong feelings.

The practitioner asks if Tina has had any lives where she participated in a happy romantic relationship with a man. Excitedly waving her hands around, Tina goes to a life, long ago, when humans were primitive hunters and gatherers.

It is hot. I am a woman with large feet. There is sand here. I do not wear many clothes. My chest is naked and, down there, I wear a cloth. We cut our hair with a knife, it hurts. We endure a lot of pain. I feel strong. I am with someone, a man.

She laughs out loud, looking powerful and proud of herself as she mentions that her man is shorter than she is and also wears a cloth around his waist.

> *My children are in the village with the tribe where we live. We wander. We take animals. We gather. We hunt. We pick what we can eat from the ground. We all sleep together to keep warm. We use skins from animals to cover our bodies. Sometimes we meet others and we stay for a longer time. We do ceremonies. We communicate well. It is an inner communication, sort of. We all know what to do. We all contribute.*

The practitioner asks about fire and the animals they hunt.

> *Yes, we have fire. The men do it! I am good at hunting. They look like bulls or buffalo or something like that. They are huge animals. I hide. Often we are many in the hunt, but sometimes just one.*

The practitioner asks about personal relationships and families.

> *The children are everybody's children. We foster all children. I have one man. We are not that interested in sex. We do not really feel up to it. We know that if we become pregnant, we will be restricted. I have children. We women help each other. When it is time to give birth, we leave the village, and an older woman helps the woman in labor.*
>
> *Our interactions between men and women come naturally without rules. It is just there. Initial sexual intimacy is after we have our first bleeding. The elder women tell us what it is. I had a ceremony with them. They took me to a special place away from the tribe and they told me stories. It was very safe. We are never alone here. Sometimes the men and women all stay together.*

Tina discovers this is one of her first incarnations on earth, saying that the tribe is very important. She comes to the end of this tribal life. She is short of breath as she speaks.

> *Ah, I am dying. I must leave my body. I must leave my tribe. They must leave me! [crying out] I cannot walk! I am wounded. It hurts. My feet and legs do not function. The tribe do a ceremony, then they leave me alone. They need to continue to wander. They need to survive.*
>
> *I see cliffs. I love cliffs. I like the colors. I have nothing now. An animal eats some parts of my body. I am leaving now. I feel just calm.*

The practitioner asks for any important messages from that tribal life.

> *Men and women were equal in that life and respected one another. We had different ceremonies with all kinds of intentions. We all made our contributions to help us survive as a tribe. Tina, in her current life, has a lot of strength and has proven that she can survive alone, unlike our need to be together in the tribe. In the past life, I was left to die alone because it was more important for the tribe to survive than to take care of a single person who could not be saved.*

Tina is very attracted to a man she is working with, but she feels great stress inside her whenever they meet. She feels inferior to him. She feels attraction, but she does not want to act on it. She thinks he is too smart. She does not dare to look at him because she feels stupid.

The practitioner asks about this inner conflict between attraction and inferiority that stresses her. Tina's guide explains what is happening for Tina.

> *She tries to communicate, but she finds it hard to talk to him. Because he is an academic, Tina cannot cope with his intellectual nature.*

Tina cries.

I can meet him on a soul level, but not on a personal level.

The guide continues with more information.

> *The guy is a challenger. He is not what Tina believes he is. She thinks of his knowledge, but while he has knowledge, she has wisdom. Tina is not familiar with his vocabulary. That is why she feels insecure and becomes silent in his presence. She does not invite him in because of her fears.*

Tina is suddenly back in her childhood years when she was only ten and in love.

> *I am in love. I have been in love with my neighbor, Mattias, for a long time. I feel very uncertain when I am near him. I feel a longing. I cannot get close to him. He has beautiful eyes and invites me in somehow. He is funny, and he laughs, but he is also sad, not realizing I know.*

Tina examines this time in her young life.

> *Whatever I did made them laugh at me. I was looking for confirmation.*

Her guide gives more details about Tina's self-devaluating views.

> *She feels that she is not as smart as the others. She cannot learn the alphabet fast enough, she cannot swim as fast as the others. She feels stupid. They laugh at her. She does not get the help she deserves. She thinks that there is something wrong with her because she cries so much.*

Tina cries for some time before suddenly becoming angry. She is imbued with a new inner strength.

> *Enough is enough! The others need to take care of their own garbage because it is not mine! I am more than they think.*

I can now take back my feminine sexual power. Men and women are equal!

Three weeks after her session, Tina writes to the practitioner.

Since my session I have dreamt a lot. The dreams have been clear and informative. I felt compelled to create an altar. I filled it with feminine symbols and a letter to my future husband. I have felt calm and my trust has increased. I am confident that I will meet a great man in this life, and we will be happy together.

During her regression, Tina's guide has taken her on a journey to change her perspective. She has felt awkward and inadequate in her recent lives, especially in the life where she was a dark man in love with a white woman. That life and her childhood experiences increased her fear of rejection.

Reliving her powerful life in the tribe helped recalibrate her energetically, wiping out much of her old pattern of feeling fearful and inferior. Then when she remembered her childhood, realizing how small and weak she'd felt, she fired up, repudiating this feeble version of herself. With a new perspective of her inner strength, she was able to build trust in herself and her future.

Overcoming Feelings of Rejection and Jealousy

Constant rejection in childhood can manifest as jealousy in our adult life. Jealousy is an awful feeling. Although jealousy is an emotion, we experience it physically in the body. People describe feeling crushed, sick, stabbed, fearful, or angry.

These strong feelings usually compel us to take some type of destructive action. We can harass our partner for reassurance, accusing him or her of being unfaithful. We can become sneaky and suspicious, crossing boundaries by examining our partner's phone, computer, or whereabouts. While we make our partner's life difficult, our life is also unbearable. We feel unsettled, desperate, and unhappy.

Augusta, age forty-two, expresses many of these jealous actions in her life. She admits she sabotages her happiness by carrying a sense of rejection into her relationships. When she feels insecure, she can become obsessed with her partner's previous relationships, even though she knows deep down that her obsession is not warranted. Her partner feels hurt and frustrated, pulling away from her emotionally.

Recently, Augusta has become more aware of her feelings and actions. She wants to overcome the feelings of jealousy she has carried all her life.

She was born to her mother out of wedlock, and her father's extended family harshly judged not only her mother, but innocent little Augusta as well. While these people later accepted Augusta's half-brother at birth, she was ignored from the moment she was born.

Although her father always treats his son and daughter as equals, and her half-brother is always loving toward his sister, her father's family have never accepted her. Augusta grew up feeling wary of other people. Her early experiences of rejection created a deep sense of insecurity within her, which can easily be triggered into jealousy and judgment.

She schedules a session because, after many years of living overseas, she is going to meet members of her indifferent paternal family. She knows it is time to heal her feelings of jealousy and rejection.

In the regression, she goes to an incident in her childhood.

Augusta and her brother enter a shop owned by their father's brother, their uncle. Her brother is given some coins, a sizeable sum for a seven-year-old in those days. He goes to share the coins with his sister when he is immediately told the coins are not for sharing. She weeps as she remembers this rejection, and the sad look on her brother's face.

Her guide takes her to two past lives, each presenting a family of differing sentiments.

> *I am young girl of about eight walking in a forest. I feel happy in this forest. I am carefree and visiting a familiar place. There is a house nearby where I live. I don't want to go back into the house. There is no love in that place. I have two parents, but the dad is not nice. He is aggressive and mean, threatening my mother. There are no other children. I don't feel safe in that house. I am neglected. My father ignores me, and I keep out of his way. He picks on my mother and he is never happy. I don't*

feel much connection with my mother either. She is sad and closed off.

Augusta is given information about her lessons in that life.

This life is about not knowing love, so the young girl goes into the forest and connects with nature. Nature is her friend.

She is taken to another life.

I am close to the ocean at night and there is a chill in the air. I am wearing boots and heavy, thick clothes. It is a cold place like Ireland.

I like to go out in the evening to a low headland overlooking the ocean. I feel peaceful. I enjoy the view and the quiet. I feel connected to nature.

There is a house close by. It is small and cozy with a fire. I feel that this home does have love, a respectful, nurturing, and peaceful love. It is just me and my wife who live here now. We are good people with good hearts. I find peace in the open spaces in nature. I enjoy time with my wife and I enjoy time alone. I am reflecting love and I am full of gratitude.

Augusta reflects on this life.

His wife left first. He is really connected to God. He doesn't feel alone, and death is not scary for him. He feels faith and trust.

The practitioner suggests Augusta step into this man, and she does.

I am feeling so connected. I know what it is to truly know God. I have been connected in past lives and I can get there again.

Augusta now remembers how wanted she was by both her parents, despite the circumstances of the extended family, and how happy her mother was at the prospect of meeting her firstborn child.

Augusta feels whole and peaceful after her regression. Her sense of security has returned. She is determined to stay open when she meets her extended family and not react with judgment in the way they have always done with her.

Jealousy can be put to rest, but this doesn't happen by focusing on others and what we think they have that we don't have. We need to look inside to heal our jealousy. When we discover what we felt we were denied, we need to acknowledge our hurt and feel our grief. Augusta did this when she remembered her brother receiving the coins that she was denied.

Later she felt the love she was missing. It had always been there, but she had forgotten. Somewhere, sometime in the past, we have all felt the profound energy of love and connection.

You don't even need to have a Life Between Lives session to reexperience this unconditional love. Once you relax deeply, gaining a state of meditation and expansion, ask your loving guides for connection. Open to the idea that profound love is there for you. A flood of loving feelings is always available and can pour into your heart.

Protecting a Broken Heart

Sometimes our sabotaging behavior has its origin in a past life. In some past lives, we experience so much grief that we close our hearts in an act of protection, and that wariness carries forward into a subsequent life. Unfortunately, we are unaware of our protective stance and look outside of ourselves for the cause of our loneliness and lack of connection in relationships. If we have a dispassionate, unengaged partner, we can blame him or her for our unhappiness. Only when we look deeper can we discover the true cause that is playing out in our life.

Tricia, thirty-six, describes her current husband, Bart, as an emotionally detached, intellectual thespian. Still, she feels a bond with this man, probably because they have been married for ten years and are raising two boys, the eldest from her first marriage. These two boys are quite different, with the youngest, five-year-old Thor, having intellectual and obsessive tendencies like his father.

Both her husbands have been emotionally absent and neglectful, and Tricia wonders why she is attracting men with these characteristics.

Tricia experiences a past life that opens in a scene in a Chicago neighborhood in the 1920s on a foggy, cold night.

> *Oh, it's 1922 and I'm wearing a pink dress. I am a woman of thirty-two. I am walking arm in arm with a man on one side and a woman on the other. We are dancing, tripping, and fumbling along the pavement because we are all quite tipsy.*
>
> *I'm a flapper in that life. I'm playful. Happy. But not really. It's fun, and I'm caught up in my profession as a successful journalist. I write about entertainment. I'm living that lifestyle, playing in it, but something's missing. I'm quite lonely.*

After exploring the ins and outs of that career, she is taken to the last day of that life.

> *It's cold and wintery. Now I am eighty-three years old. I am lying in bed in an opulent room. No one is around but the help. I am being taken care of, but I feel very alone.*

As she looks back on that life, she describes it as lonely and depressing, without love, just being surrounded by helpers.

> *Apparently, the love of my life in my twenties had gone off to war, fulfilling his patriotic duty. I never saw him again. When he left, he took my heart. Subsequently, I never let anyone get close to me so I would never have to say goodbye. I stayed alone from then on. Even though I expressed myself creatively in my work, it felt like a waste. I was never able to connect meaningfully with another human being. I learned life isn't worth living if there's no connection.*

She identifies some aspects from the past life that are active in her current life, including the solemn regret she feels whenever she is faking happiness, as well as the influence of her decision to never let herself get close to anyone.

She understands how this decision to stay detached set the stage for her relationship pattern of choosing emotionally unavailable men. She must learn to open and connect if she wants to break this pattern.

Following this understanding, she moves effortlessly upward to her life between lives. She sees an image of a sticky tar pit.

Everything feels stuck. I get the message!

The council encourages her to trust and utilize her intuitive abilities, reminding her that everything is energy. They also tell her she is a channel to lovingly awaken people on their path.

At one point in the regression, she reviews the group of souls in her current life.

My husband is off in another quadrant of souls. I feel he is disconnected from my energy. My son, Thor, is in that group as well. Now I understand why he is so bonded to his father. My other son is part of my group. He will eventually have a daughter. I can see I will be closely connected to this child, my granddaughter.

From the regression, Tricia now has a deeper understanding of the dynamics of her family. She knows why her husband is so detached and takes her for granted. She can see why her younger son is close to his father and why she and her older son feel more connected. She also knows why she chooses emotionally unavailable men. Like her husband, she too has been afraid of emotional connection. Because of her fear of being hurt, she has avoided men who can connect.

From remembering her past life, Tricia learns that trying to stay safe by closing her heart doesn't work. We attract partners who are like us. Our unresolved issues draw to us others with similar emotional patterns. We have been designed to resolve our issues. Until we do, others will be like mirrors, reflecting our distortions and dysfunctions back to us. A closed heart will meet another closed heart, until we awaken. Once awakened, Tricia remembers there is no fulfillment in a life without emotional connections.

Four years later, Tricia has left her husband. When she separated, she understood why her son, Thor, chose to go with his father. They are alike. With this realization, she avoids much grief.

Now she is in a committed relationship with a very loving, spiritual man. They are closely connected and are open and honest with each other, ensuring they do not sabotage their relationship.

There is always a reason behind the choices we make in our relationships. The cases here clearly demonstrate how decisions and experiences in previous lives can influence our choices in our current life. Nothing is wasted. Even sabotaging our happiness can be useful. An emotionally lonely life, like Tricia experienced, can be a profound and worthwhile lesson. She learned the importance of being open to emotional intimacy. Disappointment and rejection in a past life, like that experienced by Anna and Tina, can increase strength. Loss, such as that suffered by Roger, can build courage and motivation. Gaining a comprehensive understanding of our past behavior can be painful, but it is also greatly freeing. We can move on with our lives with increased self-awareness, knowing we can avoid sabotaging ourselves and our relationships.

Six

GROWING THROUGH FAMILY CONFLICT

R elationships bring us more grief and joy than just about anything else we experience on planet earth. Each of us carry within us lifetimes of peace and war, love and betrayal. Any conflict is rich with the needs, hurts, and fears of the participants. There are so many ways to relate to each other. We can be smothering or cold, uncaring or supportive, calm or aggressive, and any of the degrees between two extremes. Navigating the shoals and currents of any relationship is the work of many lifetimes.

Our wisdom is developed and refined through our experiences. No experience is more important than developing relationships with others. Our ability to relate will always reflect the quality of our connection to our true self.

Conflict is not always bad. It can work for us as well as against us. We can learn to skillfully interact with others when sharing differing views. We can build wisdom and strength. We can see ourselves through others who mirror our behavior. And we can learn to love unconditionally.

In this chapter, we examine how to create peace when conflict erupts in our families. We learn about disharmony and how to find the balance between being enmeshed and being close. We discover there are reasons for having our difficult parents or family members. We can find ways of being more accepting so we can find the true path to peace.

Dealing with Disharmony

Trying to openly resolve conflict in a family can sometimes make it worse. We like everyone to be happy, but arguing to create harmony is counter-productive. Trying to ensure our needs are met in the family might trigger hostility in other members, who may fear their needs won't be met. Even being silent and submissive can annoy some people who may read it as being disengaged.

Sometimes our inner peacefulness can rub off on others and we feel good. But often it doesn't make any difference. We will always have some family members who challenge us. No matter how hard we try, we struggle to create congenial relationships with these relatives.

Eleanor, age fifty-seven, comes to her first session because of conflict in her family. She greatly values having a close family in which everyone gets along with each other. But unfortunately, Eleanor is unpopular with her insecure daughter-in-law. Eleanor describes her son and her daughter-in-law as being hard-hearted parents who can be mean and judgmental toward all four of the children in their care. Of the four children, biologically, two are his and two are hers. Eleanor accepts these four children as her grandchildren and does her best to give love and support equally to each child.

On one occasion, Eleanor spoke to her son about the need to be gentler with the children, but this only made things worse between her and the two of them. Since her son told his wife about her suggestion, his wife shunned her mother-in-law and her son continually supported his wife instead of his mother.

During a party, the daughter-in-law accused Eleanor of ignoring her two children. Eleanor had been watching her daughter-in-law constantly pick on the youngest child, her biological grandson. Eleanor did her best to comfort the child, who looked sad and downtrodden. After the daughter-in-law's accusation, Eleanor calmly stated that she loves all her grandchildren and treats them all equally. The daughter-in-law burst into tears and ordered Eleanor out of the house. This behavior caused a deep rupture in the family.

> *We were a close-knit family. My other children don't stand up for me. They want to stay in contact with the daughter-in-law for the sake of the children. I understand this, but in a way, I am being sacrificed. My daughter-in-law has made me the problem. I see through her, but she doesn't want to be seen. Still, I feel hurt.*

During the session, Eleanor experiences a past life as a Roman centurion in charge of a group of men engaged in combat. These groups were called Centuries and formed part of a legion containing thousands of men.

> *The battle is in front of me, but I am in a safe spot, standing and watching. I feel a bit numb, frozen to the spot. I feel like an authority. Lots of my people are dying and being hurt. It is not going well.*
>
> *Now I am on a horse and galloping fast away from the battle. I am deserting my men but only so I can go for help. I have come to a tent with a big table at the front where my authorities are discussing the battle. I am reporting and asking for help. Other Centuries are fighting elsewhere, and the authorities are sending available reinforcements to them, not my men. They to say to me, "not now, not now" and wave me away.*

The centurion discovers something about the battle plan that he had not been told.

> *My group were a diversion for the main battle. We were sent as a sacrifice. I didn't know that. I feel emotional—abandoned and betrayed.*

113

The practitioner asks him what happens after he makes this discovery.

I went back to help the others. I feel a spear going through my chest. I could see it coming, but I couldn't get out of the way. I feel a sharp pain and I fall back and hit my head.

I lie there for a while, listening to the fighting. Someone comes to my aid, but there is nothing he can do. I feel myself slipping out of my body. I seem to be going somewhere.

Eleanor pauses. The practitioner asks where the centurion is going.

I am standing in a meadow and there are people around who I don't know but should know. I seem to be in a daze. They are supportive, helping me stand and walk. The chest pain is gone. Now I am floating along and it feels normal. There is a bright area that I am moving to, and now I am in it.

I am floating, feeling a little lost, in a space of nothingness. It is peaceful.

Someone is there who I know as Father and I hear, "I am here, my child." I can't see him. I am still a bit dazed. Father has said, "Come, child." But I feel I am still in limbo.

When the practitioner asks why she is stuck in this limbo, Eleanor says she feels her soul is undeserving and damaged. The practitioner suggests Eleanor ask Father if her damaged soul can be healed, and he replies.

It is done, child. It is done.

Eleanor feels emotional and struggles to accept this message because she still feels responsible. The practitioner asks for more information.

I feel responsible for the past, when I was part of the universe, part of a group of twelve. I can see us standing around a crystal and the crystal has cracked.

We were trying to increase the energy of the crystal and it unexpectedly broke. It damaged the grids around the earth.

Continents moved, and the water went everywhere. The ocean rose, and a lot of people were lost, including Atlantis. It was an accident.

The flood wasn't our intention. We were trying to increase the power on earth, so things would be better. But it didn't work.

The practitioner suggests she ask Father what can be done about this.

He said, "It was all part of the plan. It is done. It is healed." It is only my memory that feels there is a need to heal. The healing is happening. He says I took it very personally and that is why I am stuck. Taking it personally is part of my nature. I need to heal that within myself.

The practitioner asks how it can be healed.

He says, "Love. Love for the self." I feel emotional. Now I feel numb.

The practitioner asks her to remember the past life of the Roman soldier and notice if she can see any similarities between the situation of the battle and the situation with the crystal.

Eleanor sees the similarities. She took on the responsibility for the loss of the men in the past life and she took on responsibility for the devastating changes on the earth. In both situations she was just following orders. In the Roman past life, there was a greater battlefield plan that was being followed. And there was a greater plan being followed in the time of Atlantis. She agrees to let go of the feelings of responsibility.

After this realization, she is taken to a place where she senses the energy of many beings, but only sees four or five. She describes them as Masters.

I seem to be absorbing energy as a preparation for something.

The practitioner waits. When Eleanor next speaks, there has been a change.

I am feeling bilocated. I am with the group, but still in limbo.
Now the Masters are moving away.

When she regains her connection to the Masters, they explain that she moved herself away. "Limbo means losing confidence and not trusting yourself." She asks several questions about the limbo feeling, but they have only one reply.

"New journey, new path."
I get dragged back into the limbo for taking on responsibilities that aren't mine.

The practitioner asks if they can answer the questions she brought to the session. Suddenly the Masters disappear. The practitioner has experienced this before. In other regressions, clients who are sufficiently advanced are expected to use their own connection to the Masters to intuitively receive the answers.

She internally focuses on the conflict with her children while holding a desire to understand. The answers immediately come into her mind.

It is their journey. My role is to bring things up for them by
just being myself—honest and loving, letting them be. And I
am to feel okay about it. I am to trust in myself and know that
I am just as important as anyone else.

Eleanor comes out of her Life Between Lives session feeling much more at peace.

Before the session, she carried guilt from the devastating consequences of her actions. But her guilt was misplaced. Her actions were ordered by those in authority above her. When her men fell in battle and when the seas rose and destroyed Atlantis, she was not responsible. She was innocent.

No wonder her daughter-in-law challenged her. The daughter-in-law reflected her past, triggering Eleanor's misplaced feelings of guilt. The daughter in law was blaming Eleanor when she was innocent. This blame and the fracture in the family elicited the same feelings Eleanor experienced during her visit to the past life. When the authorities refused to send reinforcements and when the family refused to support her, she felt hurt, abandoned, and betrayed.

Eleanor wanted harmony in the family, but she was missing harmony within herself. Guilt was driving her. When there was any disharmony in the family, she felt responsible deep inside, even though her rational mind told her she shouldn't. The conflict outside was a mirror of the conflict she felt inside. She doubted herself, wondering if she was guilty or innocent. Her inner turmoil was unbearable whenever she was confronted with friction in her family.

Once Eleanor was at peace within herself, she saw the family conflict with new eyes. She could accept the members of her family as they were, allowing her daughter-in-law to play out her insecurities without it affecting her. Now Eleanor has the inner strength and harmony to meet any challenges with love, forgiveness, and honesty.

Dysfunctional Families

Many of us have parents who are challenging. Parents can be abusive, neglectful, or argumentative. When they treat us badly, we can feel like victims. We wonder, "Why don't I have parents like my friend's?" If we dwell on this too long, we build resentment and self-pity, emotions that add to our misery.

When we are children, few of us realize that we chose our parents. Before we are born, our soul self, plans for our life, and our parents are an important part of this plan. Our soul selves don't choose parents who will make us feel loved and happy unless such parents are part of the plan. We mostly choose parents who will challenge us in some way, teaching us what we need to learn.

Parents can teach us by many means, but the most persuasive way is by example. We can learn from the love, care, and honesty they demonstrate, but we can also learn from negative behavior. A dysfunctional parent acting violently or neglectfully can be a powerful lesson for how not to behave.

Sarina, age forty-one, has a difficult family of origin.

*My mother, father, sister, and paternal grandmother all have
personality disorders and I am, and have always been, their*

scapegoat. It has been the challenge of my life to be their daugh-
ter, sister, and granddaughter.

Despite her family, Sarina has managed well in life. She hasn't wasted their example of negative behavior either.

Fortunately, I have been gifted with psychological "normalcy"
and a great deal of intuition and resiliency, which is partially
my nature and partially learned from my experiences of life
with them. I am thankful for that.

Ironically, their negative and abusive behaviors have taught
me to value and look for the opposite in healthy relationships
with others.

As an adult I have been able to make good decisions for
myself and my life. I am in a happy marriage, raising sweet,
loving, and confident children, and doing very well in my cho-
sen profession.

Although she has overcome many obstacles, recently Sarina is more frustrated and drained than ever with her family's behavioral patterns.

The dysfunction in my family of origin persists, and I find that
coping with the slings and arrows of their disorders is becom-
ing more difficult as I age. Now I realize that there will be no
changing on their part. I need to seek more support to fortify
my spirit so that I can change the way I respond to them.

During the session, Sarina's guide appears, explaining why she has chosen this challenging family.

Her purpose is to ascend. She chose these parents for this purpose.

Her mother gives just enough love, just enough light, for
Sarina to grow. With that love and light, can Sarina stay the
path? She chose to live with this difficulty as a test of endur-
ance for her own awareness. She is testing herself.

She can draw back from the family. Find her purpose else-where. Nature is a good healer. There are other things for her. She is partially aware of what those are—but we will lead her as she goes, through her dreams and feelings from good works.

The practitioner reminds Sarina that she has felt rage at her family and then guilt. She asks if her guides can give her more information.

Sometimes rage is good. Power must be applied when it is necessary for her to protect herself and her children. It shows her that she has power before them.

Now she can let it go. Let us deal with them. It is no longer her job anymore.

Her parents chose to come into this life being difficult, abusive, and angry to help her ascend. They came as aids to help her fulfill her wish to test herself. They challenged her to stay light during darkness.

Two months after the session, Sarina writes to her practitioner.

What I am most thankful for is this sense of peace I have regarding my parents. What once weighed so heavily on my mind and heart has been lifted. I feel a miraculous difference in myself. Now I can think of them and handle contact with them.

Sarina chose her parents to test her ability to be her true self, while being challenged by the negativity of her family. Her mother was a good choice, shining just a little so Sarina didn't feel completely isolated. It takes a strong, loving soul to stay light when there is darkness all around.

Challenging Parents

Parents caught up in their arguments with each other often neglect the needs of their children. Their focus is on defending their fragile sense of self from perceived attacks by their partner. When we see these parents as indulging in frequent conflict, we judge them as neglectful. They have overlooked their child's need for a stable, comfortable environment. But appearances can be deceptive. Some children don't need a stable, comfortable environment at all. What they need is an environment that helps them grow as a soul.

Jennifer, in her early fifties, is a successful businesswoman, happily married for twenty-five years, with no children. She feels her relationship with her parents has been a struggle and she comes for a Life Between Lives session wondering why she chose them.

The practitioner guides Jennifer into her mother's womb. Jennifer feels comfortable and connects with her soul self. Now the practitioner asks if her soul energy moves in and out of the womb or just stays there. Jennifer's reply is adamant.

> *I'm just in the baby. I'm in it! I stay!*

In the womb, Jennifer feels alone, reporting that she is not receiving any help from spirit. The practitioner wonders why this is the case.

> *This makes me realize that I can do this. I did this on purpose.*
> *Help was offered, and I said no, I really want to try this alone,*
> *I know that I am strong enough. I can do this! This whole life's*
> *deal, coming into the body and my purpose, I'm strong enough*
> *to be here. I'm strong enough to be born. I'm strong enough to*
> *be in this life.*

This is a powerful realization for Jennifer, as she grew up unsure that she was meant to be here. She hasn't felt strong and wonders if this life is a mistake. She is told that as a baby she refused to eat. She assumes this means she didn't want to stay in her body after she was born.

Jennifer receives more information about her strength and starts making connections with her achievements in life.

> *I'm thinking about the determination that I always have; this*
> *is part of who I am, and I've always had it. I remember it now,*
> *the determination I have. Once I decide to do something, it*
> *will be done.*

*Now I am being shown my parents. My parents are argu-
ing and that makes me determined. It fuels me. This fire makes
me unstoppable. I can do it! Whatever it is. It's the focus that
I get sometimes as Jennifer, the same focus I had when I went
to school for acupuncture, when I trained for a marathon, all
the times I was determined to do something. It feels like fire. I
have a picture of a fire horse in my office.*

Jennifer has come to the planet in this life to stay. It seems she found
incarnations challenging in the past. But she is a determined soul and she
knows that difficult parents will give her an example of what she doesn't want
to be. In a way, their conflict inspires her.

Once she arrives in the spirit world, Jennifer meets her soul group.

*Someone is coming forward that I don't know. It feels very
maternal, like the energy of someone like Mother Mary or
Quan Yin.*

*It feels so welcoming and nurturing, reminding me I can
still feel loved and nurtured, even when nurturing is not present in a physical life. That feeling of being nurtured doesn't
come from food. It doesn't have to be your own mother that
gives this feeling to you. You have it inside of you. You know
where to look for it.*

The practitioner asks why Jennifer missed out on nurturing and love
from her mother.

*This has to do with expectation. It's a lesson around how every-
thing comes from the inside. It's okay to reach for something
inside of us when we don't have it outside of us. This happened
so I can learn not to blame people when they don't give it to
me. It's free for them to give it, but I cannot demand it.*

The practitioner now addresses the question of Jennifer's choice of parents.

It's all actually simple! They are pushing my buttons, but that is what it's all about. It's all okay. It's not about the buttons, that doesn't matter. It's all about our growth.

My mom and I are supposed to have fun together, being silly with a lot of laughter. It would be wonderful for us to spend more time together and to figure out the fun things we could do with one another. It feels good just thinking about it.

I chose to learn that nurturing comes from the inside out and to not expect it from her. I can show her how to love herself! We can have some joyful times together before it's too late. There is still space to grow.

She is happy just the way she is. Even though that's not how I would want to live my life, she accepts it. It's what she wants. It feels worse to me than it does for her. I just need to remember to be and let be.

The practitioner notes that Jennifer has been carrying around a life-is-hard attitude. She asks where it came from.

"Life is hard" is Mom's statement, it is not mine. I'm letting it go.

Jennifer now connects with her father's soul to understand why she chose him.

My dad's soul is a younger soul and a little afraid. He appreciates the determination I have, and he is sometimes in awe of that. It makes him feel insecure. He is gentle though.

We had one other lifetime together before. The main reason for this one is for me to show him that it's okay to be courageous and to just get out there. To not be afraid!

He taught me to be patient. I knew he was going to test my patience.

I am showing him different ways to live, to acknowledge the intuitive skills that he has. It's never too late to listen to his intuition if he chooses. There is still space for him to grow like that.

We chose each other to be teachers to one another. This feels good!

Some months after her session, Jennifer wrote to her practitioner explaining how her healing journey continued to unfold.

In the months following the session, I could see my parents with more compassion and a "let live" attitude. I understood that they would never be like me and that they would never be as I would be as a parent. I have accepted that. I understand that my role may be to show them how to be different, and if they see this, great! If not, that's okay too.

I also understand that this life and my purpose in this life is only a sliver, a small part of my soul purpose. Just as I chose to stay with my mom and become a living baby, so I also choose to not continue the "usual" path of becoming a mother myself. I understood that I don't have to feel guilty or like less of a person by not continuing my parents' family with grandchildren.

Overall, this session taught me that I am a lot bigger than the physical person.

Jennifer chose her parents to teach her several lessons. Their anger reminded her of her strength. She learned to seek love and nurturing from her inner self. We can beg, hope, and bully to get our needs met by others, but the shortcut is to give what we need to ourselves.

Jennifer also learned the importance of acceptance. She had wanted to change her parents until she finally realized that they are settled emotionally where they are.

We live much happier lives when we accept our parents as they are. Taking time to think about what we have learned from them is worthwhile. We learn from their love and their lack of love, from their nourishing care and their disturbing deeds. What exactly we take away is up to each of us.

Enmeshed Families

What is the difference between a close family and one that is enmeshed? An enmeshed family is like a tribe. In the past, tribes were enmeshed because they had to be. Nomadic tribes lived in harsh territory, and the survival of any individual member depended on the collective. Tribes had strict rules, and if a member of the tribe broke the rules, they were often banished.

Some tribes and clans were especially cohesive, practicing a system of payback. For example, if a member of a tribe did wrong by another tribe, any member of the offending tribe could be the recipient of the payback, even an innocent child. The hard enforcement of these rules may seem cruel to us, but tribal rules were developed over countless generations to ensure the tribes' survival.

Remnants of our tribal history are present in our families today. In an enmeshed family, we might feel the pain of a suffering loved one. Because their suffering is our suffering, we might grow angry if they don't look after themselves. We may want to control them, becoming annoyed if they are too independent for our peace of mind.

Sometime during our soul journey, we need to break away from the tribe and develop our individuality and independence. Deanna, in her mid-forties, is still single and states she is still entwined with her family of origin. She wants to know how to handle them.

Early in the session, she goes to a scene when she is four years old.

> *I feel tense. My parents are arguing. I feel frozen and fearful. I am in another room and they are in their bedroom. This is the first time I have experienced them arguing. They are very loud, and I am sensing their anger. My mother is pregnant with my younger sister. I am concerned for my mother and the baby. Now the voices have stopped and mum is crying. I feel helpless. My other sisters are here, and they are just as scared.*
>
> *Mum comes into the kitchen pretending nothing has happened. We look concerned, but she is ignoring it. My elder sister understands that something is wrong. I feel my heart beating. I am hurting and there is fear. I feel a contraction in the heart. This is the beginning of my heart palpitations. It comes*

in fearful situations and I feel like I am going to die. It is absolute helplessness.

Later, in her Life Between Lives session, Deanna's guides make some suggestions on how to handle her parents.

You are getting caught up in their stuff and it has nothing to do with you. Forget the obedient child thing. Live your own life.

Do what you want to do out of love rather than doing what you feel you must do out of duty and obligation.

It is okay to have a response to the way they are. Acknowledge that, but then move into acceptance and unconditional love.

Feeling the emotion is essential, otherwise there is no point being here in a body. Not feeling the emotion is shutting down, and that is not being here. You need to feel the hurt, but don't get stuck there.

Twenty-five years ago, Deanna's father was told by a doctor that he would be dead in a year if he didn't give up smoking and drinking. That scared him so much, he immediately gave them up, taking up soda pop and sweets instead.

Now he is old, in pain, and uncomfortable, but he won't see a doctor. Deanna wonders if he is afraid of being told he could die, receiving information from her guide.

His soul is choosing that level of discomfort. He is stubborn, and it is compounded by your mother's fear of orthodox treatments. He thinks, "Soldier on!" There are layers of history, of karmic connections, and some of it isn't your business. He knows what he could do, but it is his stuff that he needs to work on.

Let him come to his own realization about seeing doctors and looking after himself. Think of him as a child. The only things a child needs are love and time, time to work out the problem. Nothing you do is going to make any difference except alienate and isolate him.

What is the worst thing that can happen? He could die. The spirits are indicating, "So what?"

They are telling me I need to step back. If I move into judgment, that is the opposite of karmic resolution. I am to be there for him in a nonjudgmental way with compassion and unconditional love. The lesson is to move into a space of love.

The practitioner asks one of Deanna's prepared questions. She wants to know more about self-doubt, and how to deal with it.

Acknowledge the self-doubt, call it what it is. And then don't give it power. Let the doubt drain away.

When you ask for guidance, the first thought is it! The second thought is the fear, which is of a lower vibration.

An energy comes into your consciousness, such as love or fear. Love and fear are on opposite sides of the same coin. It is all just energy. Once you are aware of your reaction and its cause, move on. You can transform the lower-level resonance of fear into a higher energy of love.

Fear and love are like the same cell but vibrating at different rates. Like a cake that can be dense or light. The same ingredients can make two different cakes depending on how the ingredients are treated.

If you over-beat the cake, it will be dense, just like when you overthink and feel tight and tense. If you leave the cake in the oven too long, it will be burnt and dry. The heat of the oven is like the heat of a fiery temper. You and those around you feel burnt and heavy.

Apply this idea of experiencing life as an adventure and use the cake analogy. You have your life ingredients. What sort of cake are you going to bake?

Deanna takes on the wisdom provided by her guide.

With my family it is not my lesson. It is not mine to change. I am to enjoy my time with them in nonjudgment. The guides are saying, let that be your goal for every interaction, even those that would have previously irritated you. There is a selfless reaction and a selfish reaction.

The life lesson with dad and all the family and the tribe is just acceptance and surrender, which is unconditional love.

As we advance on our soul journey, the challenges we face in our lives become more complex. Being accepting and loving with our families can be more challenging than expressing anger and resentment, especially when our loved ones are selfish or self-neglectful. We want their attention, and we want them to look after themselves.

When we realize each person on this planet is walking a path designed to be exactly what they need, we can pull back and let go of our arrogant assumption that we know what is best for them, loving them just as they are.

Suicidal Relatives

Suicide elicits strong emotions. It means giving up and abandoning everyone. So, when someone we love takes their own life—or even threatens suicide—we feel abandoned. Anger and sadness are other common responses.

Sometimes, we feel that if we'd only offered a little more—if we'd taken that last phone call, if we'd been more aware of the signs—we could have averted their suicide. We feel worse if we've argued with someone who later takes his or her own life. Although we wanted to save them, they didn't want to be saved. They just wanted to escape.

Many people find the earth journey challenging. Research tells us that around 70 percent of people feel depressed sometime during their lives. Many of these people have thoughts of suicide. Society is concerned with the numbers of people who commit suicide, but these are small when compared with the number of people who would like to escape. Many do escape, not by suicide, but by other means, such as drugs and alcohol.

What do we do when we are faced with loved ones who tend to be self-destructive and who don't want to be here?

Colleen, age thirty-two, is a counselor to women who have suffered domestic violence. In her Life Between Lives session, she wants to discover if she is on track.

Colleen experiences a past life as a young woman, happily married, but with a troubled younger sister.

> *I am standing at my front door looking out, seeing cars in the street and the river. I am worrying about my sister. She is a lost soul who is taking drugs and hanging out with the wrong people. She is naive and trusting. While I am happy and secure, I am concerned that I can't be there for her. She won't let me. I have tried to warn her, but she doesn't listen.*

The practitioner takes Colleen to another scene.

> *I just saw her hanging.*
> *I got her to come and live with me, but she had bad depression. I had been out. I came back and found her hanging from the top bannister. I try to hold her up, but she is dead.*
> *I feel guilty. There is a big pressure on my chest. I am angry that she has done this in the house with my little girl. My husband is trying to help me cut her down. I am howling, and he is in shock.*

The practitioner encourages Colleen to breathe through the pain in her chest until it dissipates.

> *I still feel angry and some relief too. The struggle is over now. I am feeling she is at peace. The guilt is gone.*

Colleen leaves the past life and, while still in her life between lives, she receives information about how to get through trauma of this magnitude.

> *Thinking that I should be over things faster, doing more and feeling frustrated, just adds unnecessary resistance. I need to go with the emotions that arise and surrender, being in the*

present moment, allowing them, with no judgment and no resistance.

Now she wonders how she should handle negative people.

The guides are showing me a mirror, suggesting I use it as an opportunity to look at the situation. Once I discover my core beliefs about the negative behavior, I need to turn inward, bringing awareness to that core belief and letting it go. I need to create boundaries, ask myself what I expect from others and what I deserve. What I choose will reflect my feelings of worthiness. If I let go of the relationship, I don't need to feel guilt. "Listen to your guidance," they say. That is my journey in this life, to listen. I will get a sense of what is right for me and what isn't. I need to send love to these difficult people for helping me to learn, grow, and be assertive.

Colleen learns that she had many challenging past lives, including some in which she committed suicide. The guides give her more information about her soul journey.

Forgiveness keeps coming up. Forgiveness for the guilt I had. It was planned to teach me so much. I was meant to experience guilt and all that happened. Now all will unfold naturally.

My suicides and mental health problems in past lives have taught me a lot. I have good insight into others and what my clients are experiencing. I have been an abuser in past lives, but that was a long time ago. From that, I have insight into perpetrators and know they feel vulnerable and like victims inside.

Everything I have experienced has taught me insight, compassion, and understanding. I can be with people and be patient. I have experienced life from many different angles. All is valuable.

In the life with the sister who committed suicide, I had to learn to let go and let her be because there was nothing I could do. I was not to sacrifice myself or my family. In the beginning, I was really concerned, but I learned to let go and let be. My guides are clapping because I did so well.

Unsatisfactory relationships with our families can bring us great heartache. We can feel helpless because, after trying, we eventually discover we cannot change people. But the cases we have explored show us a way forward. We don't have to change others; we just need to change ourselves.

Once we really *get* this understanding, we surrender. Eleanor wanted a close-knit family. But a superficial close-knit family with members feigning togetherness is no comfort. Eleanor gave up her dream of a close-knit family and large family get-togethers. She saw there were other ways to have happy times with her family members.

Accepting the reality of our parents can be freeing. Sarina and Jennifer felt more peaceful when they understood why they chose their families. And Deanna was able to step back from worrying about her parents.

Acceptance also worked well for Colleen. Her loved ones were struggling with negativity and learning how to adjust to being here on the planet. When Colleen realized her loved ones were in the process of finding their own way to love and happiness, she could let go. With this new understanding, Colleen knew her role was to give unconditional love.

The guides often advise "let them be" to anyone having difficulties with family members. When we look closely at our own motivations, we often find our concern is more about us than our loved ones. We are worried we won't cope if something bad happens to them. Our fears hark back to our primal sense of looking after the tribe. We want them to be happy and peaceful because we feel more at ease when they are happy.

Unconditional love is acceptance. Each person is on their own soul journey. Once we honor the choices of our loved ones, even when it hurts us, even when it keeps us awake at night, we will eventually find peace.

Seven

NURTURING RELATIONSHIPS

The word *nurture* originally came from Latin and means "to feed and cherish." Food is a fundamental need. We need it to survive. To grow into healthy adults, we also need to be emotionally cherished. Once we are adults, we need to nurture and care for ourselves. But even when we are strong and independent, there are times when we need the love and support of others. At such times, we feel small and vulnerable, much like a needy child. Before long, with some care and attention, most of us are back on our feet, moving on with our lives.

We want to be there for our friends and relatives when they are vulnerable and in need. We want to know how to cherish them and pick them up when they fall. To fulfill our roles as caring friends and relatives, we need to be strong, resilient, and loving. How do we ensure we have the emotional resources needed to fulfill this role?

This chapter is not about duty. It is not about trying to be good. Trying to be good and dutiful takes effort. It doesn't have to be this way. When we are loving and caring toward ourselves, our love and care for others comes naturally. In this chapter, we explore cases that illustrate the wisdom needed to nurture each other.

Balancing Needs

Many of us believe we should always assist others. This belief is fine when we are helping someone in an emotional crisis, knowing the crisis will pass. But it is not a good idea with those who are always in one crisis or another. Such people can come to rely on our help, reinforcing their feelings of powerlessness. In the long term, we do not benefit either. We'll grow tired of always picking them up. We may even deteriorate into illness or resentment. How can we support them in a way that is empowering? Achieving this balance between weakening and empowering others can be tricky.

Keith, nearly sixty, has a successful career in the computer industry. Quietly spiritual, but not affiliated with any religious tradition, he is in the habit of doing his best to keep people happy. Keith comes for a Life Between Lives session feeling he is ready for an undefined change in his life.

In the session, Keith feels surrounded by his guide, sensed as a spiritual, calming presence. The guide has not been getting through to Keith and lets Keith know.

> *It seems I haven't listened to my guide. I'm sorry I didn't listen! He says it's okay. I want to say thank you to him. He is so understanding. He has been with me a long time. He is embracing me. It feels so good! He tells me to calm down.*

The practitioner offers some calming words to Keith, suggesting he can listen and understand more easily when he is calm.

> *My guide wants to take me someplace. He is going to show me something I do not want to see. I do not want to see it!*

The practitioner suggests Keith ask for help.

He says it is okay. But I feel that I was killing people in some war. I do not like it. It is not right, and I should not have been doing it. I am hiding. I am underground over a hill.

What am I to see? Oh! I asked to do this. I need to be more aggressive. Those people [I killed] are okay. They are soldiers. Why did I have to do this?

Keith discovers he planned to be more aggressive in this past life as a soldier. He doesn't feel comfortable with aggressive, masculine energies. But this discomfort indicates he is out of balance. He needs to be stronger and less submissive, admitting he allows people to manipulate him now, and in many past lives too. Keith is now taken to a past life where he is female.

I am the mother of a child, a little girl, Anna. I love her and I am very gentle with her. I am combing her long, dark hair. She likes it, and also likes it when I bake.

She dies young by running out of the house and being hit by a car. It is my fault. I should have watched her. [crying]

The practitioner asks what Keith is meant to understand from seeing this.

I am to understand what it is like to lose someone I loved. But she is okay. She is with me now [as his present mother]. She is in my heart. I protect her. I would die for her. [cries] She is with me and she will be with me forever.

I don't know why I don't understand these lessons.

I was told she would be with me a long time and she is very connected to me. I now understand why I have been so protective of my mother. I've had many lifetimes with this soul.

I still don't understand the war, something about manipulation. Oh. It is about protecting. I like to protect.

The practitioner wonders if protecting is a natural quality of Keith's.

Yes. Sometimes to protect you must be aggressive. To be less aggressive is to be manipulated. You cannot protect if you are manipulated. The same way you protect yourself, you protect others.

Keith likes protecting and looking after others, rather than himself. He is told, quite clearly, that the guides do not want him to keep doing that.

My guide says I do not need to be physical. I can use my words, as I am good with my words.

Keith needs to feel more powerful, but he doesn't know how. The practitioner suggests he ask to be shown.

Listening to others deviates me from my path. Ahh! I need to protect my path. My guide is telling me now that I don't need to do what others tell me to do. I do not need to please others or protect their feelings. I am to do what my heart tells me and follow my path. I am not to let others manipulate me or distract me. I don't feel that they are manipulating me, but I do defer to them often. I just want them to be happy. Like with Anna. I wanted her to be happy for a long time, but I failed. She died so young.

The practitioner asks if there was a soul lesson and soul choice for Anna in that short life. Keith reports that there was an agreement between them. She was meant to die young. The practitioner suggests Keith sense the power of that agreement, allowing any feelings of remorse or guilt to be released.

It is okay. Anna is laughing. She says it took me almost a whole lifetime to understand. She is in this life to let me protect her as my mother, and I am doing well. I love her so much.

To defer to others is easy for me. I wanted to make Anna happy. Then I wanted to make everyone happy and keep them from bad things.

In the past life, Anna's mother expected her daughter to grow up and have a happy life. When this didn't happen, she blamed herself, feeling she'd failed her child. The need to make things right was so strong that it affected the soul, like an imprint of a traumatic memory. This imprint manifested into Keith's life as a need to make people happy. It gave him a feeling of setting things right. But sometimes, instead of helping, he weakened those he wanted to help. He took on responsibilities that belonged to others, not him, thereby sabotaging their opportunity to build strength. Keith begins to see the connection between the past life and his need to please.

> *I can do both, protect AND be strong. Others don't have to influence me, and I don't need to let them.*
>
> *There are people who will be put before me and who will show me what I need to do. I am to be patient. I do not need to be all or nothing, all passive or all aggressive. My guide says to notice how his colors are mixed. I am like his colors, I am mixed, a little bit of this and a little bit of that. I think that refers to some song. He is laughing.*

The guide now takes Keith into another lifetime to consolidate his new realizations.

> *I don't see anything; I just feel cold. There is ice all around, like in Alaska. I think I am in in an igloo. So cold!*
>
> *I am wearing lots of fur. It smells good. This is where I learned to love dogs. He is showing me one dog I had. He was special. I was happy, though I did not like the cold. But that is the way we lived. I am male again. I don't like that.*

As explained earlier, Keith doesn't like experiencing masculine energy, seeing it as aggressive. The practitioner asks about the lessons of this life in the cold.

> *It is about being without, having nothing, and having the fear of being without. It's about surviving. Yes. So much ice, so many people died, so hungry. No fish. Too much ice to get to the fish.*

I don't like being hungry. My guide is telling me that is why I have excess weight now. I carried the imprint of not wanting to be hungry on my soul.

Keith now becomes strongly emotional.

We can't eat the dogs! Some want to eat the dogs. I won't let them. I tell them NO! I am very angry.

The practitioner points out that Keith is protecting the dogs, using his power and his voice.

Yes. They listened to me. I said we must wait. I told them to wait. We were okay. It was the dogs who led us to the fish. We all laughed about that. It was good.

The practitioner notes that Keith was a leader, suggesting he sense the strength of his voice and power.

Yes. They listened to me. It was one of the first times I said NO! like that. I loved the dogs. Our people listened to me from then on. They wanted to listen to me, and I like people listening to me.
  My guide said, "See how easy it is to follow your heart."

Keith touches his heart.

Your heart can protect you like the gun. You do not need a gun. The heart is what protects, not a gun. I learned that from being a soldier. It's what you believe. It's not what you do, not what you kill. You do not have to kill if you believe. I like that I learned that. That gives me goose bumps. Your heart protects. So many died, but they are okay. They all learned so much. Their lives were not wasted. No life is ever a waste.

Keith realizes he had a sacrificial life, a life where he played a role for someone else to learn an important lesson.

Did I learn a lesson in that life? My guide says I am learning it now. Sacrifice. It is not all about me. Sacrifice—such a short life, but a BIG lesson for the other soul. Like Anna in that life with me when I was learning about loss. She sacrificed herself for my learning.

He says that there really isn't any loss. We are all here together forever. I understand our journey is about loss, the painfulness, and the lessons, and it is all okay because you survive it. He is filling me with that feeling of there being no loss. Wow!

The practitioner asks if there is a universal message here.

Think with the heart. We think with our heads and it is not necessary at all. Every decision can be based in the heart, every single one. It is simple. Follow the heart. That is what the world needs now. I should tell people. Think with the heart, not the head, not the ego. He says it is truth and he is filling my body with truth. Wow! It is so simple.

The practitioner follows up with Keith several times after this session. A year later, he describes the session as life-changing. He lost several fears, including his fears of rejection, making wrong decisions, and disappointing others. He is happy in his work and has been promoted. Another year on, he feels called to move across the country to a place he has never visited. He follows this call. Now he is happily relocated and open to do whatever spirit wants for him. He is living from the heart and sharing that with others.

Keith's case tells us we should follow our heart. This means following our feelings. To trust our feelings, we need to clear the emotional baggage we carry. Keith did this. Keith felt some change was imminent and it was. The old imprint that had him running around trying to make everyone happy was gone. Now he could trust his feelings to guide him. He knows when to lead and when to pull back, when to give and when to say no.

Tough Love

Finding the balance between weakening and empowering when helping others is especially delicate when the person we want to help is close to us. Chad, a thirty-year-old horticulturist, loves working outdoors. Chad comes to a session wanting to know what lessons he needs to learn. He is falling into the same trap as Keith. During the pre-briefing, the practitioner learns that he has a specific issue with his sister.

Chad describes his sister as angry, impulsive, and in the habit of over-spending. She is always in debt and rarely pays off her loans. Being a generous soul, Chad is easily manipulated, repeatedly lending her money. In the session, he asks his guide what he should do about this.

> *It is not for the highest good of all to keep lending. I am enabling her. I would be helping myself on my journey if I stood up for myself more. I don't like people getting angry at me, but their anger is about them, not me. I am to walk away from angry people and go somewhere nice.*

When Chad is with the council of elders, he receives further information. Their advice is about using our intuition. This is another way of expressing the guidance Keith received about thinking with the heart.

> *I need to think more positively and be grateful, putting myself in other people's shoes.*
>
> *Intuition helps me stay on my path and make decisions. Feelings don't lie. When a decision feels good, it is right. It is intuition and that is how our guides help us. I don't use it often enough. My mind is too busy. I talk too much in my head. They are suggesting I meditate, mindfully meditate. I am to clear my mind and be aware of the thoughts that come in, quieting the mind so I can listen.*

Chad learns that his self-talk distracts him from listening to his intuition. He is trying to be perfect and worrying about making mistakes. Calming his mind will allow his fears to arise with a deeper understanding. He will feel more in control when he learns to either release or manage his concerns, whichever is appropriate in each situation. His guidance will support him, so he knows when to be generous with others and when to pull back.

By following our heart and the guidance of our intuition, we tap into wisdom and compassion. We can see what is in the best interests of our loved ones and follow through with the appropriate approach. Sometimes we need to look after our own needs, even when others do not agree and want more from us. Other times we are called to sacrifice our needs to help another. We need flexible, wise boundaries to balance our needs with the needs of others.

Healing the Unloved

There is one message that is often repeated by various guides during regressions: we need to fill our hearts with love before we can really help others. The case of Mary demonstrates the importance of this message.

Mary, nearing sixty, felt haunted by the thought that she had failed her mother. These unsettling thoughts became more intense since her mother had died recently.

Mary's mother grew up in a violent household. As an adult, she married an aggressive alcoholic who beat her. Taking her children with her, Mary's mother left her husband when Mary was ten years old.

They moved into what Mary described as "an old, dumpy house" and times were tough. Even though Mary was young, her mother expected a lot from her. Needy and critical, her mother said one day, "How could I be wanted?"

Mary had to grow up quickly, as her mother needed Mary to take care of her. Being a devoted daughter, Mary tried to meet her mother's needs and expectations, but this was impossible; her mother was "an unfillable well of sadness, shame, and unworthiness."

After her mother died, Mary thought about her mother's life, concluding that it was very sad. Then she wondered if she did enough for her mother, worrying that perhaps she hadn't.

Mary never felt loved by her mother. As she talks about the passing of her mother, tears well up in her eyes. Coming for her Life Between Lives session, Mary has only one thing on her mind.

I just need to know if my mom really loved me.

Soon after the practitioner begins the session, Mary experiences a past life as a happily married, wealthy woman with several children.

Home feels good. There's nothing to want for.

A few years later, her peace is shattered. Her nine-year-old daughter in this past life suddenly dies. She is grief-stricken and struggles to give her other children the attention and love they need.

> *It feels like part of me is gone. The other children need me, but I can't be there all the way. I never got over the loss of my daughter. I couldn't give my children what they needed. The love was there but it couldn't be expressed.*

Mary knows what it feels like to have a mother who is emotionally empty and cannot connect with her children. It is exactly what Mary experienced in her current life with her mother.

During this past life, Mary is the mother who emotionally neglects her children. And she doesn't understand the hurt inside her children caused by having an emotionally absent mother. But now Mary realizes she did love her children. She just failed to express her love, caught up in her own grief. Now she sees her mother was the same. Of course her mother loved her! She just couldn't express it. Mary not only knew the answer to her question, she felt it reverberate through her body.

A week after the session, Mary wrote to the practitioner.

> *It's the most unusual thing. Because of our session, I know my mother loves me. I always felt she didn't love me because I thought she saw something in me that was not lovable, not worthy of love.*
>
> *I have been given a gift from my higher self. It's the gift of knowing I was loved by my mom. I was unable to know this deep down. Knowing is the only word I can think of to use, yet it doesn't feel like the same knowing as everyday terms.*
>
> *I am so grateful. This is the most valuable of gifts.*

Mary didn't feel the truth of her own mother's love until she relived her past life and remembered the true depth of a mother's love. Mary realized that because her mother was full of grief and emotionally empty, she was unable to express her love.

Insight into the pain and struggles of our loved ones gives us power. We see their behavior in a new light, realizing we are not bad or unlovable after all. We can feel love and compassion for ourselves and for those who are still hurting. When we are filled with love, nurturing our relationships with others is easy and natural.

Forgiveness Heals

Forgiveness is healing. Little else is as nurturing as being forgiven and feeling redeemed. But forgiveness is not something we do just for others. When we forgive, we free ourselves.

We are not talking here about feigned forgiveness. Feigned forgiveness is avoidance. Some hurts are so deep and painful that we want to put them out of our mind. We think if we forgive the perpetrator, the pain will go away. But we are mistaken. We might have put the incident out of our mind, but it hasn't gone away. As soon as we encounter a situation like the betrayal from the past, we find ourselves thrown back into the original pain.

To forgive, we not only need to look at the perpetrator's actions, we also need to look at our own. If we are cloudy about our own motivations, we do not have the clarity to see the truth. Instead we justify our own actions and blame others. We need discernment and much courage to see the truth. Only after we have seen into our soul and the soul of the other, do we know the truth. Forgiveness comes from a deep understanding of the perpetrator and of ourselves.

The case of Natasha, a forty-year-old woman, shows us this path to real forgiveness. For nineteen years, Natasha was sexually and ritually abused by her stepfather. After he raped her at age six, she fell under his power. The abuse caused turmoil in Natasha's life and she spent many years in therapy, healing her shame and self-hatred. Despite her emotional work, Natasha was still suffering feelings of rage and sadness. She came to her Life Between Lives session wanting to understand the deep reasons for her stepfather's abuse.

Early in the session, Natasha experiences a recent past life as a man named Max. Max is married with two children, but he would like to be free of his marriage. He is rich and money-driven. He has no respect for his wife, is sexually "cold" toward her, and beats her and their children. His only interest in his wife is to maintain their social status. He is totally caught up in all the material external things, including money, fame, and social recognition. Max never reflects on his behavior, becoming more and more abusive toward his wife. Although they hate each other, they hide it from their social acquaintances.

His wife sees no way of protecting herself and her two young children other than killing him. She knows carbon monoxide is deadly, quick, and painless, so she poisons him with this gas.

Until he passes over, Max is not aware of the impact of his behavior, but Natasha soon sees through the man she was in that life. During the regression, she reflects on his behavior.

> *Being like Max doesn't give you anything good. I was playing out what I thought I had to do. "WAKE UP!" I look into his eyes and tell him to wake up. Weirdly enough, I want to say this to the man I was: "I forgive you. Max, you were like a child. And thank you."*

Natasha reports that Max now feels respected and acknowledged. He knows he didn't lead a great life and did need to be forgiven. Now Max's wife appears, and even though she made a sacrifice to be his wife, she agreed to do it. They forgive each other. Natasha, as Max, has another realization.

> *I also need to apologize to my children, for leaving them and beating them badly. Somehow, I thought that I was a good father, but I see it differently now. They were really damaged.*

After reviewing her life as Max, Natasha is no longer bothered by that lifetime. She meets her council of elders, and they give her information about her progress as a soul.

They say that Max's life was an important one, because [cringing] I didn't learn anything. So now I have a choice to really buckle down if I want. I can discover what my lessons are, learn, and wake up, or I can just continue down that path, kind of circle around the drain, and then go down it. It is important for me to understand that I did not move forward as Max. It was an opportunity for me to make different choices, and I didn't.

The practitioner asks how Natasha feels about this.

I understand exactly what they say. I kept the lid on the box the whole time. I refused to open it.

They used to call me Butter Flower and they are doing it again, saying, "Now you're getting it, Butter Flower!" They say I was sitting on the fence for a long time. I thought about it a lot and in the last three years of my current life I buckled down.

The abuse in my current life was to wake me up! It was forced. They tell me that in other lives I had all the ingredients to be more conscious but, in that life as Max, I overrode my awareness.

The council points out that the abuse in her current life was brutal and painful for a reason.

All that pain made it much more difficult for me to stay complacent. The abuse was meant to create a crisis.

The practitioner asks for more details about this arrangement with her stepfather's soul.

We both agreed to play our parts. We made an agreement before we lived this life. And I knew, going into it, that it would hurt. He was chosen because he could do it.

The practitioner questions Natasha about her stepfather being capable of abuse and if there were any other reasons why he was chosen.

His soul was capable of abuse. That is why he was chosen. We did not really have a strong bond when we made the plan. My guide and his guide were there when we signed the contract. My father is on a very different path than I am. They show me his soul, and his light is very dim.

The practitioner wonders about the essence of the lesson from the abuse. Natasha exhales slowly and pauses several times as she receives the information.

Compassion. Forgiveness. And awakening in consciousness. Yeah, and waking up, I just hear, "waking up, waking up!" And experiencing the other side of the coin. I have been in the role of the abuser before.

The practitioner asks how the council is rating her progress.

The heavy lifting is behind me. [she smiles] And they are very proud of me! They know it was a big test.

Natasha has a deep-seated fear of men, and the practitioner wonders how this can be healed.

My fear of men comes from having experienced both sides, the lifetime when I was the abuser as a man, and this lifetime when I am abused by a man. For a long time, I turned a blind eye to it, and I did not want to look at it. I agreed to clear up a lot of this stuff in my present life and the abuse by my father is one of the biggest parts.

I must learn to go within and look inside. They say part of my work is to have faith and trust myself. Forgiveness is first, and not just for other people. I came in with very specific work to do, and the biggest piece is about men. It's learning

to respect men, while knowing my own value. Also, I need to
confront my own pain around this.

There are all these emotional places I did not want to go
to, but I do have to go. It's the only way. I just need faith. They
show me that I am turning a corner. They tell me to remember
this conversation.

Natasha's forehead is gently touched by the practitioner, to help her remember, knowing she will need this memory as she moves forward in her life. This helps her integrate the learnings from the session and clears any remnants from the past.

Natasha now understands the reasons she suffered the abuse. Her soul was stalled and, in Max's life, had made no progress at all. The abuse was designed to force her to wake up. Her suffering set her on a path of searching for answers. She has been working on self-improvement for several years, and this healing path guided her to her Life Between Lives session.

She also discovered she had been a perpetrator in her past lives. She forgave Max, and this helped her begin the process of forgiving her stepfather. As she and Max shared the same soul, she was effectively forgiving herself, as Max was a part of herself that she'd disowned. Forgiving and embracing the lost parts of ourselves brings us to wholeness, expressed in religions as holiness. Forgiveness is the heart of our soul journey. We cannot be whole without it.

A few years after the regression, Natasha had forgiven her stepfather, enabling her to begin dating and to open to love.

The forgiveness I feel toward my father is a huge relief. I know
it was my soul that chose what happened to propel myself for-
ward. And it has worked so successfully.

Forgiveness is one of the most powerful actions we can take to nurture our relationships. When forgiving feels out of reach, ask to understand the greater perspective of the hurtful behavior. Once we fully understand the highest perspective of the situation, any need to forgive disappears. Forgiveness is automatic and all our pain melts away.

Severed Bonds

Connection is fundamental to relationships. And yet we can be in relationship and feel disconnected.

How do we connect with other people? We connect in pairs. This means the fundamental connection with others is always one to one. Even when we are with a group, each person connects to all the others individually. It is like a network. If three people are friends, there are three relationships. If four people are in the group, then there are six relationships. Even though a relationship is between two people, a third person can influence the quality of their connection.

Our sense of connection is not stable. It comes and it goes. Still, the quality of our connection to others greatly influences our relationships. This is profoundly true of the connection between mother and child.

During her Life Between Lives session, Valentina, thirty-six, describes her sense of disconnection from her mother.

I am coming through the birth canal and there is a lot of disturbance. It isn't peaceful, too much is happening. It is stressful and painful for my mother. Everyone is worried. They are trying to get me out. She is afraid, not able to trust the process and connect with the baby that is arriving.

Looking back on her birth, Valentina describes the environment as hostile, saying she didn't feel much connection to anyone.

As she grew, there were other times when she felt disconnected. On one occasion, when she was a little toddler, she wasn't cooperating with her mother, who wanted her to get dressed. Instead, Valentina was playfully jumping around in her cot. Her mother became angry, worried about being late for an appointment. Suddenly she grabbed Valentina's hair and threw her down. Valentina recalled how she felt.

I hit my head on the rails on the cot, on the right side of my head at the back. I have a feeling of fear. I feel scared and vulnerable.

It is a feeling that makes me want to go into my own world to feel safe. My trust in her to protect me and my feeling of being secure is disturbed. I get a sense of closing down, feeling safe within myself and needing to be self-reliant.

Even now, feeling insecure affects my confidence. It is important in early childhood to feel secure and connected.

Valentina describes disconnection as a sense of closing into her own world. Others have described it as a sense of contraction, rolling up into a ball, and distancing themselves from others.

Connection was one of many themes running through Valentina's seven regressions. She discovered that reconnection is achieved from experiencing both sides of the coin. Like Mary in an earlier case in this chapter, Valentina learned from her past lives that she too had disconnected from her children. She forgave her mother and became a more loving and connected mother from understanding the nature of connection and disconnection.

Many parents do not understand the nature of connection. They think they are being helpful when in fact they are pushing others away.

Importance of Self-Love

Attachment and connection are different. When we are attached, we have expectations of our loved one. We think we are connected but we are not and we end up trying to control, manipulating our loved one to give us what we need.

Connection is different. When we are connected, we have no expectations. Our love is much bigger than that. We see the humanity in our loved ones, their vulnerability, their strength and their protective stances. Nothing they do can permanently break our sense of connection to them, even though they may deny it and go their own way.

Marie, a fifty-seven-year-old nurse, feels disconnected from her loved ones and wants to know how to re-establish relationships with them, especially her son. She felt connected to her son until his early teens, when he started isolating himself. He is now eighteen.

The practitioner asks Marie's guides why Marie is having these problems.

Marie has preconceived ideas about what love is. When her experience is different from her expectations, she is unable to stay open. She closes herself off and cannot receive love. She doesn't understand that you automatically deserve love. You don't have to earn it.

Many humans hold this misunderstanding.

Unconditional love is a like a sense that you know is there. It is not a thing that you can prove, and it is not actions. You may have an inner knowing of love or you may not even be aware of it at all. You just trust it is there.

When people are close emotionally, it is easy to trust that the love is there. You sense their sincerity and you don't have doubts.

You need sincerity and honesty to build trust. This comes from the heart rather than the mind. It is sensing rather than thinking. When you love, any action you take comes from a sense of sincerity. You might give, because your heart tells you to give, but you don't expect anything back.

Wanting proof of others' love is not actually important. In fact, wanting proof gets in the way of connecting. It pushes your loved ones away. Marie tries to provoke a reaction from her loved ones, thinking she will then know they love her.

The practitioner notes that Marie will go to her son, pleading to help him by asking what's wrong. Usually he is not interested, saying with hostility, "Leave me alone." She will then often provoke him, making a scene, crying or yelling, hoping to get his attention. The guide explains why this is happening.

When she does this, she is acting from her needs and not his. She must stop this if she wants to be sincere in her relation-ships. She needs to know that her needs and the needs of her son are both important. And this applies to all relationships.

She must understand that the love we need the most is the love we give ourselves. When she is her own closest com-panion, she is no longer dependent on others. Then she can focus on just being, instead of trying to manipulate others into meeting her needs.

Here we accept that everyone is perfect and exactly as they should be on their journey. Humans need to accept themselves. This means loving and nurturing yourself instead of supporting others in the hope that they will love and care for you.

When Marie acknowledges and nurtures herself, then she can extend this to others, no matter what their circumstances and no matter what choices they make. That is unconditional love.

Valentina helped us understand the deep pain of disconnection from those we love, particularly when children feel disconnected from their mothers. Marie's case gives us direction on how to connect to our children as parents. Both cases remind us of the power of present time: unconditional connection with those we love.

A Gift of Unconditional Love

There is nothing really to say to introduce this case. Its power resides in the story itself.

Kelly, age forty-nine, comes for a session seeking wisdom and guidance in her personal, professional, and spiritual life. Kelly is a soul who is strongly connected to her higher self. This is evident from her recent past life as a nine-year-old Jewish boy, Joseph, who lived in Austria during World War II.

Joseph and his five-year-old brother had a happy life with their family in Austria until the Nazis came. They were separated from their quiet, loving parents and taken to a concentration camp. Joseph stayed calm in the camp, looking after his brother, observing and comforting the others. He watched the guards and wondered how they could treat children with such neglect and cruelty.

We feel mostly fear. We fear we will never see our parents again. And we fear the hunger and cold, having no blankets or coats, or anything. There is a lot of yelling from the guards. They don't look at us; they try not to look at us. But

I look at them in their faces anyway. I want them to see me. I know they have children. I don't understand how they can do this. They can't all not have families of their own! But no one takes care of us. I have a girl, Ellen, as my friend, and she talks to me. She is not always comforting because she brings all bad news. She says we won't be here long. It will be over soon.

Joseph notices one guard and senses an uneasiness inside him.

There is a guard. I see his face. I feel like he hates his job. I know he does, and he hides it with his yelling. But I know inside he doesn't like what he does. He feels pity for us. I try to stand near him. I feel like I remind him of his own son. My brother and I are always together, always holding hands and I never take my arm off him, if I can help it, to keep him warm and to keep him safe.

Joseph describes what happens when he, his brother, and Ellen are taken to the gas chambers.

There comes a time when they move us. They move us to a building and Ellen tells me we're going to die there. She says they call it a shower, but it's not. It's poison. She says to not fight it. Just breathe it in and make it fast. She asks us not to scream. She doesn't want to hear us scream. My brother and I promise not to. So, we go inside and it's very crowded. We are all pressed together. Some adult people are with us too now, but I don't know where they came from. We are waiting, it seems like forever. We know this is the end. I am praying. I pray to God that it's quick. Then, the mist, it is like a shower, but it isn't. I take a deep breath and ask God if I can go at the same time as my brother, so we can go up to heaven together. It's very fast! I come out before my body is done living. I feel no pain or suffering in my death.

The practitioner asks Joseph to describe what happens after he leaves his body.

> *I'm lying on the ground. I am naked. Everyone is falling around me. But I don't see other souls. They each have their own way. I know my brother is safe and Ellen is safe. And a light is there. I pass right into the light. It folds around me. I'm instantly okay. I felt bad for the guard. Pity was the last thing I felt, not fear, and I am in the light. It's very, very bright, and I feel at peace.*

Joseph passes into his life between lives and is welcomed by an angel. He soon retains his soul consciousness and is given insight into the reasons for this short, challenging life.

> *My last life was so short. Oh! I only went to teach the guard compassion. And that he should overcome the coercion to do the job they wanted him to do.*

Kelly is told that Joseph was brave and did what he was supposed to do. The practitioner asks for more information on Joseph's purpose.

> *I was to give comfort and compassion. It was so scary. There were so many people panicking. If I didn't panic, it would comfort them. I showed strength and courage so that they knew they could do it too. By accepting, it would be easier, and it didn't have to be so bad. To show acceptance demonstrates that, no matter what, you are okay.*
>
> *And I see that I looked at the soldier, looked at his face, as I was going into the gas chamber. I knew I was going to die, and I saw that he regretted everything. He wished he could follow us in there. That he could go too. But he says in his mind that this is his punishment. He will endure it then, whatever he must, to the bitter end.*
>
> *I see now that he is my father in my current life!*

There is a pause as Kelly takes in this revelation.

Joseph energetically connected to the guard, reading the guard's emotions, and seeing that the guard's aggression was just helplessness disguised as power. Joseph also connected to each of the children, calming them with his serenity in the face of great adversity.

Kelly is still connected to the guard who shares the same soul as her father. She mentions that her father refused to discipline her or her siblings, wanting to be the fun-loving parent. And he completely avoided watching any war movies.

During the session, Kelly discovers that Joseph's life was a sacrifice. She could have finished incarnating several lifetimes ago. She volunteered to help the souls of the guard, the brother, and the children on their soul journey. While incarnated, Kelly and Joseph are connected to their higher self.

Just as we have a one-to-one relationship with each other, we also have an individual connection to Source Energy, often referred to as our *higher self*. Joseph felt this personal connection to God, and the peace it gave him was significant. He was able to positively affect others. Although we are always connected to this energy, we can deny it. When we are afraid or negative, like the children and the guard in the camp, we feel alone and abandoned. This is disconnection. Because Joseph still felt connected, he became a conduit for the loving energies from above that were able to calm the inmates of the concentration camp.

Sometime later, Kelly writes to her practitioner, expressing some of the insights she received during and after the regression.

> *I realized how we are all one, all interconnected. Then this message came to me: We are collectively like a pond of water. If a stone is thrown into the pond, only a few drops of water touch it, but the whole pond experiences the stone. Our individual souls are the drops of water that make up the pond. What the pond experiences, we ALL experience together, even if the event doesn't touch us directly. What we do to one another, we do to all and do to ourselves. Thus, it is so important to treat each other as we wish to be treated. This is how we are all connected by God's love and energy. In the regression, I saw how*

all souls seem to be individuals, yet completely connected at the same time. To think we can somehow be separate and alone is impossible! We just couldn't exist if that were true.

––––––––––

Each of the cases we explored in this chapter demonstrates the importance of opening to our soul journey. Keith and Chad teach us the importance of building strength and resilience, so that we can act from the heart, balancing our needs with the needs of others. Natasha shows us a way to forgiveness through understanding her own soul's journey. Valentina teaches us the importance of feeling connected to others. Mary demonstrates the power of seeing both sides of any trauma, which leads us to compassion. Kelly, through Joseph, demonstrates the power of our one-to-one connection to love energy, thereby reassuring others in need.

When we are open to connect to others and we are living from the heart, we are our true selves. Our true self naturally nurtures others. We are calm, even in challenging circumstances. We are accepting and not judging, expressing unconditional love to those around us. We know what to do because our heart tells us. And we trust the universal plan, understanding that whatever happens is ultimately for the highest good.

Eight

BALANCING CAREER AND FINANCES

Acquiring money and support for ourselves can be an obstacle or a help as we move along our life path. It could slow our spiritual progress, if we put too much time and attention into it. It's an obstacle if we spend the bulk of our time and energy creating a successful career, securing recognition, or becoming wealthy, at the expense of the goals we set while still at home in the spirit world. Also, it may be difficult for us to find the right balance between career and family responsibilities.

Some of us have trouble getting started and just aren't sure what we want to do with our lives. Money can seem like a necessary evil and something that we just can't master. Problems with those we work with can be a nuisance and make us very unhappy. Or the fear of not having enough money can keep us in a situation we can barely tolerate and prevent us from following our passion. Struggling with a job we don't like or having a problem making ends meet could be an obstacle to our spiritual growth.

Fortunately, these situations can also be a help. They provide wonderful circumstances for achieving soul growth. These opportunities, however, are not be easy to spot and often appear to us as frustrations, difficulties, and challenges, unrelated to our personal development. We may even view these struggles as getting in the way of our spiritual growth. But what looks like a problem may really be just the right circumstances to achieve one of our important life goals. As the following cases demonstrate, the gift in these experiences is a chance to achieve significant growth.

Career versus Family

For any of us, balancing family and career responsibilities may be an issue. In today's modern world, this can especially be a problem for women. Child-rearing years can overlap with the important early years for building a career. Such is the case with Stephanie.

Stephanie, a thirty-three-year-old woman, has already met all the educational and certification requirements for becoming a therapist and has a successful practice. She is interested in advancing her career and is considering returning to school to obtain a doctorate. However, at thirty-three years of age, she worries that going back to school will interfere with having a child, something she also wants to do. Can she handle both? She feels stymied and unsure about what to do. Stephanie schedules a Life Between Lives session to gain some clarity.

During her session, Stephanie is guided to the library, where she is shown a picture book with images of lifetimes involving the loss of a child or dangerous childbirth experiences. She is an English knight in the year 1200. In that lifetime, the knight's wife dies while in childbirth with their third child, and the baby does not survive either. He stops living when his wife dies, becoming bitter and resentful toward their two remaining children because they remind him of his wife whom he had loved so dearly. He chooses to remain bitter in that lifetime and does not move on to a happier state.

The most significant lifetime Stephanie is shown is in the mid-1800s in America. Here, Stephanie incarnates as a female who suffers damage during a difficult childbirth. This results in lifelong physical pain and the inability to have any other children after this first one.

This is one part of living that I hate, I don't like to experience pain, death, fear, wars, and nothing compares to the difficulty and pain of birth. I hate being a girl. That is why I must give birth. It's an opportunity for me to be nurturing.

The previous death and injury sustained during childbirth in previous lives had created an unconscious fear of the childbirth experience for her. This fear manifests in her ambivalence about pursuing career advancement or starting a family. However, having a child is something her soul really wants to experience.

Stephanie's guide reassures her that her fears surrounding childbirth are not hers but are carried over from another lifetime. He tells her that she need not worry about whether she'll be able to conceive. This time it will be easy, and her body is getting ready for it. She will conceive in another year and have a daughter named Mandy. They have been together many times before. He suggests she consider an alternative birthing place because hospital energies are affected by the death, sickness, and germs there.

Stephanie is reassured that she is on the right path now, but that she needs to connect more and feel more. She is told not to worry, that she will eventually go back to school to get her doctorate.

Before, the time wasn't right for school, she explains. Things are in the way because it isn't the right time. The roadblocks are there because I'm supposed to be stopped right now, learning patience.

Stephanie learns that she and her husband Gary have been together before, and that he is the right one for her now. Last time they were together he died before they could have children. He's ready for fatherhood now.

Several years transpire, and when the therapist contacts Stephanie to follow up on what has happened since her Life Between Lives session, she is reluctant to report that she has not had a child as she expected. She admits she was newly married at the time of her initial session and wasn't ready then to have a child. She wants to enjoy time with her new husband first.

After the news she received in the session, Stephanie kept busy with her work and adopted several dogs, admittedly as a distraction because she just wasn't ready for her life to change, as she knew it would when she became a mother. She even made another attempt to go back to school for her master's degree but was thwarted when one of the dogs fell ill and required surgery at a great expense.

Stephanie shares that at one point she and her husband tried to adopt a child, but the adoption fell apart at the last moment when the birth mother changed her mind. She decides to do a follow-up session to find out more about the situation.

During the follow-up session, she learns that her situation is a lesson in choice and free will. Guides provide information and give counsel, but we have the freedom to follow the advice or not.

Stephanie confesses that she doesn't want to go through the pain of childbirth. She is her own block. She is informed that she must do it to clear the block. She still isn't sure she's ready to have a baby, but she and her husband truly want a child. She discovers that the role of the dogs has been to provide happiness, patience, and unconditional love. They serve as placeholders to heal the cracks in her heart.

Stephanie is shown the past life in the 1800s when she again experiences the difficult childbirth which results in her only being able to have the one child. She is reminded that science and medicine have advanced a great deal since then and that she and the baby will be okay. She is also warned that she doesn't have much longer or it will be too late. She feels a sense of pressure to rush to get it all in, along with feelings of failure for not completing her life's mission.

Stephanie's guide shows her a large switch and tells her that it's up to her to pull it. By pulling it, she agrees to move forward with plans to be Mandy's mother. Stephanie pauses a bit, thinking over the situation and its consequences from all angles, still uncertain she is ready to move forward with having a child. Stephanie finally is ready and pulls the switch. Mandy appears, clapping and giggling.

The guides explain that there is always a lesson to be learned. Everybody's lesson is unique. You can learn from what appears to be a mistake. There is so much more out there than the human brain can conceive, but the soul can know it all. You

just need to be open to that understanding and that percep-
tion. That's when free choice and free will come into play. She
is advised: free will is a tricky one; it's like walking a tightrope.
Stephanie experiences doing things her own way, pursuing her
other interests but with time to get pregnant. The timing pres-
ents a challenge, though. She will not be able to become preg-
nant after a certain age and she is getting very close to that
time.

With the insights from her sessions, Stephanie is now ready to move forward with a pregnancy. She leaves feeling excited about the future.

Choosing Money over Passion

Mike is a divorced, forty-three-year-old inspector for specialized construction
with an eight-year-old-son. Mike is tall, handsome, physically fit with well-
developed muscles, and very well-groomed. He has temporarily relocated
away from home to take this current job, because he feels he needs the money.
He doesn't like the work he is doing but views it as a financial necessity.

He feels under pressure at his job and guilty over being so far away from
his son. He is usually very strict with his diet and exercise regime, but now
finds that hard to continue because he works long hours and lives in a temporary situation. He yearns to do something more creative, preferably nowhere
near a construction site, but does not see how he can do it with child support to pay and other financial obligations. Over the past several years, he
has become a spiritual seeker and wants to learn more about his life path and
his current situation.

During his session, he sees himself at his current age, sitting at a computer, and makes the following comment.

I'd rather be doing work in a relaxed atmosphere than doing
what I am currently doing. I want to be working for myself—
that's my aspiration.

Then he receives the following information from his guide.

Just relax. Let things happen and don't take them personally. You're getting comfortable with being uncomfortable. There probably will be some stress when you make your next career move. You need nourishment such as fruit. You need to follow a diet in alignment with the person you are trying to become. You need raw fruits and vegetables, smaller meals, fish. You need a diet that supports life, and you also need to eliminate distractions. Stay focused and recapture your "kid energy." Turn things into play with adult wisdom added.

Next, he sees himself at age sixteen, puny, weak, and shy. He is a meek teenager who is bullied. He is much stronger and more powerful now and no longer needs to worry about body image. His is shown that he is much better with the opposite sex now too, and no longer needs to worry about approaching women like he did back then. He is told that he is too serious and needs to lighten up a bit and that it is okay to eat desserts occasionally.

Then, he finds himself in a scene when he is age eight, the same age his son is now. He sees that his father shows much more interest in him than he is showing his own son. He sees that he can be more intimate with fathering. Speaking as a soul through his higher self, he shares the following comments.

I should do more things with my son, be more present. Let go of troubles. Do more artistic, creative work. Try to balance the logical left brain with the creative right brain.

The scene changes, and he finds himself in purple clouds, looking up at a beautiful golden tower.

It's very warm and peaceful here. I look different now. Alien and bluish. I can feel the energetic presence of other souls. Oh, I'm visiting my soul family! They're telling me, you're safe—we have your back. If you leave your current job, everything will be okay. You know that when you've been worried in the past, you always pull through. It is your choice. It is up to you this time. Your purpose for this life is to heal others, leading from a platform of communication about what you know and what you have learned.

> *My soul family is telling me that I must act. I must let go of things I let get in the way, such as fear and lack of self-worth. I need to feel the fear and do it anyway—I need to move forward.*

Mike recognizes that his grandfather who passed away is one of his soul family members. He also sees his grandmother there. He learns that his guide's name is Maximus. He's told that he is experiencing an expansion within himself. He is learning to hold the space of light worker energy in a harsh environment, such as the one that he is currently working in. This enables him to learn more about what others are going through and to be positive and inspiring. He wants to be a light worker in a difficult environment and receives additional guidance.

> *Don't worry so much about work. Make personal connections. Be present and meet people where they are at and be an inspiration to them. These are lessons being learned and they are part of the plan.*

Mike realizes that being away from his son is a problem. He feels ready to plow through the barriers that are there.

> *This is not what I want. This is a wake-up call to do what I want!*

His guide gives further advice.

> *Move forward with focused energy, but do not force things. Working alone feels positive, but you need to get out of your comfort zone and meet people. You need to find your tribe; it is preplanned. You must find a way to connect. You need to stop being a perfectionist! Mike, you've got it!!*

Mike thinks the girl he is currently dating may offer a way to move out of his comfort zone. He can go out and be social with her and meet new people.

Next, he goes to a past life as a Nordic man named Jeb. Jeb points to the ocean. He shows no fear, and just wants to go out and explore the unknown. Jeb tells him:

You can be afraid, but when you get there, it can be bliss, just great!

Jeb tells him to move in the direction of healing.

Just get started, you don't need to know where you're going— just explore.

Jeb tells him that he would rather have an adventure than a mediocre life. He says to get in touch with that past.

The practitioner asks, when did Mike lose this sense of adventure? His guide gives the following answer.

In this life, some caution comes in. His grandmother is very frugal. To her, money is everything. From this, he develops the attitude that he must make money. The need for the security of having money overrides the feeling of adventure. Also, he begins to strive for perfection in body image. Eating healthy, taking vitamins, cooking his own food, and going to the gym on a regular basis to keep the right physique. He is worried about body image and his health, because when he was a young man, he was scrawny and got bullied. Women are not very interested in him. He needs to clear his apprehension about his body and his ability to attract women. Those doubts control his mind. He needs to let go but can't do it. He can't get out of his mind and into his heart.

Mike sees a pyramid and steps into its energy. It is drawing energy from the earth, pointing toward the heavens. He sees an image.

It's creating my own reality!

Mike leaves the session feeling much calmer, saying that he has some reflecting to do about all that he has learned. He reports two weeks later that he is feeling better than he has in a long time. He has quit his job and is heading home to spend time with his son and plan a career change.

Money Woes

You first met Eleanor, age fifty-seven, in chapter six. Eleanor came to her session for several reasons, including past difficulties with her property and finances. A few years before her session, Eleanor had over a dozen properties. Most were rented but a few were being developed or renovated. She had nearly a million dollars in cash and reasonable equity in the properties.

Eleanor was a confident investor, full of trust in her business ability and her spiritual guidance. However, with no warning, her properties were all greatly devalued. None of this was her fault. Not long before, a bank sued a property appraiser for overvaluing a property. Word spread quickly amongst other property appraisers, who quickly reassessed their appraisals, wiping millions off the value of property in Eleanor's estate.

Suddenly Eleanor had little or no equity in many of her properties. Eleanor's financers insisted on more equity against her properties. Her cash was soon eaten up and she was forced to sell, often for less than what she paid. She avoided bankruptcy but ended up with nothing. Her financial position has not significantly improved since then, although she manages.

During the session, she discovers she is carrying guilt from her previous past lives, but that is not the main factor in her financial loss. When she lost her property, she was with a lovely man, Louie, who eventually became her husband. Louie has many desirable qualities, including a good balance of masculine and feminine energies, a great sense of humor, and a sensitive and romantic nature. Eleanor describes him as a wonderful support to her, like a knight in shining armor.

But Louie has one major defect. Within him, he carries a deep fear of financial insecurity. Before the session, Eleanor wondered if his poverty consciousness was affecting her. She had been with him only a few years when she lost all her financial security.

During her Life Between Lives session, her loving guide comes through. We ask him about the loss of her properties.

You chose to lower your energy level because of love. It was a choice. You could have moved on from Louie.

The practitioner clarifies what the guide has said, wondering if there was any way Eleanor could have stayed with Louie and kept her financial security.

No. It was not possible to change him to keep the properties. She must match his vibration on this issue to be together. She chooses to do that and gradually she is helping him to raise it. Before her wealth was lost, he had a taste of what could be. That helps him to raise his vibration up now. Eleanor could have left Louie but chose to stay. She wants to help him.

The practitioner asks if Eleanor can do anything more to help him.

Trust. Louie is getting the help he needs, in his sleep and dreams, and in time he will raise his vibration for finances. All you need to do is trust and you will be brought into financial security again.

There is a purpose in everything, in every hardship. Know your journey is the right journey. Remove your fears and just trust.

We learn from Eleanor's case that to create a compatible romantic relationship, vibrations must be aligned. Eleanor's soul knew that Louie's poverty consciousness would affect her financial success, but she chose to be with him anyway. She chose to help him learn to move away from his poverty consciousness. Her role now is to trust as their vibrations concerning finances realign.

Not Living Up to Your Potential

Erin is a thirty-three-year-old married mother of two young children. In her twenties, she was considered among the best and the brightest enrolled in her graduate program. She is now feeling pressure both from herself and from those around her to use her ecological and analytical skills to help "save the planet." The high pressure and other aspects of academic life, however, are not a good fit for her. But the lingering feeling of failure and the sense of untapped skills seem to haunt her.

As a young mother, a debilitating injury affected her ability to do many basic tasks of daily life. She became interested in a Life Between Lives session to understand her life purpose and the meaning of her injury and subsequent disability.

During her session, Erin visits a past life in which she is a leader who is very concerned with protection of the environment and maintaining harmony in the society. Later, when she visits her council, Erin asks why she has sustained her injury and is now disabled. Erin relates the information she is being given by the council.

> *They are very pleased that they have come up with this solution of an injury and a disability. As a soul, I have already experienced being a leader and change-maker on a large scale. I have developed a deep resonance for the earth and culture. In past lives, I have been a leader in protecting the earth and creating connectedness and coherence in the culture.*
>
> *What I have not yet developed is an exploration of body intelligence, a slower pace, and an inner attunement. The limited mobility offers me many possibilities for learning this. Their hopes for me are that I will be forced to go more inside.*

Erin asks the council:

> *Shouldn't I be using my knowledge to help fix things? This drove a lot of what I worked on in my schooling. Can't I bring that in somehow?*

Her council replies.

> *We can see how you got so confused, but no. There is a compelling aspect to that idea, but that's not what you have come to earth to learn. You've had responsibility before and you thought maybe you should have a similar role in this society, but no! These health problems are an intervention to stop you,*

to keep you from doing that. This is fine, it's just your body, not your core energy. Think about how much progress you'll be able to make developing your inner resources.

Erin asks:

There is this sense of my heart knowing that things aren't right out there, wondering what I can DO. It's not wrong to want to help, is it?

Erin translates the council's response:

And they're saying, well, in a way it is wrong! Laughter follows. It's not your job to go fix the world in some concrete way. You don't have that kind of power here. You're not a decider here.

Erin ponders this and then responds.

But there have been times in the past when I have just been receptive and that was easy to do when I was receiving good things. Then I could be active in a practical way after being open to that larger level goodness. But now I need to be the opposite. NOT receptive to the chaos around me, and just active practically in a very small and local sense. I must use my memories of coherence and connection and really filter out the bad stuff. And remember the gratitude. Finding the good things and really focusing on them with gratitude in my heart. I should use selective attention and ignore the bad stuff. That's what you must do to create a coherent subfield. You can't be receptive to all the bad things.

The practitioner asks the council if Erin knew this was going to happen before she incarnated.

No, we hid a little bit from her. It is better that way.

Erin reacts to their answer and responds.

Well, no wonder I'm confused! And having these memories, knowing where we are off track as a culture. There's no turning back now. They started to reference it, but then stopped and put up a shroud. I don't know if earth is completely going away, but the train is rolling down the tracks and no one can stop what's going to happen. But they put the shroud up and I'm not supposed to think about that. But I see it, I know the earth. I don't need them to show me what's happening. I'm living here now, watching it happen. I've been wondering what I can do to help. And they are giving me lots of compassion now. Of course, it's hard for me. No wonder I want to help.

The work I am doing now is just about me, just my energy, just the immediate vicinity where I happen to be. I have very little responsibility for anything else right now. This seems so small, but also totally overwhelming. It looks easy, but it's hard when you really must do it. Release the responsibility! NO responsibility. That's the new classroom for me—not in charge of anything. Just try to do the first little project within myself.

The practitioner thinks that it will be difficult to tell a young mother that her disability is her "medicine," but is surprised at how Erin calmly accepts the rightness of this information. Erin has embraced the inward journey and reports feeling a freedom from the old sense of what she ought to be doing. While her family does not always understand this, she feels more at peace and has become stronger.

This example is unique because we so often hold the outer accomplishments, those recognized by others, as most important. But here, the inner state and a more refined sensitivity is what is seen as a better accomplishment for this soul.

Always Second

David, a seventy-one-year-old married man with adult children comes in for a Life Between Lives session after reading Dr. Michael Newton's books. He is a successful musician who performs with many well-known rock artists. However, David is not in the primary role. Instead, he is mostly in backup.

While he is happy to support others, this experience is making him question why he is not more visible, in a more ego-gratifying position. David lives a good life, but like many, he comes to the session looking for answers about his life.

In his past-life review, David experiences the life of a dogmatic and fiery Catholic priest named Bruno, who exhorts people to repent and worship or face the wrath! This life of Bruno is the last in a succession of five Catholic priest lives, all filled with aggressive behavior. Toward the end of the life of Bruno, a higher soul embodied as a young and very beautiful woman visits with Bruno. She points out the futility of the fiery attitude and reminds him that this work is over. It is time to move on.

After the death of Bruno, his soul chooses a short, ego-gratifying life as a dashing German biplane aviator. This life is a materialistic, ego pleasure trip. It is a life of people fawning over him, receiving great accolades and hedonistic enjoyments.

Immediately before the war commences, he meets the same higher soul he had met as Bruno, but this time she appears as an English noblewoman. She looks into his eyes, making him feel introspective, and wakes him up to his soul's calling. It is time for him as a soul to give up the hedonism, to stop wasting time, according to her. Shortly after, in a fiery airplane dogfight over France, he dies in a fusillade of bullets and is shot out of the sky.

In returning to Spirit, he connects with his main guide, who asks him the following questions.

> *Alright, did you get that out of your system? Can we get to work now?*

David discovers that his relationship with his guide has been changing over his recent lifetimes. Now he is less a guide and more of a mentor. His guide conveys that David is very close to crossing the finish line, and that it is time for him to escape the bondage of the incarnation cycle, to give up the small ego, the small "I," expand into the universal "I," and to be a guide himself. His guide shows him that all it will take is a "leap of faith," and that he is ready for it.

Next, he visits what at first appears to be a council of elders, yet he begins to understand that he is part of the council as well. All nine members of the council wear similar deep purple robes. He learns that they have all advanced, and now, in the life of David, he has the golden opportunity to advance as well.

All in the council are loving toward him, yet he can feel their impatience and their sense of urgency, knowing he is so close to advancing beyond the need to reincarnate. He understands, from the council, that some attachment to ego and materialism is all that is in the way. He also understands from them that the opportunity he has in the life of David will not be available for several future lifetimes if he does not apply himself now.

In the past, he experiences a lifetime with his guide when they were both disciples of Christ, about six lifetimes prior to his current life. In that earlier lifetime, he witnessed how his guide had attained liberation. He learns that he might have achieved it at that time as well. However, both he and his guide saw that the gap between being a fisherman and liberation was a big leap, and that he needed more incarnation experiences. He has had those experiences now. He can attain liberation in this lifetime. His guide repeats the same message.

> *You have the choice to be a guide now! Extend yourself, your awareness.*

David, as his soul self, cries.

> *There's a barrier, the personal ego, which says, "Don't leave me"; it's freaking out, afraid of being left behind.*

The practitioner asks if it is possible to let go of the personal ego, yet not make it feel left behind. Perhaps let it go to a safe place?

David, as a soul, affirms that this needs to happen.

> *I cannot take the girlfriend with me [euphemistically meaning that the personal ego must be left behind].*

The practitioner suggests that he ask for some help from the advanced soul who has visited him in previous lives. He reports that she soon appears as an overwhelmingly beautiful being, twice as tall as he and his guide are. She kisses him on the top of his head, places her hands on his shoulders, and tells him the following information.

Listen to him, all you need right now is to let go of the ego.

David, as a soul, reports what he is feeling as he lets go.

All awareness is floating, it feels just neutral now. It's just me, awareness… it's not blissful… there are no properties, but it's me… it's pure awareness… and all in the council are cheering!

My guide says my leap of faith is accomplished, and he and the council all say STAY!

I'm feeling the need for vigilance with every breath. Everyone in the council is clapping. I've regained something I've always had but didn't realize, something I just forgot.

A long period of silence follows as David absorbs this experience.

My guide says, stay with this feeling, it's a fun new experience! This is just the beginning of the experience, and as you continue, layers of communication will open to you. All in the council say, "Be patient, STAY in this state, and feel."

David comes out of the session feeling clear and directed. He says he feels able to let go of the personal ego and continue to grow into expanded awareness.

In the follow-up, David reports that he downloaded the recording of this session and took it with him to New York for a music gig. On the way home, he had the opportunity to listen to the recording, which brought him right back to the experience and sensations he felt during the session. He says he feels he is growing in awareness from having had this experience. He no longer has any concern about filling only backup roles in his music career.

We see from this case that David's secondary role in his music career is a step away from his previous ego-driven past lives. It is also a step toward a role he is to assume when he returns home to the spirit world and becomes a guide.

Gifts from the Past

Dennis is in his fifties and serves as a minister in the Christian church. He chose this career path because it felt very important to him. Recently, he feels that the framework he is working in is limiting him, because his beliefs are more expansive than those of his church. He wants to understand why he chose this career path and why he has trouble sleeping and has the habit of studying late at night when he really needs to sleep.

During his Life Between Lives session, in response to a question about why he chose his current career, he is guided to a past life.

> *I'm inside some building. I'm standing on the floor and looking up at the ceiling. The ceiling is made of glass, small pieces of glass—purple, blue, green, a lot of colors. I'm wearing brown sandals on my feet, and I can see my bare feet in them. I'm wearing a long dress-like brown thing. I'm a man, my name is Louis, and I'm thirty-five years old. It's a holy sanctuary I'm in. I've been here for many years. The year is 1783.*
>
> *I walk out into the sun and there's a cobbled path lined with trees. There's a crowd of people looking at me positively, and I'm glad that so many people like me. They know me from the holy sanctuary. It's white with a black roof and has towers. There's a crescent moon beside the entrance. People greet me and I greet them back while I walk down the path. It's lovely weather and I'm smiling.*
>
> *Now I am in a dining hall at a long table sharing a meal with my brothers. I feel safe being with them. We are eating porridge and drinking beer out of large mugs.*
>
> *Now I'm sitting and reading a book, I have grown old and have a long grey beard. I feel good, but I can feel that my life is about to end. I'm about to die. I'm in my room. There's a window*

with small panes. The room is small, and there's a bed, a table, and a chair. I'm reading an old book. I like the books that I get from the library. It's the best place.

The practitioner guides Dennis back in time, to an important scene in the library.

I'm talking to a brother and we're recommending books to each other. We're exchanging experiences with leather-bound books about deep wisdom. I use the wisdom to live my life. I have this calling that I must live with my brothers and it couldn't be different. It's a divine wisdom. I've got it good here. It's a good and safe existence.

My interest is mostly with books about God, and the creator of the universe. Love is extremely important. The love is in everything, in everyone, everywhere. The aim of our lives is that we become one with it. It's important not to keep the love to yourself; it must be turned outward to the world. The world and those closest to us need prayer. They need us to pray for them.

The practitioner asks Louis to go back to the time he arrived at the holy sanctuary.

I'm eight years old and I'm being dropped off by a strict woman with an acute nose and grey hair. She's my aunt. I don't understand why I should be here. There's a large man with a round head and red cheeks who greets me. He's gentle and nice. I can feel him take my hand. He has a big, warm, soft hand. I'm happy to get away from my aunt, but I don't understand why I have been brought here.

They aren't interested in having me anymore. My aunt and her husband don't want me and it's my aunt that decides it. I live with them because my mother died when I was three years old. It's the husband who has ties to my mother. I think it's her brother. There are a lot of rooms, and many stairs in this big beautiful house. It's lonely here. There's no one for me to talk to here, and I'm not allowed outside. My aunt says nothing can happen to me when I'm here inside, but I don't believe that. The kids outside aren't proper enough to play with me. I can see them when I sit in the window. They have ragged clothes, and I want to play with them.

There are no other kids. The others are all kind to me. I like the garden. I must work in the garden, but here I'm allowed to play amongst the big trees. There's love here.

What's the religion called, here in the sanctuary? Does it have a name?

It's only talked about as the wisdom. There are olive trees, and I can smell the herbs and hear the cicadas. There are mountains in the background and the climate is lovely.

Now Dennis goes to the last day in the life as Louis.

I'm eighty-five years old. I'm lying in my bed and there's always someone at my bedside. There's a little light burning, and it's quiet. I'm lying with my hands folded on my stomach. Life is as it should be. It was a good thing, coming to the sanctuary when I was eight, because that was meant to happen.

I have left the physical body. It is peaceful. I'm hovering a little above the body. The death is peaceful and pain free. I am ready to die. I think about never experiencing love for a woman, and therefore never having any children.

I learned in this life that my goal was to surrender to God. Then everything will be as it should be. Next time, I will do it even better. I must focus on reaching my goal and getting closer to God.

The practitioner says, "I know Dennis does a lot to live up to that goal. But he also suffers with trouble sleeping at night, can you tell me about that?" The soul as Louis's higher self gives an answer.

I sit in my chair at night and work a lot. It's important to be something for someone. It's important to pray and to read. There's no time to sleep, because I have many chores. Every hour there is something I must do. It is important work, both the physical and the spiritual.

Dennis's guide offers further information.

Dennis's purpose is to maintain and deepen his spiritual contact. He is striving to live with love throughout his heart. He lives in another time now, and so he can study and learn, and immerse himself in silence and prayer more easily. In this way, he can explore the congruence of ancient wisdom he has acquired with the framework in which he is now working and find his way forward. He does not have the physical work now that he did in the previous life, so he has the time to rest and sleep as he chooses.

The information about his previous life confirmed for Dennis that as a soul, he is on a spiritual path in which he is choosing devotion to religious study and teaching. Thus, his current role in the church is not surprising. He is learning to deepen his spiritual contact and demonstrate and spread love in the way he lives his life on earth. The guidance he received suggested that through further study, especially of ancient texts, prayer, silence, and contemplation, his next phase of spiritual growth can be realized. This will allow him to feel less constrained in the framework in which he currently works.

Dennis also learns that his difficulty sleeping is likely a carryover from his previous life. While Louis had so much work to do during the day that staying up late at night was his only time to study and learn, Dennis has more choice in the matter. He can sleep at night without neglecting his spiritual quest.

Dennis reports that since his session he feels at peace and has been doing some research about the past life that he visited. He also reports that his sleep is improved; not perfect, but better.

Loss of Identity

Wanda, a sixty-year-old dentist who works with children, was loved by her patients and their parents. She was so popular with her young patients that they didn't even mind going to see the dentist. She, in turn, loved her work and made it a point to get to know her young clients and their families and do special things for them. She had assembled a loyal staff that shared her values and warmly welcomed and served the children and families.

Wanda is also an excellent artist, and her paintings made her office a delightful place. She is unmarried at the time of her session and had no children or close family in the area, so her work was always like her family. This was a blessing for all concerned, but then trouble arose.

Wanda had long suffered from periodic back pain stemming from an injury she sustained in a boating accident when she was much younger. The pain would flare up from time to time, but rest and self-care measures usually cleared it up in a short amount of time. However, as she got older, the problem became worse and was aggravated by her long hours of standing as she practiced. Soon, the pain became so severe that she was forced to stop practicing dentistry. She was devastated by this, as she hadn't even given much thought to retirement yet. As she left her dentistry office for the last time, fear about the future and a deep depression set in. She came for a Life Between Lives session to gain some insight into this situation and what the future might hold for her.

After entering the spirit realm, Wanda's guide addresses her concern over no longer being able to practice dentistry. She describes a scene from the past that she is being shown.

> I see an old grey-haired man in raggedy clothes standing on the edge of a stream. He's a farmer and he's kind of smirking and laughing at me. He says I should persevere like he did. He says I should keep going and keep my business running. He has NO pity for my pain at all.
>
> He is not wise, and I disagree with him. I have been like him for years and just plow through, as my stoic upbringing has taught me to do. Now I see the damage that I have done to my body by trying to keep going all the time. My body is in

pain, but I squelch it as much as I can so that I can keep work-
ing. I feel that I must, for my patients and my staff. So many
people depend on me. Is this pain telling me it's time to let go?
As I look back at my practice over the years, I am very proud
of what my loyal staff and I accomplished. I'm proud of our
success, but much prouder of how we all loved and cared for
our patients. But I must let go!!

Now I'm on a beach and there is a dragon here—all green-
ish and breathing fire! It has no fear because it knows that
nothing can harm it.

Wanda takes some time to absorb this experience.

Oh, I get it. I should make friends with my fear!

The practitioner assists her in doing this by encouraging her to approach
the dragon in a friendly manner. As she does, the dragon becomes smaller
and smaller, until it is the size of a small frog. Wanda decides to keep it and
puts it in her pocket.

As she continues moving along with her guide, she enters another scene.

I see these brown, formless blobs. They remind me of a car-
toon. They are in my body for a reason. I have been work-
ing with patients for thirty years and I've been holding them
inside, to keep them close to me. Wanda paused to contem-
plate this insight. But I need to let them go! I've been holding
on to the negative things, like their pain and their fear.

The practitioner assists Wanda in releasing the negative things she has
been holding on to for so long. Wanda imagines standing under a golden
energy shower that cleanses her completely inside and out. As she does so,
the brown blobs completely disappear. Wanda noticeably relaxes.

The practitioner continues, addressing Wanda's guide: "Wanda feels
uncertainty about her future. Do you have any guidance for her?"

She knows that she has done well, but it is time to move on. She now needs to develop other parts of herself. This will give her the opportunity to do so. She can go back to her art if she chooses to do so. She now has a decision to make. She can let her pain take over and give up or she can make the best of her situation and take care of herself, as she knows how to do. Working to accept the situation will help to relieve her depression. Then there is energy to spare and energy to continue to serve. She has all the resources she needs. This is an opportunity to expand.

Wanda left the session feeling more hopeful. The pain was still there, but she felt more confident about managing it and less like a victim. She also felt some excitement about getting back to her art.

A later follow-up finds Wanda engaged in an active program to manage her pain, taking art classes, and seeing a counselor for her depression. She plans to do commissioned art work in the future and has plans to marry her long-term partner.

Having to figure out how to support oneself while incarnated on earth provides an excellent opportunity for learning. In the modern world this means having a job and making money or finding someone to support you. While this necessity offers many opportunities for growth, it can also derail you from pursuing your spiritual goals.

In addition, family responsibilities must be considered. Achieving the right mix among these competing life demands is not easy. Finding balance in modern life can be further complicated by carryovers from the past. It is no wonder that we can become sidetracked from what we came to earth to learn.

Stephanie reminds us that we have free will to allow us to achieve a balance that is right for us. But a carryover from her past regarding childbirth made discovering the right balance for her more difficult. Dennis, too, discovered his sleep problems, which interfere with daytime functioning, are related to a past life.

For Mike, the perceived imperative to make money kept him from following his passion. It also kept him from forming a close relationship with his son. Eleanor, who was comfortable with making money, chose to be with a partner with poverty consciousness, thus lowering her own capacity for attracting money. But with guidance, all of them can find the right balance.

Too great an emphasis on any one area can keep us from developing other parts of ourselves and can lead to unhappiness when things change. Wanda became depressed when she could no longer continue in her profession, which had been the center of her life. However, this change led to many positive developments in her life.

Erin and David were concerned about not living up to their potential in the careers they had chosen. However, both were working on other aspects of themselves that others might not understand.

Fortunately, when we stray too far from our path, are laboring under a carryover from the past, or are confused about how to proceed, guidance is always available. Finding the right balance between making a living, developing a career, nurturing family relationships, and pursuing our own self-fulfillment and spiritual goals not only leads to contentment, but to spiritual advancement.

Nine

BREAKING FREE

It is quite common to consider habits a normal by-product of our busy lives. Inundated with tasks and responsibilities, many of us develop routines that create efficiencies, save time, and make life easier. Simply stated, habits are formed when a behavior is repeated so frequently that it becomes automatic. Despite the benefits, some habits are limiting at best, while others precipitate life crises.

Releasing Habits

Habitual behaviors can impact our health, as is the case with smoking and eating habits. Understanding their origin and how they serve us might free us to break the habit.

During a poignant point in a Life Between Lives session that is focused primarily on healing childhood sexual abuse, Nancy leaves her body as she begins to transition to her life between lives. She notices that she is breathing deeply. The physical sensation is powerful. She feels free! She realizes that breathing deeply is a reminder of freedom, whether she is breathing in fresh, clean air or her favorite brand of cigarettes. Within an instant, she understands that in pairing the two she has developed a lifelong habit that is financially costly and will ultimately impact her health. Now she is free to make another choice—a choice to break her smoking habit. It's one that she happily makes.

Habits are not limited to behaviors. They are also automatic reactions to specific situations. As such, they create fixed ways of thinking and feeling. Habitual beliefs solidify perspective and outlook, leading you to patterned behavioral and emotional responses. At a communal and societal level, habits that become customary practice are formalized as customs, norms, traditions, and ultimately laws.

Habitual behaviors and beliefs create both positive and negative effects. For example, if you have a habit of always looking on the bright side of things and seeing the best in others, you will likely usually find that your beliefs manifest positive feelings. You may even notice that your generally positive attitude is contagious, spreading to others you interact with. Conversely, you may have a habit of avoiding interacting with others because of your belief that people are not trustworthy and will likely betray you. Habitual behaviors and beliefs don't discriminate; they work both ways.

Over time, habitual behaviors and beliefs are hard to change. They become almost involuntary. As such, they provide fertile ground for the soul as it seeks to learn or to heal during a lifetime on earth. In his seminal research documented in *Journey of Souls* and *Destiny of Souls,* Dr. Michael Newton highlighted multiple ways that the soul is challenged through the habits it has formed.

Emily, a middle-aged woman, is stymied in her new career as a nurse because of paralyzing self-doubt about her competence. Seeking understanding of the purpose in her life, Emily learns of successive lifetimes spanning five hundred years in which she lives as priests and nuns in cloistered environments where she is insulated from the hassles of connecting with society at large. When she appears before her council in her Life Between Lives session, she is challenged about whether she is ready to break out of her rut and finally get involved with outside society. The succession of cloistered lives has served to balance what Emily described as a long prior history of excessive noncelibate lifetimes. With gentle understatement, council members remind her that too much repetition over too many lives can hold the soul back.

Testament to the patience of spirit guides, Dr. Newton wrote of two other cases in which the souls were slow to break long-standing patterns. One soul had been working on envy for lifetimes spanning 850 years. Another sought authoritative power over others, on and off. A habitual behavioral tendency can be especially difficult to give up, especially once it has shaped beliefs and character traits. Eventually the soul will be faced with balancing these propensities.

Patterns of Belief

In Lily, we see how even a behavior that has created a positive character trait can restrict the soul who is working to achieve balance. Lily is a thirty-four-year-old well-educated, professionally employed, financially secure woman. She is divorced from Robert, who has bipolar disorder. She is calm, patient, rational, and has extraordinary empathy. The latter trait is not surprising given her 752 lifetimes, most of which were dedicated to serving.

Lily has worked hard in the last decade to strike a balance between service and self. She hopes to learn how to relax more and build more pleasure and fun into her life. Surprisingly, despite the importance she places on finding direction for her career during the Life Between Lives session, her guide gives the following advice.

> *Her career is intended to give her stability. It is a means to an end so that Lily can focus on the other things. There is a tendency and drive to do more because that is what everyone else is doing, but balance is what her soul is seeking. She is not living to work but is working to live.*

During her return to the life between lives, her guide emphasizes Lily's habitual lives of service. He points out that Lily's drive and tendency to prioritize the needs of others comes from many lifetimes when serving others did not allow for the luxury of focusing on herself.

Most of her lives have been lives of service, taking care of people. Newer experiences take her out of her comfort zone. In this life she needs to set boundaries.

Marrying Robert, who struggles with bipolar disorder, provides Lily with the impetus to practice taking care of herself. During the planning phase before this current lifetime, Robert agreed to a role that would help Lily transition from service to self-care. He has not reneged on their agreement. The guide explains further.

His behavior is so extreme. He makes it so difficult for her to take care of herself that she has no choice but to set boundaries. That triggers her learning more about setting appropriate boundaries. She hadn't really heard of boundaries until then. It isn't a concept that she was taught growing up. Her soul plan for this life is meant to set boundaries, and being married to Robert gives her a perfect setting to learn and practice prioritizing herself. He pushes her to where her only choice is to focus on self-care. And now she is learning to balance self-care and serving others.

The guide stresses how once the pattern started, repetition reinforced it time and again.

She wanted to be of service in all those lives. Caring for others was easier. She's used to it. It was more natural. It was a habit to care for others. She wanted to be of service. She was motivated to change because she got tired of serving others, but she really couldn't keep doing it without constantly recharging energetically. She was getting burned out. The plan that she developed for this lifetime was to break this habitual behavior out of necessity.

The guide elaborates, striking a hopeful note.

Through this session, Lily is learning that she has been overly devoted to service in these many lifetimes. This insight will help her put things in perspective in this life, but the change will not come overnight. And it will not be automatic. It is something that Lily will need to work at for some time.

The guide's realistic evaluation is a reminder to us all that insight alone does not change behavior. Change requires determined focus and a willingness not to give up, especially when there are setbacks. It requires reinforcement. Changing habitual beliefs requires new beliefs to be formed and acted upon. Breaking habitual patterns takes considerable work, whether those habits are positive, like Lily's devotion to others, or negative, as is the case with addiction to substances, sex, or gambling. As we see in the following cases, even negative behavioral patterns offer the soul and their loved ones opportunities to grow spiritually.

Addictive Echoes from the Past

Those addicted to drugs and alcohol have developed a habit with an impact that is far-reaching. In fact, the widespread availability of drugs and alcohol, and abuse of them by young and old, has made addiction one of the more common problems people struggle with today. Drug or alcohol abuse may greatly impact your life even though you might not be personally suffering from the addiction. It exacts a heavy price on the one trapped in its grasp and has a major impact on family, friends, job, and community, as well as society.

The personal costs of addiction are enormous. It robs a person of health and vitality, contributes to accidents, disease, and, if left unchecked, death for those under its control. It affects daily functioning by obscuring judgment and clouding the memory.

Addiction strips people of their ambition and damages reputations, costing many their jobs, livelihoods, and careers. Financial hardships often leave individuals and families bankrupt of financial savings and stripped of security.

In the case of Baldwin, we see a crossover between habitual beliefs and habitual behavior. Baldwin is a thirty-eight-year-old draftsman with deteriorating health due to chronic alcoholism. Although schooled in architecture, he has never felt confident enough to seek commensurate employment. He is not married, acknowledging that he never quite learned how to overcome his insecurity about dating. He shares that his low self-esteem and self-doubt have been debilitating for as long as he remembers.

During his sessions, Baldwin re-experiences several lifetimes in which his dreams are short-circuited by his low self-esteem and self-doubt. He dreams of marriage and a lifetime of shared love, financial security, professional success, and recognition.

In an emotionally charged return to one "failed" past life, he sees himself dying alone at a young age of liver disease, having developed an addiction to alcohol in his teens in order to cope with paralyzing insecurities. As his body transitions to his soul state, his guide reminds him that, despite his best efforts, he still needs to work on changing his beliefs and habitual behavior.

> *You will have to try again. You cannot give up, either on life or yourself. You already know that the path you travel is not easy, but you must continue to seek the confidence and success that you deserve.*

Later in his session, the same message repeats when Baldwin meets with his council.

> *I have the sensation of being wrapped in their love. It feels warm and reassuring. I am being told that they have confidence in me. I am blocked by my lack of love for myself. They will never give up on me. I need to learn to not give up on myself, to value myself and to build confidence and a sense of my worth.*

Baldwin's emotional Life Between Lives session has helped him to understand why it has been so difficult for him to realize his dreams and why he has again chosen to dull these painful thoughts with alcohol. He has come face-to-face with his truth. Until he changes his opinion of himself and his view about his talents, skills, and lovability, he will return time and again to the destructive pattern of addiction that has gripped his life.

Armed with this profound insight and carrying forward the acceptance and unconditional love of the higher beings, Baldwin is ready to embark on a different path. As his Life Between Lives session concludes, Baldwin affirms both his desire and commitment to break the patterns of the past and to write a different ending to his current life on earth. He knows that he has much work to do but is ready to abandon the patterns that have not served him.

Addiction tests and challenges relationships. Over time, drugs and alcohol become more important to the addicted individual than their loved ones or associates. Deceit becomes commonplace, fracturing the trust that is foundational in healthy relationships. In advanced stages, addiction causes blackouts, dangerous enough for the one left with significant gaps in memory while also being disastrous to relationship longevity. Unresolved, these relationship cracks ultimately destroy friendships, partnerships, and families.

Habits That Limit Growth

Bret is a tall, athletic, forty-five-year-old dentist. Since his early teens, he has been gripped by anxiety and a profound sense that he is not in control. At age seventeen, he discovered that marijuana calmed him. In his own words, he became addicted to this chemically induced tranquility.

Despite this, Bret has managed a highly successful dental practice, employing a staff of eight, including another dentist. While marijuana does not lead to addiction, his use of it has become a habit that limits his growth, and it is illegal where he lives. Thus, he uses it behind closed doors, and his sense of integrity is affected. His capacity for appearing to have everything under control seems to help him fool most who know him, including his colleagues at work.

Bret decides to schedule a Life Between Lives session after he is broadsided by his wife's decision to divorce only a few months after they purchased their dream home. He describes Gena, his wife, as a weekend binge drinker. He credits her with having greater control over her habits than he does. At the same time, he blames her behavior as the cause of their marital problems.

At the outset of his work with the Life Between Lives practitioner, Bret shares that he cannot imagine being able to forgive Gena for her decision to leave him. He finds himself bouncing back and forth between rage and crippling numbness. He and Gena have been married for seventeen years. In addition to his anger, her decision leaves him feeling abandoned and betrayed. Understandably, he describes that he's floundering about what direction to take in his life.

Early in Bret's Life Between Lives session he sees himself as an officer in the Army prior to and during the American Civil War. His wife in that life is now in the role of his wife in his present life.

Bret sees how his military responsibilities kept him away from his wife and child for long periods of time. Despite his wife's fidelity, he recalls betraying her numerous times by having brief affairs with prostitutes while on leave. On one visit home, he infected Gena with gonorrhea, which in those days was deadly. Eventually, it weakened her so much that she died at the age of forty. He was not with her at the time because he was leading his company during a decisive campaign of the war.

Bret learns when he comes home after his wife has died, that their thirteen-year-old son has been sent off to an orphanage. Despite a frantic search, no one knows where his son is. He is devastated by both losses but can't let anyone know how sad he is. It would be a crack in the persona he has created to bolster his authority. Any sign of weakness would damage the image that he has projected to the outside world, particularly with subordinates.

This reflection back in time leaves no doubt about the issues of integrity, abandonment, and betrayal that characterize Bret's current situation. Even within his hypnotic trance, he clearly sees an old pattern being played out in his relationship with his wife. He is now on the opposite side of the dynamic. And, from this expanded perspective, he will now be in a better position to achieve the learning that his soul desires.

When he taps into the between-lives realm, he hears the same message repeatedly from different spiritual sources.

You are here now in a place of unconditional love and acceptance. Allow yourself to unburden yourself from these difficult emotions. Release them, free yourself. Have compassion for yourself. Learn to accept yourself without judgment. Learn to love yourself deeply as we do.

Bret's Life Between Lives session helps him to understand that while protecting him on several fronts, his marijuana habit is limiting him. His use of an illegal substance is making it impossible to be fully present for his clients, causing him to fail to act with integrity. He worries that over time his dental practice may suffer.

More importantly, his marijuana habit numbs his emotions. Not only has he buried emotions from the loss of his son and wife in the Army officer life so long before, but Bret has been burying his emotions in his current life as well.

At seventeen, Bret's decision to begin using marijuana allowed him to feel more in control. Ultimately, it worked in just the opposite way. From a higher perspective, Bret can understand how issues of integrity, abandonment, and betrayal are influencing him. Releasing these subconscious memories through his sessions brings a sense of internal power, resolving the need to numb himself and manipulate others. From this perspective, Bret can see how he and Gena have been mutually responsible for their pattern of interaction.

He comes to understand how he and Gena enabled each other's limiting habits, keeping them both emotionally stuck and contributing to their breakup. In addition to insight about how his marijuana habit helps him cope, he now understands that on a spiritual level, Gena is assisting him in growing spiritually.

Bret has now not only forgiven Gena, but he appreciates the gift she gave him as she kept her part of their soul agreement. The breakup and divorce forced him to look deeply within himself, to release the pain from the past, and to heal his heart. Embedded within the experience is the opening for self-forgiveness that will serve him in this and many future lifetimes.

Limiting habits and addictions take over lives, destroy happiness, and shatter dreams. The damage is far reaching and long lasting. And yet for the one struggling to break free of its grip, it can eventually become a pathway to great insight and personal growth.

Like many other problems that exact great personal and interpersonal costs, coping with the addiction of someone you care deeply about presents an opportunity for tremendous spiritual advancement. Because the soul learns through upheaval and opposites, we are led to establish a new pattern of thinking and behavior.

Addiction in Families

Another way that the soul chooses to grow is to place itself in life circumstances that are opposite of an earlier life. This provides an opportunity to see and experience the very same circumstances from the opposite perspective for learning purposes. Doing so offers the soul a chance to balance the impact of earlier decisions and actions.

Samantha's experience coping with a loved one's addiction illustrates how this plays out. Samantha is a sixty-year-old married mother of three adult children. She comes in for a session to gain some insight into problems she is having with her youngest daughter.

Karen, a beautiful, talented, and intelligent young woman in her mid-twenties, is seriously addicted to drugs. During her childhood, Karen became an accomplished ballet dancer, but started taking pills she obtained on the street at about age sixteen. With support from her family, Karen managed to graduate from high school and college despite actively using drugs.

During those years, Samantha, a nurse, did everything she could imagine to help Karen. She exhausted her retirement savings and ran up huge credit card debt paying for counselors, rehabilitation programs, bail, and attorneys. Nothing worked. This all put a tremendous strain on her marriage as well. Now Karen is using cocaine and heroin and living a very chaotic life.

Samantha knows, from all that she has been through, that she is enabling Karen by continually rescuing her. She realizes that it is time for her to let go and show some "tough love." However, she is having a very hard time doing so, and is plagued with guilt and fears about how all this has happened to her daughter and what might happen to her in the future.

During her session, Samantha finds herself as a samurai warrior in feudal Japan. In response to questions regarding the situation with Karen's addiction, Samantha describes the following past-life experience.

> *I am a great warrior; my name is Miamoto. I follow Bushido, the honor code for samurai. I fight bravely and gain much respect. I am rewarded well and now retired; I have nice home and servant.*

Miamoto goes on to describe that his servant's daughter dies, and she is left to care for her daughter's baby. The live-in servant has no choice but to bring the baby to live with her in Miamoto's home.

The baby cries, and the servant does not do the work right. The baby must go away! I am very angry and I lose patience. I tell her the baby cannot stay here. I tell her to get rid of the baby!

Due to Miamoto's decision, his servant is forced to sell the baby. Although this is possible to arrange, the transaction is shrouded in secrecy. Nothing further is known of the infant girl's whereabouts or fate. The infant's grandmother is devastated. Despite living a life of honor, Miamoto's insensitive and self-centered action causes great emotional distress for his servant, and likely much more suffering for the infant girl who is dispatched so callously.

As Samantha recalls her prior action during the life of Miamoto, she recognizes the servant's baby as her daughter Karen.

Samantha next ventures to a life in England in which she finds herself as a female ruler. Her husband dies, and since she has only a daughter and no sons, Samantha inherits responsibility for the land and its workers.

I am now the queen and the responsibility for the land is mine. We have rich land, many workers and a fine village. The guards protect the castle and patrol the borders. There are many who would take this land if they could. They see me as weak, because I am a female ruler. But the people are loyal to me.

Things are peaceful for many years, but then the ruler from a neighboring kingdom becomes more aggressive, threatening to take over her land.

Things are getting more and more dangerous and my advisors feel that an attack may be imminent. I make a visit to that kingdom to try to form an alliance. We agree that my daughter will marry his son and then we will be allied. That will bring peace. However, when I return home and tell my daughter, she is angry and wants no part of it.

Samantha realizes at this point that the daughter in this lifetime is again her daughter Karen.

Things keep getting worse, so the pressure mounts. Eventually my daughter agrees to the marriage, although she is not happy about it and resents me for it. The wedding takes place and she moves to his land. Things are peaceful for some years, but I hardly ever see my daughter. She doesn't answer the messages I send her.

Trouble starts brewing again. I try to reach out to my daughter, but it seems she has joined her new family and turned her back on me. Soon we are attacked by them and we cannot hold them back. They storm my castle and I am killed in the battle.

Samantha is weeping now. She feels guilt over how she has treated her daughter in past lives and sadness over how her daughter has betrayed her. She fears she may lose her daughter again in her current lifetime.

Now I see why I have been feeling so guilty and have had so many fears about the future, given how I've treated Karen in the past. No wonder I have not been able to let go even though it is draining me physically, emotionally, and financially. I am trying so desperately to help Karen, to assuage my guilt.

As Samantha moves into the spirit world, her guide addresses her question about how to handle the situation with Karen.

You must remember that she is on her own path and has her own lessons to learn in this life. You have been repeatedly rescuing her and robbing her of the opportunity to find her own way. Just love her. Love is always the answer.

Remember your own path and your own self-care. Love yourself.

Inspired by the revelations and the loving acceptance of her guide, Samantha went home after the session and, as she described it, did some powerful soul searching.

Samantha concluded that it was best to stop rescuing Karen, even if that amounted to letting her go. She later reported the following experience.

> *The decision did not really make acting any easier for me, but I knew in my heart that it was the right one. It was the most loving thing to do for Karen.*

When Karen showed up the next time at her house, high on drugs, broke, wanting to come back home to stay for a while, Samantha mustered all her strength and courage and said no. Not surprisingly, the following weeks were filled with anxiety and doubt. Given her history and not knowing what was happening with Karen, Samantha imagined the worst and struggled not to accept responsibility for the decisions that Karen might be making and the danger that she might be in.

When she finally did hear from her daughter, Karen was living with a new boyfriend. Samantha's decision had been a turning point for both her and her daughter. Karen's new boyfriend was supporting her in her efforts to get off drugs, and she seemed to be doing much better. Eventually the two married.

Samantha's decision and action had a positive effect on her daughter's life and a major impact on her own. Her days are no longer filled with drama and worry. Life for Samantha has become much more peaceful, enjoyable, and free. She is trying to consciously love and care for herself.

A follow-up several years later finds Karen married, off drugs, and expecting a baby. Samantha's days are now filled with a new excitement as she prepares to welcome a new baby into the family. Sadness and angst have been replaced with joy and anticipation.

The clues to your soul's intention for a lifetime lie within your patterns of thinking, your behavior, and your relationships. If you struggle to resolve life problems and to achieve a sense of inner peace, you will find that your habits offer a road map to your future. Your challenge is to decode the clues and then to use this understanding to make the needed changes—to break free.

We have seen how Nancy, Emily, Lily, Baldwin, Bret, and Samantha used the wisdom gleaned during their Life Between Lives sessions to do just that. They broke free of the patterns of the past. Each achieved the learning, balancing, and healing that their soul yearned for by breaking free of the patterns that had long held them captive. Each reached a place of inner joy and serenity through the spiritual work they undertook to cope with life's suffering. In doing so, they answered the whisper of their souls, which sought problem resolution through spiritual growth. Their lives improved while their souls advanced.

Ten

TRANSFORMED BY A BRUSH WITH DEATH

Nearly dying, or finding ourselves in a situation when we could die at any moment, can have a profound effect on our lives. Some of us may simply feel great relief to have made it through the incident, and end up with feelings of joy or exhilaration, no longer afraid to die. Others are left with less positive feelings. Those who have survived such an event can be left with feelings of anger, resentment, guilt, or fear. They may need assistance in releasing the negative emotions remaining after the encounter.

Another confrontation with death is what has come to be known as a "near-death experience," or NDE. The term generally refers to situations in which an individual is clinically dead for a short period of time and then revives or is successfully resuscitated. While their life functions had ceased, they report events such as out-of-body experiences, encounters with deceased relatives or wise beings, or significant messages.

These experiences are of great interest to the public and more recently to medical personnel and researchers. Few people doubt that the situations are real to the person experiencing them, but there is still controversy over what causes them to occur. Some researchers believe that they indicate survival of consciousness after the death of the body, while others believe the experiences are generated by chemicals or neural responses of the dying brain. Additional research is needed to answer this question, but there is no doubt that these after-death encounters can lead to psychological and spiritual healing.

While most near-death experiences are reported to be positive, we have learned that not all who undergo a near-death episode have a clear or constructive experience. Research on patients having a cardiac arrest during heart surgery have revealed that some patients report confusion or anxiety following the episode. Some may need assistance to integrate the episode into their lives in a positive manner. Others may fear what this may mean for their future and desire healing.

Those who have had a positive near-death experience may wish to recapture the feelings of unconditional love and oneness they encountered during the event. Or they may wish to regain access to the source of wisdom they encountered, but are unable to do so on their own.

As we reported in our previous book, *Llewellyn's Little Book of Life Between Lives* (2018), experiences described during a positive near-death experience are remarkably like those revealed in a Life Between Lives session. For most individuals, both experiences are life-changing. However, the Life Between Lives session is longer, offers more depth, and gives the opportunity to gain answers to questions. Thus, these sessions offer a way for individuals who have had a positive near-death experience to reconnect with the spiritual realm to gain clarity, healing, and additional wisdom. The sessions may also bring clarity and comfort to those persons who have fragmented memories of their near-death experience or some uncertainty and anxiety about it.

We believe that the spiritual realm is where we plan our incarnations on earth and where we return after our earthly death. We presume that individuals who have near-death experiences visit this realm briefly. The Michael

Newton Institute continues to conduct research and collaborate with other researchers to expand our knowledge in this area.

This chapter presents cases that describe the healing from a Life Between Lives session, which can occur for individuals who have survived a life-threatening situation or who have had a near-death experience. We begin with the survivor of a violent event.

Rape at Gunpoint

Debra is a forty-eight-year-old hypnotherapist who has a Life Between Lives session. She gives the following history.

> When I was eleven, my mother married a man named Charles who was half her age, and only fourteen years older than me. I can only conclude that she was flattered by a younger man's attention, and he was good at presenting a positive and caring facade whenever they were together. It was a pretense that came down after they were married. The truth was that Charles was a narrow-minded man who believed that women were second-class citizens and that he was the most important person in the family. He had a love of guns and believed that they solved all problems.
>
> Charles was a violent person. He beat my mother, he beat me, he beat my dog, and he attacked my older sister and broke her glasses. He created a state of siege in our home. The marriage only lasted two years, but all my memories of those years are in black and white. There is no color, no joy, no sense of really living.
>
> When I was twelve, he started to come after me, first subtly, but when he didn't get the results he wanted, he became open and determined about it. I was able to fend him off, sometimes with unforeseen luck or pure strength. But he kept trying. Eventually, the final attempt was rape at gunpoint, and I was afraid he was going to kill me. I managed to get away from him, but he told me that if I told my mother he would kill her. I was too young to know any better, so I believed him

and kept my silence. From that point on, he left me alone. But for some unknown reason, he told her.

After that I was sent away from the family for my own safety. My mother filed for divorce and moved out of the house not long afterward, and we all moved to another area. Thus, a whole new and amazingly open life began, and those black and white years seemed as if they belonged to someone else. Sadly, when Mother and I were gone, Charles shot my dog and her cat.

When I was twenty-nine, a trusted medium told me that someone on the other side was asking for me to forgive him, so he could move on. I NEVER told anyone what happened, except my husband, who has been a huge part of my initial healing. The medium, however, was able to tell me the name of my abuser and the circumstances of my abuse, so long ago. I realized I had been hanging on to my anger and it was still hurting me, so I went through some healing- and anger-releasing processes and came out in a better place. But it was still there, deep inside.

Debra got training to become a hypnotherapist and healer when she was in her early forties. She found that many of the men and women who came to her were survivors of the same kind of abuse that she endured. Because she went through similar things, she had the extra understanding and empathy to truly help them.

From a spiritual perspective, she understands that the childhood abuse was part of her path as a healer. But there are times when she still feels anger and resentment from all that she has been through. During her Life Between Lives session, as soon as she enters the spiritual realm, she is met by her soul group. She hears music, and they all move together as their energies blend into one flowing circle of love. Then a master joins them in the circle and they all dance together, joined as if one being.

From there she moves to a lovely park with huge trees and lots of pavilions. In each, there are different groups, as if each family has their own spot to picnic and play. As she walks past, those she knows come out and say hello. It is a wonderful bright sunny day in an incredibly beautiful park full of people having a good time.

Eventually, someone gets up and comes to stand in front of her. At first, she doesn't recognize the person. Then she knows who it is. It is Charles, the man who was married to her mother and the one who abused her. Her gut reaction is alarm. But his image fades and she sees who it really is. Charles, on this higher spiritual level, is a soul mate, someone she knows and loves. He is someone she trusted enough to ask to do those awful things, even if, as a human being, we would judge them as negative and evil. He agreed to be the person who abused her. Because she asked him to play the role of abuser, he did not take on any negative karma. She asked for the experience of being abused so that she could become a better healer. As her soul self, she explains this further.

> *I asked to learn about being abused and molested, because being a healer is my soul's path and this is part of the healing process. I wanted to have a 360-degree understanding of it so I could truly help others facing similar situations. It is part of my work in this lifetime and he agreed to that sacred contract for my sake. As Charles, he did not have a happy life—he was beaten and abused himself as a child and died before he was forty.*

After the session, Debra stated that she believed that this was the final piece of her healing from her "brush with death." She gave the following explanation.

> *Prior to my session. I would not have been able to share this story or even speak his name. It took me years to get to a place of normalcy and balance. However, the final piece, the true release and forgiveness and healing, came through my Life Between Lives session. This work heals on many levels and it is real. It was only during my session that I realized the complete truth of what happened to me, and remembered that I, in my soul state, had asked for this experience to help me grow as a healer.*

This session allowed Debra to truly release the episode and forgive her abuser. She now looks forward to returning to her soul home one day and being able to thank him "face to face" for acting out of love and divine truth to help her become the healer she wanted to be in this life.

Global Tragedy, Personal Awakenings

Earth school offers countless experiences that create a range of negative emotions. Experiencing personal or global tragedy, for example, can create tremendous anxiety. If there is no relief from the stress caused by these experiences, both physical and emotional health are jeopardized. Yet even amidst tragedy, there are opportunities for growth and renewed perspective.

Laura, a forty-year-old-woman, lives with her partner, Fabian, whom she considers to be her soul mate. Chilean by birth, she migrated to another country with her family as a small child. As an adult, she suffers with depression, which depletes her emotionally. This impedes her creativity, something that is crucial to her career as a film producer.

Laura schedules her Life Between Lives session after being on the site of a terrorist attack in 2017. Five people were killed and fourteen others were seriously injured after a truck careened down a crowded street and burst into flame upon crashing into a department store. Laura was unhurt but was badly shaken. She has questions about her soul purpose, her depression, and the meaning behind her presence at this tragedy. She is also hoping to eliminate the blocks to her creativity.

During her session, Laura experiences a past life as Bree, a woman born into a well-to-do family. She claims that she felt stagnant in that life, as she describes below.

> *I am independent, no partner, no children. I chose this way of life. I am not like other women. I never dream about a partner and children. I want to see the world, travel. I still have the same character as when I was running around in our house when I was a child. I learn how to play the social games and I do not want any conflicts.*
>
> *Women must fight for their independence now. I was born in a good family, I have support, so they leave me alone. But it*

is difficult to become someone in society. In a way I live inside hidden walls.

Upon her death, Bree describes her life as wasted.

I did nothing. I had money and status, I had all I ever wanted. I could have married someone like me who could have helped me and supported me. I could have explored the world as much as possible. Although I died in peace, my soul is frustrated and irritated that I did not do more.

Entering the life between lives, we hear from Ariel, the eternal soul of Laura. When asked by the practitioner to describe Laura and Bree's similarities, Ariel gives the following answer.

They both feel trapped. They do not use their full potential. I think that Laura has developed a bit more than Bree. Unlike Bree, Laura has a partner. Not only that, she has more insight about herself and about her life. She lives life more fully.

Ariel responds to the practitioner probing about Laura's attraction to writing and filmmaking and about what is behind the depression which is holding her back.

She has stories that can touch so many people's souls. She has the wisdom now to explore her creativity to the fullest. When she goes inside herself it's like diving into a deep well. It's like a treasure chest and she can dive right in and pick up the details like treasures and gems. The gems are her stories that will touch people.

If Laura wants to do something, she can just do it. Nothing will stop her. If she adds some patience and peace, she can do it. She can soar like an eagle, like the one in her recurring dream. She can create whatever she wants on earth. She is free! She is competent. She has great inner power. She must tap into her higher perspective. The time for this is now!

In response to the practitioner's question about the deeper meaning of Laura being at the scene of the 2017 terrorist attack, Ariel explains.

> *I was so frustrated. I wondered if it was time for me to leave earth, because I wasn't getting anywhere. But at the last second, I realized that there is more to explore here.*

Ariel goes on to explain the broader context of the incident and how it relates to the experience of others who are both directly and indirectly affected.

> *It was not only about Laura but about the people who were there. They needed to experience the same thing. It was the easiest way to do it. There was a much bigger picture to it than you see. Much, much bigger. We see it as sorrow, but all who were there needed to be there. Even those who died. They are fine now!*

Elaborating on how collective experiences such as this terrorist attack are organized from a higher perspective, Ariel adds further explanation.

> *Those who participated were meant to be there. I am not sure how they all got there at the same time. I just know that Laura needed to be there because she was stuck. I was so frustrated. I couldn't make Laura go forward in life. The recurring dream about the soaring eagle did not work. I tried to stir her using other techniques; even the depression was meant to get her to move forward. I thought, I give up! I cannot do anything more! It did not work. Then I wanted to shock her into waking up.*
>
> *I had to find a way. Laura was stuck. She was difficult to reach. She was not able to break free from the malaise that had overtaken her. So that was why I needed to put her into a collective awakening like that. It worked. It woke her up. It did!*

However, just because Laura and the others at the site of the attack could potentially benefit from the experience does not free the terrorist from responsibility for engaging in destructive actions. Even though some good came from this collective awakening, it does not give us permission to do bad things.

For Laura, her brush with death at this attack forged a path for her to move forward. It offered her a chance to break free from the despondency that had gripped her for so long. Seeing others die reminded her that she is still alive and still has a chance to move forward. Realizing that life can be over at any time jolted her awake to the sense that time was passing and she was standing still. The lessons that she learned from the experience provided fuel for her next steps as well as her dreams for the future.

We're reminded from Laura's case that our time on earth is valuable. It's a time to explore, to experience, and to grow. Negative emotions, however, can make us feel stuck and prevent us from moving forward and enjoying our lives. Our souls and our guides try to help us get back on track through such things as recurring dreams, depression, illness, injury, or even close calls with death.

Surviving Life-Threatening Events

Tiffany, a thirty-three-year-old hairdresser and single mother of a seven-year-old child, comes in for a Life Between Lives session to gain a better understanding of the recurring life-threatening events she has been experiencing. She also hopes to gain some insight into the depression she has developed over the past several months for no apparent reason that she can identify. Tiffany owns a hairdressing salon and continues to train in the latest styling techniques. She travels throughout the world and leads a very active life. Tiffany has four siblings. Her parents work diligently. Her father is an artist, and her mother is totally submissive to him.

> *My father does not love my mother with all his heart. At home there is poverty and a lot of violence. My siblings and I often run away from home to our grandmother's house while our parents are quarreling.*

Nevertheless, as is customary in her home country, she and her siblings now financially support their parents. The father of Tiffany's child was a foreigner. She said that he had a dark energy within him. He was also aggressive, and when she was pregnant, he quarreled with her frequently. She left him.

Tiffany reports that she is saved each time she experiences a life-threatening event, at the last minute. The first event was during her birth. After the umbilical cord was cut, she was accidentally poisoned. She doesn't remember this event but has been told about it. She describes the second event as occurring during her teenage years, when she was hit by a car and had a near-death experience. Then years later, she was rushed to the hospital for an emergency appendectomy, just in the nick of time. Her near-death experience had the greatest impact on her and she is still somewhat troubled by it.

She describes it as starting with an incident with her parents, when she was fifteen years old. They were quarreling because her parents had forbidden her to go out. Refusing to conform, she made good on her threat to run out in front of a car. Observers reported that she was hit by a car and thrown almost nine feet into the air. Nobody believed that she could still be alive after that.

She was rushed to the hospital. She saw herself from above as this emergency operation took place. While she was above her body, her beloved grandmother, who had passed away earlier, appeared to her. Her grandmother told her to go back because she still had something to do, but she did not tell her what that was. She saw herself then in the ambulance and saw a cross that shone like a monstrance from the church. At that moment, her vital signs got better and she started improving This is the moment when she began to believe in divine protection. Now Tiffany really wants to find out what the task is that her grandmother had communicated with her about during this experience.

During the Life Between Lives session, Tiffany goes back to the time when she is hit by the car.

> *I wanted to run in front of a car because my parents did not allow me to go out and then I ran out and was accidentally hit by a car. I said that to my parents. [she sobs] I want to apolo-*

gize to my parents because I did not mean for that to happen even though I said that. But it happened. [cries loudly]

They did not want to let me do what I wanted to do! [continues sobbing]

Next, she goes to the womb and experiences her mother holding her lovingly in her arms right after her birth.

There is a lot of light there. I am so happy that I am with her. It is very warm here. We want to go home, but we cannot, there are complications. They take me away. My mom does not want to let me go away. It is dark. After a pause [sobs] mom is here. She takes me and loves me. I want her to never leave me again.

Tiffany experiences her death in a past life and, as a soul, goes home to the spirit realm to reflect on the life that she has just lived.

I walk, I shine with light, there are many buildings, bliss. I look at all of this and admire it. There is someone here, but I do not see him. The light flows through me. This is like a light shower that cleanses me. I have been here, but I admire this place and see if anything has changed. I feel someone near me, an elderly, wise man in a purple cloak with a long stick. He has bright eyes, long hair, a beard, and a hat that looks like a pope headgear. I go with him.

There is my grandmother. She looks majestic. She emits a lot of light. She's beautiful! She says to concentrate on my family. She tells me she worries about me.

I want the man who hit me with his car to come. He is here. I look at him with compassion. He still has so much to learn. Sad. I am told to pray for him. I thank him for the lesson. [crying] I have learned humility! I feel that what does not kill me strengthens me. I have become more determined, braver. He stands there. We hug each other. My spirit guide and grandmother are proud. Me too.

I want to apologize to my parents. Mama is holding me. She promised never to leave me, never. I feel strong gratitude. I thank you [crying]. My parents are here with my grandmother and I feel the love.

Tiffany reports that she experienced great healing from her session. She was particularly touched by the love she experienced from her mother during the session. She stated she now understands why her mother never left her father as others thought she should have. I wanted my mother to never leave me and she kept her promise and stayed with my father, and thus with me. I am now relieved of the troubled feelings that I had about my near-death experience. Love and forgiveness are so healing.

Traveling Through the Tunnel of Light

Zola, a sixty-seven-year-old woman, is retired from a career as a writer and editor. She was very involved with the theatre in her younger days. Because of a head-on collision years earlier, Zola traveled through the famous tunnel of light in a classic near-death experience. There she met with a council of beings of light, who were wise and humorous. They are guardians of humanity and the ancient wisdom, and shared with her the meaning of life and the secrets of the ages. She referred to them as Lion People, based on her own inner experiences. She said that these beings have been her companions for years.

During her near-death experience, Zola was given the choice to stay or come back. She cannot remember or imagine why she decided to come back, since during that time she felt such love and joy. Zola comes in for a Life Between Lives session to reconnect with the wise beings she encountered during her near-death experience. She also wishes to learn why she had this encounter and why she decided to come back.

Zola goes through a past-life journey that takes her to the life of Elsa, who lives somewhere in Germany at the start of World War II. She becomes involved with the resistance fighters to the Nazi movement. Elsa is captured in 1936, while they are trying to block a road as the German army tries to move into their town. She is taken to a camp of some kind, where she remains until she dies of malnutrition in the winter.

After the last breath, she realizes she isn't cold anymore. She feels free but sad for the woman she has been, and she understands that she is no longer alive. She sees that Elsa had such a valiant heart, very fierce.

> *I am being bathed in love and light. I want to stay for 10,000 years! There are other beings around me, beaming and surrounding me with love. It's like a party going on, but I have mixed feelings. I am still sad for Elsa, what she went through, and I am proud of the things she did to try to help. The Nazis did some horrendous damage! I feel like I've been away for a long time, now that I'm back. They are all telling me I did a great job. It's a fast mood change.*
>
> *I am walking around and talking to all the other people who are there and died first. We are talking war stories and patting each other on the back.*
>
> *Wow! I'm glad that's over! But wasn't it fun!? We really lived! We were this group that was totally engaged with the life and all that was present to us, we just plunged in! I am starting to feel like it was all just a play. It isn't really who we truly are.*
>
> *Now we are all backstage at the cast party. Now there are more here than are in that life. Many of them are the ones who are there to meet me, not in that life, just friends who are in the audience.*

Zola sees another soul coming forward that she calls the director.

> *He is very tall. He has been standing here the whole time, next to me. Good job, he tells me. I remembered the script, the plan. [pauses and gasps] We were betrayed! Someone in our group who we trusted informed on us. It was not done to hurt us; he was just trying to save himself. It was done out of desperation and self-preservation.*
>
> *What was the purpose of that life? It was putting myself on the line for what is right. This was a deep truth for me. I see a picture book with flipping pages, different times and clothes*

and faces. It is people standing up for what is right and being punished for it. I'm done with those lives now.

Elsa reappears and addresses Zola.

Elsa tells Zola that everything was complicated in that life. But it was okay, just plunge into life! The water is fine!

Zola responds to Elsa by telling her she did well and that she showed her a lot. She tells Elsa that she didn't hesitate!

Now Elsa dances off, wearing the same dress she did at a dance party when she was younger. She's twirling around and moving into the light.

Zola is now about to enter the spiritual realm. As her soul self, she reports on what she is experiencing.

It is very expansive. There is a lot of movement and activity, but I don't really see anything yet. I feel others around me, I am not alone. I see a series of meeting rooms. I will meet with somebody. The rooms get nicer and nicer, now I see an executive meeting room.

Now I am back at the pavilion I was at in my near-death experience and I am choosing whether to stay or go back. Next, I find myself back in the executive meeting room again. I sit down at a big rectangular mahogany table and chat with the others who are there. At one end of the room there is a wall of windows. The room is very bright and sunny, and there are potted white lilies and big potted palms.

Everyone sits down now, and I realize that I have dreams of this place. I see myself and see that they are doing it again. They unroll plans that look like blueprints, the plan of my life, for discussion. I am the architect; these are my plans. There is a general feeling of congratulations, validation, and self-love. I see that the foundation of my life is strong, even though it was so hard to build. Looking at my life as the house I'm building on that foundation, now I can complete it and put on the finishing touches. It's amazing!

Why did I come back from my near-death experience? I wanted to see my house finished. At the time, the foundation was not complete. I see that the purpose of the near-death experience was to help me connect. I was about to give up, because I had spent half of my life working on that foundation, but I couldn't get it right because things kept going wrong. They showed me how to fix the foundation.

I am in a new phase now. My house is finished and it's perfect! I get to do decorations, flowers, find beautiful things to put in my house, bring beautiful people into my home. I love my house. It has a three-sided wraparound porch. I see myself putting tables and vases and lamps from all over the place. I can travel and collect. I understand that the message for me is to lighten up! I've finally finished it!

The practitioner asks, "Who are the Lion People?"

They are me; I am them. They are a clan of beings, my people. We have lived in many worlds. We are helpers and guardians. We guard the truth and humanity. Around thirty of us are here on the earth plane. It's hard for us to be here, the vibration is too low.

I am exactly where I am supposed to be, doing exactly what I am supposed to be doing. They show me the image of a lighthouse shining the light to help people to avoid the rocks, even though I get smashed by the waves in the process.

A check with Zola six months later finds her doing very well. She has purchased a new home and is busy decorating it. She received the answers she needed from her session and now understands why she came back from her near-death experience. She still had work she wanted to complete on earth. She received assurance that she was right where she was supposed to be, doing what she came here to do.

An Out-of-Body Experience

Dana did not even remember that she had a near-death experience, which she refers to as an out-of-body experience until years later. She tells her story in her own words.

> *I had a serious accident. I was bicycling and a vehicle hit me. I do not recall anything about the collision, except for a flash of realization that I was going to die if the vehicle hit me head on. I remember screaming to alert the driver that I was in the path of collision, and then I experienced a knowing that I wouldn't die, as the driver altered the course. That is the extent of my memory.*

Dana's body healed in time, but she had been traumatized by the accident and sought counseling to help her adjust to life after her accident. She continues her story:

> *Over time, my counselor eventually took me back to the moment I was hit by the vehicle. To my surprise, I recalled that I had an out-of-body experience. I was part of a beautiful black space, which was very peaceful. In this rich, spacious, loving blackness, there was no "me." I sensed others in this space and had no desire to leave. There was a lot of chaos outside of this black space, and I sensed that someone really needed help. I felt so content and peaceful and continued to rest in the blackness. Time didn't exist.*
>
> *Again, there was more commotion down below and I sensed that the person was really in trouble. Then a beautiful silvery-white rope-like cord caught my attention. I felt curious to see what it was and lazily followed the swaying cord down. Later in discussion with my counselor I felt that I was tricked into leaving the peaceful black place. This lovely silver cord was placed in my awareness so that I would follow it down to my body. When I got close to my body, I felt like I was falling fast and then slammed into my body. My first thought*

was "holy cow, that person in trouble is me!" And my path of recovery began.

Through my recovery, I worked on reconciling my out-of-body experience with my life; I am alive! A big hurdle I had to get through was the realization that I was okay with others having an out-of-body experience, but not me! It took me time to accept and process the experience, especially the feeling of the space when there was no me. The philosophy of Buddhism and meditation helped ground me in the process.

Years later, I discovered Life Between Lives sessions. I was nervous about trying this out and initially felt that I was straying into nut-ball territory. But after I learned more about the process, I felt that it was an opportunity to better understand the context of the accident in my life, reconnect with the black space, and learn more about my out-of-body experience.

During Dana's regression, the practitioner guides her back to the time of the accident. Dana's guide is there, showing her what has happened during the accident. She is describing what she is experiencing.

My guide is showing me energy. He is putting on massive wings. He is showing me that he caught me when I was flying off my bike. I have a sense that he was flying so he could catch me. Others helped to catch me too.

My guide looks out for me. He is very strong and he is caring for me. I have nothing to worry about. He is a great guy. He has a powerful, strong light. I can feel the light in my body.

The practitioner guides Dana to let the light and energy do what it needs to do. Dana explains what she is feeling.

It feels different. It is a heavy energy that is healing all through the body. It's like liquid gold, like white and gold light. It is a very firm energy. My guide is working very hard and all I need to do is let go. He is working on my fracture site and doing a body scan. Now he's working on my head and checking the energy. My head energy is expanding, and it is sweeping all over my body. There is gold and white light with a thick cloud of red, gold, and silver sparks.

My guide is very stern and serious, and he appreciates the opportunity to work on me. I know I have a stern guide who never says much. I have seen him before. I am connected to him. I have an image of a crystal in my head that is helping me to heal. It is lighting up my whole body and I can feel the energy. He tells me that the reflections from the crystal are helping me keep out unwanted energies and letting me reflect energy in. This light is like a map because it shows me where to do more work.

The light of the crystal is important to me, as it helps me connect outward and inward. It's like a clothesline to my higher self. It gives me light, so I can see and heal the shadowy parts of myself. I know I can heal myself after the accident. I know my body can do it. It is more important for the emotions to heal and I have been doing that work with my counselor. After I release the emotions, things that are cloudy become clear. My guide is done. I feel a completeness now.

The practitioner guides Dana to a quiet place to integrate the healing she has received. She is instructed to breathe in peace and light and return to her body. Dana makes the following comments during a follow-up to her session.

As I reflect on the Life Between Lives process, it was an incredibly powerful experience for me, which continues to offer new insights. The experience was not static. I came home to my body on a deeper level and feel more grounded on earth. As a human. I know that I am never alone and that I am deeply loved. But often I forget and then remember again. I feel a much greater respect and empathy for people now, recognizing that each of our paths as humans is uniquely individual. Love connects us all together.

A Troubling Accident

Judy, a thirty-five-year-old married woman, was on vacation with her husband and five-year-old son in another country when tragedy struck. They were driving along a mostly deserted road on a warm, sunny afternoon, on their way to another town, when they were hit head-on by a large truck. The last thing Judy remembers was hearing a lot of noise. Her husband was killed instantly and she was badly injured, but miraculously their son sustained only minor injuries. Adjusting to the loss of her husband and recovering from her injuries has been difficult. She is still troubled by the accident and its aftermath. During her Life Between Lives session, the practitioner takes Judy back to the time of the accident. She describes what she is experiencing.

> *I see my husband in front of me and he says that he is sorry. Now I see myself lying on the ground in an unnatural position. My hand is crooked, and I do not feel anything. Now, I see a bright light. It feels very soothing. I recognize my father, who is no longer living, and he is smiling. He tells me, "Be brave."*
>
> *I still do not feel anything. Somehow I know that my husband has died, but I want to come back. I want to come back for my son and for my dance career.*

Next, Judy starts to feel some pain and tries to look around for her son. She is unable to move and can't see him. She tries to call him but can't seem to make a sound. Then she sees him walking around, looking as if he is trying to figure out what is going on. She tries to call out to him again, but he doesn't seem able to hear her. It looks like he has a small cut on his forehead, but otherwise he seems okay. She feels very helpless because it is starting to get dark. There is nobody around, no cars and no light. She starts feeling hopeless and very afraid for her son.

The next thing she remembers is being picked up and put on a stretcher. Then she is aware of being in an ambulance, and her son is sitting right beside her as they make their way to the hospital. She is in and out of consciousness during the ambulance ride, but she recovers fully from the accident.

As Judy enters the spiritual realm, she receives some additional information from her guide.

My husband lost control of the car. The purpose of the accident was to help me connect with my strength. I see a picture of a tiger and I look directly in his eyes. I feel the strength and hear my father telling me to be strong.

Next, she goes back to a past life in India in 1857.

I'm a male around thirty years of age, wearing my dress scarf and sitting on a large, ornate chair on a raised platform. There are many people down below, looking up and waiting for me to speak. I'm the king and they have come to receive my opinion. They are parents who are fighting with each other and not taking care of their children.

The king takes seven of the children away from their neglectful parents and brings them to his palace to be raised. He says the parents are relieved rather than upset by this. One of the children is Judy's son in her current life. While the servants provide daily care for the children, the king loves them and spends time with them frequently.

A few years later, the king marries, and he recognizes his beloved wife as Judy's husband in her current life. They have no children of their own and are devoted to the children that the king is raising in the palace. There are many wars over the years, and through his strength and endurance, his kingdom survives and flourishes. Between battles he loves spending time with his wife and the children. His wife becomes unhappy and leaves him, but he remains content spending time with the children. He lives a long life and is dedicated to the welfare of all the children in his kingdom. Judy's guide explains why they have visited the king's life.

He is telling me that I already know how to be strong, I just need to remember it. The king regained contentment after he lost his wife, through spending time with his children, and that will be of help to me as well.

Judy reports that her session has really brought her peace. Revisiting the accident and the time spent waiting for help to arrive helped her fill in the gaps. Encountering her father during her near-death experience was very special to her. To remember her strength as she adjusts to life without her husband, she recalls the eyes of the tiger and his encouragement.

Tiffany, Zola, Dana, and Judy achieved emotional healing and peace from revisiting their near-death experiences. This relieved anxiety and allowed them to integrate these episodes more fully into their lives. They now see the purpose behind these occurrences.

Cosmic Healing

Kai, a retired professional woman in her sixties, has been suffering from a debilitating chronic illness since childhood. She has become so ill at times that she is transported to emergency rooms and has endured several near-death experiences. Somehow, Kai's inner strength and determination have pulled her through, for, despite her physical limitations, she has accomplished a great deal in her life. She has more projects that she wishes to complete, and further aspirations. So she is seeking some understanding or perhaps even some intervention regarding her underlying health conditions.

In her Life Between Lives session, Kai easily flows into an exalted soul state. She communes with spiritual beings of startling immensity and power, including her own soul's mother, that great and loving spirit who nurtured her as she was first created. During the session, Kai encounters several advanced beings who perform energetic restructuring and healing on her.

> *I see the earth itself and it shines like a jewel. It is so rich with experiences and all the light. It's gorgeous. So beautiful! Oh my gosh, there are so many faces, and they look like giants. All these beings of light are much larger than people on earth. They are looking lovingly at this planet. Now they're piercing through my thoughts and my barriers; it's like they washed through.*

Kai laughs with delight.

> *I'm being turned on a giant circle. Slowly, as if allowing me to watch all the stars above and all the stars below. It's like saying hello to a new vision. I feel myself rising. And the earth and*

the large beings are helping me to create a translucent pattern of a new body that I will receive. As it solidifies, it will carry me through this life. I'll need it because this life is going to last longer than I thought, by far. All this light, it's taking different configurations around me and forming in different patterns. I don't know what this is, but I like it! It has to do with healing. Lights and colors and shapes, I feel it all over. Different beings are bringing different specialties of healing.

It's as if I have tiny light beams moving through all of me, at different frequencies and colors and vibrations. It's changing moment to moment. I'm receiving these infusions. This is fabulous. This is a gift. And I won't be the same.

I'm feeling these very wonderful pastel colors, but with a warmth and life. The body interior is changing into something more coherent and integrated. I can feel this restructuring coming from above, down into all parts of Kai, in my hands. It's like a burst of celebration. I'm having an internal feeling that's different. I don't know what to call this. In my lower legs there is a feeling of pulling, increasing my bone and muscle.

I am shown an image of a box-like structure, stacked like pancakes, and it glows as if it's made of stars. It's a healing device.

The practitioner asks, "Is this an actual earthly or physical device?"

It will be. It's being worked on right now. It will be known. It balances to a degree we can't imagine. The energy, the cells. It creates an alignment of harmonious interactions within the body. We do not have this understanding, but it's coming sooner than we think. This device uses chakras as portals. I feel this light energy traveling through me, I feel like a mountain, and a stream, running by trees and the sky in sherbet colors. I'm being disintegrated, taken apart, being restructured head to toe, everywhere. Harmony, integrating the systems at an energetic level.

I am balanced so precariously on my own. I am getting help all the time, but not the help that I just opened to; knowing, only now, there is so much more to ask for! And this is the first baby step.

Some weeks after her sessions, Kai writes the following note.

My first intention for seeking a Life Between Lives session was to help revitalize my body back into a state of functional health. During our session, I experienced sensory, palpable, vivid sensations of internal integration, calmness, deep peace, joy, and evidence of healing within my physical being.

One of my meditation group members said that during the spiritual healing part of my session, when I saw multicolored pastel lights comprising the inside of my body, and no longer a chaotic jumble that represented a life-threatening condition, that I had experienced a reset of my original essence energy.

Afterward, those expansive feelings of connection remain. My health continues to improve, and I have been presented with some exciting new opportunities. I feel as if we opened another doorway to source and love, which is where all true healing comes from.

Kai's experience shows us that self-healing is possible, even for those who are very ill. A connection with the spiritual realm, such as that experienced during a Life Between Lives session, is one way to facilitate this self-healing.

Revisiting a Mystical Experience from a Coma

Nora is a sixty-three-year-old biologist who had an infection that shut down her brain and put her in a coma that led to a near-death experience. Free from the brain and body, she experienced extremely expanded states of consciousness and returned to consciousness completely cured from her condition.

Nora seeks a Life Between Lives session to return to her out-of-body time to reexperience the expanded states of consciousness. She hopes to recover more of the gifts, learnings, and insights from her time in a coma. She has been trying to do this on her own for many years but has been unable to do so.

During the session, the practitioner gently guides Nora back to the time when she is free from her body, but still connected.

> *There is an illuminous umbilical connection, an illuminous filamentous strand that comes into the navel and is an eternal connection. The physical body in all stages, in all times, is connected to this awareness. The physical body is a light, an ideal. And there is a connection to that. The final connection between light, the light form, and the physical body is one of projection. There is never an actual existence of the physical body. Always, it has been a projection, but the light body is very real and eternal and yet fleeting, eternally morphing from one basic awareness. Projected from the perspective of the light form, the light form, the ideal is always perfect, is always one. All is part of one process.*

The practitioner asks, "Can you help me understand, if the body is a projection of this perfect light form, how is it that there are times it becomes ill?"

> *These are attunements to instruct. The apparent imperfections are all a perfect part of the plan. Always perfect and only when viewed from the proper perspective; we're just more inclusive. Illness can be addressed. In recovering the love and the oneness, all apparent imperfections evaporate. All in a perfect oneness exists.*

"And can you help me understand how, when your body is so ill, you make this journey into this oneness? How does the healing of the physical body come about?"

> *It is the only possible outcome. Once the decision is made to return, the healing occurs. There are no other options, given the willingness to return. It comes from simply knowing that it is the only possible state given the choice. The choice is the important connection, and all the rest flows.*

So, I am seeing alternative futures, because the past and the future are similar. All of them exist, but in potential form only. It's by connecting the dots that the optimal future, the pathway to healing, becomes the only possible pathway. The free will choice involves only one of an infinite number of possible futures. It's the connection with the higher soul that is all oneness around eternity, infinite dimensions, all existence visualizing the pathway.

The practitioner asks, "How do you make this choice?"

Simply the recognition that it has always been exactly like this with complete free will to determine your pathway. All is possible through choice.

The higher perspective is from the direction of the oneness, and only by originating in the oneness can one begin to perceive how the actuality functions. You cannot see it from the other side, this side of the veil. It's like a one-way mirror, but the connections, the apparent separation soul-to-soul viewed from the proper perspective, the origin of the oneness; this perspective knows that the free will of the one mind does direct actuality out of an infinite cloud of potentiality. It's all done from pure unconditional and infinitely all-inspiring love and connection. A love of creator, creation, it's made of pure gratitude, love, bliss, joy, and the original actuality.

The practitioner asks, "When there is disease in the human body, is there a way to connect to this realm to bring about healing?"

Yes. It is through trust, trust and fearlessness. Trust in complete abundance. The universe always gives us everything that we need. Trust, gratitude, acceptance. Knowing that we have nothing whatsoever to fear. We must overcome the false sense of limitation. Know with complete and absolute assurance, with no doubt at all. Believe in infinite power, unveiling of wisdom, and becoming whole. Know and trust. Gratitude. Gratitude.

The practitioner asks if any other information was given that might have been forgotten, missed or not clearly understood during the out-of-body experience.

There are themes between lives that focus on learning the same lessons. These lessons repeat and grow more complex as the soul group progresses. Through this process, patterns are built up and amplified, resulting in growth. Over time this leads to extraordinary evolution and awakening of consciousness to the highest levels. Nothing is ever lost. All that we reap we must sow. This occurs in repeating patterns of growth, knowing, and connectedness. All is fueled by a pervasive, loving force, everywhere throughout the universe.

It's all a part of a much larger plan, a plan of infinite perfection and growth. The realization of oneness, sacred bond, and perfection.

Nora tried in various ways for almost ten years to attain that same expanded state of consciousness she experienced while free from mind and body. She was elated to have finally reconnected with this state. She finds it easier to now connect on her own. She is also much more aware of the amazing gifts and profound insights she received during her "dead" time and is now writing about her experiences so that others may benefit.

Coming close to death is a life-changing experience. While such events are traumatic, they contain within them a great potential for spiritual growth and healing. There is a reason behind these events. Debra's brush with death helped her become a better healer, while Laura's experience jolted her out of being stuck in her life.

––––––––––

Near-death experiences can be life-changing and bring peace. However, not all of these experiences are reassuring. The cases in this chapter illustrate the power of Life Between Lives sessions to promote healing for those who have had a near-death experience. Visiting the spiritual realm during a session can assist these individuals to gain clarity, find peace, and integrate the experience into their lives. It can also provide them with the opportunity to return to the unconditional love and wisdom they received during their "dead" time.

Kai, Dana, and Nora received not only wisdom, but physical healing. While all healing is ultimately self-healing, Life Between Lives sessions can bring the guidance and insights to empower individuals to promote their own wellness.

Eleven

AGING AND DYING

We incarnate on earth to learn various lessons in each lifetime. No matter the focus of our mortal journey for each life, one experience is inevitable: our death. Some of us will die in our prime, suddenly and early. But many of us will face the challenges of old age, noticing our bodies deteriorate and our minds dim as our time on earth ends.

By living to an old age, with its health challenges, we have an opportunity to mindfully come to terms with our impending mortality. This is important in an age when death is not easily or gracefully accepted. In time past, early death was common. Infant mortality rates were high, and most of those who became adults still did not live long lives. Advances in sanitation, improvements in nutrition, and the success of modern medicine means that now most of us do not encounter death until we reach middle or older age.

We arrive on earth to grow as a soul, and leaving earth is another opportunity for our soul to grow. The decline of our physical body reminds us that the material world is impermanent. As we face the ephemeral nature of our body, some of us will open to the existence of our immortal soul. Reviewing our lives helps us come to terms with the choices we've made and the way we have lived. Instead of fearing or denying our approaching death, we can find peace and acceptance, ease and grace.

How each of us faces aging and approach our mortality varies. In some cases in the previous chapters, people experienced death at the end of their past lives. They left their bodies in different ways, passing slowly, quickly, easily, or while resisting. Knowing what may await us and deciding ahead of time how we would like to approach our death can be comforting.

In this chapter, we will meet Gayle, Jacquelyn, Frauke, and Stan as they experience their past lives and their life between lives, giving us wisdom about the very human process of aging and dying.

Losing Independence

We can become grumpy and angry when we feel that our body and mind are letting us down and our productive years are over. Growing old is challenging when we know that success in our modern world is associated with strength, beauty, intelligence, and, above all, independence. Age therefore becomes the great betrayer. The more we are attached to this belief, the rougher the ride to the end will be.

Gayle, an extremely positive, worldly woman of ninety-one, decides to check in on her soul's progress and satisfy her curiosity about the Life Between Lives work of Dr. Newton before she leaves the planet. Having had two close brushes with death earlier in her life, accepting her mortality was easy for Gayle, but losing her independence was not.

Assisted by her younger husband, Ben, Gayle arrives for her session with a list of questions that include, "Why do I have such pain in my feet and such terrible balance?" While she is grateful for Ben's assistance, she is indignant and annoyed that she is losing her independence.

During her regression, Gayle is reminded that her childhood lacked love and attention from her parents. Yet she did recapture some tender and loving early childhood moments with her nanny, Alma, and Hooti, the cook. She then progresses into a past life as Elizabeth, a twenty-one-year-old woman of an aristocratic English family. There, standing surrounded by the wood-paneled walls of her father's library in a fine mansion, she is hot under the collar. Her parents have chosen a man for her to marry that would forge family alliances. Her father let her know that she was expected to comply. Riding gloves in hand, she storms out of the house, calls for her horse, and rides hard through the countryside.

I won't marry that man! He is almost twice my age and I just won't do it. No man can own me. I won't have it. I don't care about family alliances. Father can't make me. I have my own means. That is one good thing about being an aristocrat. I have my grandfather's endowment.

And with that, the decision was made. Elizabeth leaves her childhood home with her mother in tears and her father offering nothing other than a stony glare. She would never return.

Elizabeth went on to create a very independent and self-sufficient life. She never married and never had any children of her own. Although she used her wealth to support a local orphanage, she didn't spend time in the orphanage; rather she occupied her time riding and spending time with her intellectual friends. We meet Elizabeth on the day of her death at the age of sixty.

I feel very weak. I am not sure that I am sick, but I feel very weak and tired. I am in my bedroom sitting in a chair. I don't want to be in bed. I am beside my bed and I have a chair and small desk. I am sitting at that, playing with a pen and looking across the bed to the window. Just looking outside toward the daylight.

The practitioner asks what thoughts and feelings Elizabeth is experiencing and if she understands why she is dying.

I am thinking that I am just tired. Tired enough to go to sleep and not wake up. It's time for me. I have had a good life. I have enjoyed the life I have led. But now it is time. I don't really know what is taking my energy; I think it is physical, but nothing obvious, except my body is quite thin.

Her practitioner asks how she feels about her life as Elizabeth.

It was a good life; I enjoyed my life. Because I am so tired, I don't mind a bit that I am leaving. I have left a trust fund for the orphanage. I have done what I can for them, and they will go on being taken care of. Strangely enough I didn't get emotionally involved at all with the children.

I have decided that I might as well lie down on the bed and just drift. I slip off my shoes and get comfortable on the bed and it is restful [sighs heavily]. I am just so tired.

Gayle becomes quiet and is asked about what she is experiencing.

I seem to be... well, I am not in the body anymore. I am looking down at the body. It's very quiet. Elizabeth is alone. I just say goodbye to my body, quite unattached. Sooner or later someone will come into the room to check on her or bring her something, and they will find her and take care of things.

Gayle's Alma and Hootie soon come to greet her for a beautiful afterlife reunion. Although they were only part of her early life for a few years, Gayle understands that they are part of her soul family and were there to make sure she wasn't alone as a child.

It is not surprising that Elizabeth calmly faced the moment of her death, given her independent, strong, matter-of-fact nature. Having completed her reunion, her practitioner asks Gayle if she has any thoughts about her life as Elizabeth.

Why should we talk about that when my questions are far more present?

Gayle seems to want to avoid any discussion about Elizabeth. However, later in the session, when Gayle meets her council, her practitioner encourages her to ask them about her soul's progress as Elizabeth.

Oh God, what a question. They are a bit noncommittal. They say I did well enough. They are pointing out that there is still a very strong independent streak in me, in this life, where I prefer to be rather like Elizabeth. Strong, independent, and able to row my own boat. There is a lot of that in me still.

The practitioner inquires whether the guides can help Gayle understand if this is a quality that she is developing or if there is something she is learning from this characteristic.

It's very much a learning. Um, they are saying that I need to learn when to let go and let somebody else do something for me. I don't have to be so independent. There is nothing wrong with being independent, but it shouldn't be the "be-all and end-all" of my life. This is something I need to learn.

I'm at the very end of this life and I am learning to accept dependence. I have been thoroughly independent most of this life. But for the past year, I have had to accept a great deal of dependency and it sticks in my throat. Fortunately, it is Ben I need to care for me, to depend upon. My car was taken away from me and that was a great loss of independence. I can't drive the family car! I am literally not big and strong enough to physically drive it. They are telling me, quite definitely, that my loss of balance is part of the lesson.

Gayle now understands why she is shown her life as Elizabeth and explains that, while she can accept it with her head, her heart has trouble with letting go of the desire to be independent.

I can see that it probably won't happen in this life, but at least what I can accept at this point is that I have an opportunity to internalize the acceptance of dependence and experience it. This is hard, because come hell or high water, I will be independent in many ways. I have never been dependent before. And if this is a lesson I must learn, well, FINE! I must learn it.

I needed to know there was a point to it. There clearly is a point to being dependent as I am. And thank God it is with Ben.

It has been almost like living two lives in one life. I needed the independent experience of that first half of my life, which could have been a whole life, but now I get to learn about dependence. It was clearly arranged that Ben would show up later in this life to assist me this way.

Although I have far fewer years to live than the ones that are behind me, I still need to accept dependence, and there is still learning to be done. And I am not being told exactly what that will look like. That's for me to discover. My council is showing amusement and saying, "Isn't it high time you realized it?"

Gayle thanks her council, acknowledging that it has taken her a long time in her current life to realize that every challenge is a lesson. She also explains that having her partner, Ben, show up later in her life was a brilliant life-planning choice. She knows that she could have never allowed herself to be dependent on her first husband. Four years after her Life Between Lives session, Gayle expresses her deep love and gratitude for having Ben in her life.

When Alzheimer's Is Healing

The emotional and physical strain of losing our cognitive abilities, or watching a family member fail in this way, is very difficult to experience. What we may not appreciate is the service the afflicted individual is offering to the family, or what they themselves are experiencing.

Frauke, a woman in her mid-forties, married with two adult children, is suffering immensely watching her father's Alzheimer's condition cause him to deteriorate. The situation is further complicated by a long-standing family conflict stemming from tensions between her mother and siblings in their childhood. Frauke seeks to understand and heal the family conflict and to connect with her father in her Life Between Lives session.

Frauke's mother favors her oldest brother, holding him up as the perfect role model. He is inaccessible and arrogant to Frauke and her younger brothers. They become insecure and obstructed in their own development, lacking inner strength. Her father, feeling helpless, has stayed outside of the conflict, often being away at work. In adulthood, emotional coldness and estrangement develops between her and her younger siblings on one side and her mother and oldest brother on the other. Their father's Alzheimer's disease has brought the unresolved tensions to the surface.

After arriving in the spirit world, Frauke recognizes and senses the timeless, loving connectedness of all that exists. She meets her guide, who assists her to experience her luminous spirit self, a very bright multicolored energy, pulsating with spiritedness. She expands into an all-embracing, deep respect for all other souls and an honoring of All That Is.

Frauke's guide takes her to meet with her soul family, where she recognizes her oldest brother.

> *He smiles, a bit cheeky yet lovingly, and says, "Hi little sister, you bullhead."*
>
> *My father is here too, with an expression of love and compassion. He wonders if I know that he can still hear me, even though he has not yet passed over to spirit.*

The practitioner inquires whether she wants to ask him about the meaning of his Alzheimer's disease.

> *He says that we all must leave this planet one day. That the physical body dissolves and the soul light becomes free. Yet love continues and stays with the family, like a light ball. It is his love which can reunite us all into a new whole unity.*
>
> *You are all doing it well, he says. Think of your younger brother who cried at my bedside recently. It's very unusual for him to express his feelings. You saw him like that for the first time. This is one of the messages of my disease. He says that it is a bit difficult to explain.*
>
> *He is telling me that there is always an energy residing in the disease that can transform the people close to the sick person. I could see that for my brother's soul when he cried at my father's bedside. My father now says we should understand*

*that we all dismantle while passing, and the freed energy has a
special function for those left behind.*

The practitioner suggests that she inquire whether her father's energy is
already in the spirit world.

*He says that sometimes he is in the light; however, he can't yet
leave because something down here has still to be completed.
The conflict between my oldest brother and me is holding him
here.*

The practitioner asks whether her father can assist her in any way to support the healing between her and her brother.

*He is showing me that I can see my brother's emotional inju-
ries, his traumas.*

    *Now, we are building a ball of healing energy; it is not yet
whole. I am putting my arm around my father, and at the
same time embracing my mother. We bring my brother into
the circle and my father strokes his head. Through this gesture,
he tells me that I can forgive my brother. I shouldn't restrict
my perception of him to what I see on the outside but see him
instead from inside and connect with him there. Then the circle can close.*

From the perspective of our immortal soul, forgiveness becomes the
healer, as Frauke was shown. All human anger, resentment, and hurt just
melts away, as we come to know, directly, that there is only pure love when
we meet soul to soul. In the physical world, the old stories of who did what
to whom can come back. Putting this forgiveness into action on earth can be
challenging. The practitioner checks that Frauke has embraced the teaching
of her father's spirit and asks whether she can now hold the experience of
seeing past her brother's hurts and traumas to forgive him.

*Yes, I can, and I do see my brother in a new light. My father
says he hasn't much time available on earth, however, he*

doesn't want to leave before this will take place. He wants to contribute to this peace. Although he is well inside, he wants to go home and return to the "light."

Turning back to the question of the impact of Alzheimer's disease on her father, the practitioner asks whether her father is suffering in any way from developing the disease and from the symptoms.

He tells me that his soul is clear. His physical symptoms are unpleasant but, he says, we perceive them as much worse than he himself does. The aches are inconvenient, yet they are not real pains, because he is still luminous inside. Through his eyes, he can see very clearly. He tells me that our belief that the mind doesn't work any longer is not correct. The light inside understands everything. I see him now with a clear, keen expression. The confusion and craziness we often see in his eyes, and the others with this disease, doesn't give the complete picture. He says his inner self is full of light. It is true light.

One year later, after the passing of her father, Frauke wrote to her practitioner.

I had given my father a promise, whose fulfillment he had desired before he could leave this earth. I made good on this promise, of course not alone, as the souls of my brothers have been partners. The way it happened still moves me to tears. One week after my father's last wish, of having our family reunited, he found peace at home in his bed, holding my mother's hand. The souls know better than the human minds; they know what to do and what is essential. His dearest wish was immensely important to our family. When I stood with my brothers in front of his coffin, I felt the same image as in the session and I knew this meant the fulfillment of my father's longing. It was a true legacy given by him to our family. He clearly knew the meaning it had for us. I feel such deep gratitude for everything he had gifted me in this life, and also on the soul plane. My Life Between Lives journey has helped me more than anything else to understand the meaning of his years-long suffering and pains.

Checking in with Frauke two years later, we see the lasting value of her Life Between Lives experience.

Today, our family relationships are very good, warm-hearted, and familiar, even if our older brother still has difficulty expressing this. We have regular contact with each other. Meanwhile, I have a deep and loving bond with my mom. My Life Between Lives experience has been the key to this change. Without it, I wouldn't have found a way of understanding and processing it. However, this atmosphere of compassion and love needs to be lived every day anew. I must learn this as well. Through my father and his disease, which I call the dementia "gate of light," I got a soul-level, deep understanding of the world.

Whether physically, mentally, or emotionally, an ailing parent, sibling, or loved one often brings the issues of family conflict, resentment, pain, and trauma to the surface. Estranged siblings meeting at the dying one's bedside can squabble about what mom or dad would want, igniting old family dramas. Yet the situation also holds the opportunity for healing. Perhaps the dying one resists passing because of the discordance in the family, or perhaps they chose the suffering itself to bring healing. Frauke's experience in meeting her father at the soul level revealed a deeper purpose and more hopeful understanding about how we choose the manner and timing of leaving this mortal plane. Offering the opportunity for our loved ones to heal though our deaths may just be our final act of service.

Dying with Ease and Grace

Jacquelyn, an intelligent, healthy, and active woman in her early sixties, decides to explore a Life Between Lives experience in preparation for the next phase of her life. She will be retiring from her career as a counseling psychologist and wonders if there is a new purpose for her life energy and time.

During Jacquelyn's first past-life regression, she explores her life as a young, orphaned girl named Teresa, living on the dirty streets of old London, surviving only through the kindness of others and an inner determination. In her teens, she meets a loving man and marries, making a simple life in the small community where they settle. She is respected in her community as a wise woman and offers her council freely and lovingly.

When guided to move to the last day of her life, she finds herself resting in her bedroom. Her practitioner asks her to explain what she is experiencing.

> *I feel chest pain. It's been around for a while and getting worse. It really hurts today, so I have come to lie down. There are others in the home, but I am alone. I feel comfort in hearing voices around.*

Jacquelyn is guided to review some of the key aspects of her life as Teresa.

> *That first part of my life, when I am an orphan living on the streets, wears me out some, but it's been a good life. I'm tired. Tired of living. I do know that I felt love when I was young, before my parents died, and I am able to carry that into the loving relationship with my husband. But I feel some melancholy generally, like "woe is me." It is about the loss of my parents so early. I didn't 't know how I was going to survive; I was only five. Someone looked out for me for a while. I might have had a brother, but we were separated after a while. It is as if that grief never leaves me.*

Teresa acknowledges that her early experience of losing the love of her parents and her ability to carry on, assists her to become a beautiful, wise elder that people seek for counsel. She also finds love with her husband, inner strength, and a good moral compass of knowing what is right and wrong. She fondly remembers people bringing her reciprocal gifts for her compassion and counsel. She lovingly remembers the lunches that she made for her husband and his gratitude for her kindness. She expresses a sense of pride for conducting herself well in life and acknowledges that others saw it too. Teresa, the pain in her chest intensifying, knows that she will soon pass.

I'm lying here wondering whether to call others or not. I am mostly thinking about my nephew, wondering whether he would like to be here as I die, but also considering what I want. I am kind of enjoying the peace.

I decide to call him. I want to tell him one more time that I love him and thank him for caring for me. I have talked about my life somewhat to him, but I will share a bit more. I mostly want to tell him I am glad to go now.

I sense that I am detaching. It's kind of weird now, because I have a sense that nothing has changed in who I am, but I am no longer aware of being in that life. It is now just fuzzy. I am not aware of my body. I just rise, of course. I can feel myself drifting up, like a beautiful relaxation after a physical exercise.

With opportunity to reflect on her life as Teresa, and a passing that could be described as present, calm, and peaceful, Jacquelyn is not prepared for what her council will show her next. Jacquelyn has identified a reoccurring problem with vertigo, or dizziness, due to an inner ear issue. It is getting worse as she ages, having the potential to limit her very active lifestyle. After asking the council her most pressing questions about her upcoming retirement, she asks if they can assist her to heal the vertigo. The council takes her to another past life.

There is a sense of being on a boat and being in trouble. It's wild and stormy and the boat is sinking. Um, I thought water was my friend but WOW, it is such a big force. I am so anxious and fearful. I know I am going to die. I feel sick, nauseous.

We are on a smallish boat, like a fishing boat. There's a couple of other people and we are all in this together. We have worked together to try to ride this out, but the boat is breaking up. Things are crashing everywhere. Oh, I am in the water now, terrified.

Slipping beneath the waves, Jacquelyn leaves her nauseous body, fearful and anxious and feeling an overwhelming sadness. What a powerful death imprint. She did not have the ease and confidence she experienced as Teresa.

Her last thoughts were about her family and the distress they would suffer, never knowing what happened to her after she left for that fateful fishing trip.

Jacquelyn's practitioner intervenes and asks her to go back to that moment in time when she was standing on the sinking ship. While there, she is guided to remember the truths she knows from dying in other lives. She remembers she is an immortal being, that dying is the process of awakening to her immortal self and returning home means returning to all those she loves.

> *I am calmer this time, but there is some nausea. There is chaos everywhere, the ship is rolling, and the waves are crashing. We all know there is a risk of being in the ocean. We have done what we can and now we just see if we will survive it or not.*
>
> *I am back in the water now and I am sensing the sadness and loss of dying young. I know I will be able to reach out to my family once I am home. It is quiet as I slip under the water. I am not feeling the nausea, but my head is feeling quite "dizzy" as I feel myself floating up. It's like my head is releasing the residual energy of the trauma I experienced.*

Several months after her session, Jacquelyn writes about her experience of dying.

> *The biggest surprise of my first past-life regression as Teresa was the experience of my death. It felt like a non-event! I, my consciousness, did not alter as I became detached from my body. Leading up to this peaceful death, I did experience some fear—of the unknown. Lying on the bed with pain in my chest, I came to know somehow that it would be okay to die and that I could drift off when I chose.*
>
> *I felt sorrow at saying goodbye to my family, but then knew that I would be able to still love and touch them energetically, more than they would be able to interact with me. In my life now, I am heartened to realize that my father and others really do love and support me from their world in spirit, more easily than I can be conscious of connecting with them.*

Jacquelyn was able not only to gain confidence in her ability to come to her natural death in this life with ease and grace, she was able to understand where that momentary hesitation when fear arose was imprinted. Not only was she able to "redo" dying calmly under the traumatic circumstances of drowning at sea, but she was able to clear the fear imprint and cure her propensity for sea sickness. She confirmed this later in an email after taking a summer boat trip. She was also left with a deep respect and honor for the forces of nature.

So often, the power of a Life Between Lives session unfolds over time as we take the experience into our daily lives. This is the case for Jacquelyn regarding the stress she is feeling to know what she should be doing once she retires. In her follow-up email, she shares this beautiful insight.

> *The other aspect of my session that particularly stood out for me is how perfectly it spoke to my current life situation. I'm on the brink of retiring. I feel vulnerable, as I wonder who I am without my professional identity as a counselor. In my life as Teresa, I was a farmer's wife whose days were spent doing mundane tasks. Reflecting on that life I feel comfort in the mundane. It was and is enough to be an ordinary person.*

Welcome Home

Regardless of how we leave the body, one thing that is universal is the love and support available to us as we enter our immortal home. Through many thousands of Life Between Lives sessions conducted all around the world with individuals from every culture, with belief and even lack of belief of an afterlife, we know that our soul is welcomed home. We are welcomed, regardless of whether we have led a life of virtue or not, whether we are young or old, ready or resistant. This is demonstrated in the case of Stan, who receives just what he needs at the end of his life.

Stan experiences a past life as an indigenous elder who is injured and lying on his deathbed after defending his village. He is in a longhouse with his daughter, Tisha, expressing his sadness at letting down his tribe. He failed to provide wise advice, advice that would have avoided the loss of so many of the tribe in the battle. He grieves leaving his daughter and the tribe. Stan describes the gentle welcome he receives from those on the other side.

> *I'm sensing Tisha is holding me in great comfort. We have such faith in each other. It is beyond words now. I am feeling a kind of sadness for all that has happened. I remind her that I will always look out for her and that, if ever she calls upon me, I will send my love and guidance. I feel confident about that. I am now feeling a bit more at ease.*
>
> *It's good to know that I can leave. My body could live on a bit more, but I don't have to. It is nice to go when ready. And it's happening, I am drifting off. Now I don't see her in front of me in that way. There is a lightening of my body and the intensity of sadness is gone.*
>
> *I am feeling so much love. There are open arms all around me. I am getting closer. I am taking my time to be embraced. It is all so overwhelming. They all know what I have been through [crying]. And the love that I feel is that love of absolute acceptance, but also appreciation. They know that life is hard, that it has its challenges. It is kind of like they are saying "well done, and now we are all here to welcome you back." Well done, as if they would all write me a good reference [laughs]. Those open arms are so touching.*
>
> *I no longer feel the tiredness. My energy is restored to what feels like a natural flow. I'm just basking in the feeling now. There is a sense that they are all there for as long as is needed. There is no urgency. It is like being totally supported to go at my own rhythm.*

Stan is moved by the welcome he receives in his past life. Like those who die and return after a near-death experience, Stan knows how gentle death can be even when we carry guilt and sadness at the end.

Preparing for our death is wise, as is emotionally accepting our decline into old age. The cases in this chapter offer great wisdom for facing our decline and death with grace and ease. Gayle showed us how to let go of our independence, which is a task assigned to anyone who lives a long life and who seeks to be content.

Diseases of the elderly such as dementia and Alzheimer's appear to be greatly debilitating to sufferers. Relatives feel sad and disturbed watching their loved one's decline. Frauke's Life Between Lives session is most reassuring for anyone whose loved ones are suffering from these conditions. Her father's message tells us there is no need to grieve.

We have no need to fear death either. Jacquelyn, in her life as Teresa, was afraid of death right at the end of her life. In her other past life, she was not ready to die. Fear of death is common in our world. Even those with a strong belief in an afterlife, like Teresa, can remain under the influence of this fear energy. Jacquelyn's two past lives taught us how to let go of our fears, accept our death, and pass over peacefully.

Some people struggle with death because they regret decisions they made in their lives. Stan's case shows us how to let go. There is no judgment on the other side, just welcoming arms.

Coming to terms with death while we are still alive is a sagacious choice. We prepare for other events. Why not this one which is waiting for all of us? The cases in this chapter show us that there is nothing to fear. Being prepared helps us pass over peacefully, gently, and gracefully.

CONCLUSION

Earth has many pleasures and is a beautiful place to be, but that is not why we, as souls, choose to incarnate here. We come here to learn and to experience. It is a school where we can grow and develop under the protection and tutelage of wise, benevolent beings. With the assistance of these wise beings and our soul companions, we make careful plans for each life that we live on earth. There is a whole system of support and guidance in place to enable us to do this. An explicit set of principles governs activities within the earth sphere.

When we incarnate on earth, an amnesia settles upon us that allows us to believe that we are the character we have chosen to be in any one lifetime and that our current experience is all that there is. We become immersed in the drama that unfolds before us, a drama that was chosen by us so that we could have certain experiences and learn specific lessons. There are also special challenges built into an earth incarnation that aid in our development.

Earth school requires us to adjust to being in a human body and negotiate with an ego we believe to be our real self. We are challenged to care and provide support for ourselves, to connect and cooperate with others, and to live our lives meaningfully. We are given free will and the ability to create our own experiences. There is tremendous potential for love, joy, peace, fulfillment, creativity, and achievement.

However, all of this plays out in a setting where we are vulnerable to illness, injury, natural disasters, isolation, conflict, and violence. We experience fear, anger, and other strong emotions. Challenging situations occur, and we observe good and evil in action. It is under these conditions that we have the potential to make rapid spiritual advancement. By facing the difficult, painful situations in our lives, we can find the gift of wisdom contained within them.

Life Between Lives sessions offer a way to connect with our real self while immersed in the human experience. The cases have demonstrated how to receive guidance from our higher self, guides, and wise beings, and how to gain a unique perspective on our lives. While the cases are personal, the life situations are not. We have explored problems that many of us have faced or that we may face in the future.

The guidance has passed through many hands to reach you, conveyed by souls and spirits, received by generous clients who pass it on, and contributed by Michael Newton Institute practitioners. All have one aim: to help you with challenges that confront you as an incarnated soul on this demanding planet.

We hope you have been touched by some of the cases in this book, that you have received knowledge and wisdom that will lighten your load and encourage you to connect to your own inner wisdom. We wish for you a joyful, fulfilling existence as you continue to live your life on earth and, in due time, return to your spiritual home.

CASE CONTRIBUTIONS FROM NEWTON INSTITUTE MEMBERS

Listed below are the chapters to which each Newton Institute member has contributed cases.

Aurand, Paul: Chapters 1, 3, and 10

Barklie, Gayle: Chapter 5

Blankinship, Bryn: Chapter 8

Borenstein, Rita: Chapters 4 and 10

Christopher, Eric: Chapters 2 and 7

Clark, Ann: Chapters 1, 2, 4, 5, 8, 9, and 10

De Tamble, Scott: Chapter 10

Dhanowa, Morgan: Chapter 4

Fares O'Malley, Patricia: Chapter 6

Fuckert, Dorothea: Chapters 3, 5, and 11

Halls, Laura: Chapter 2

Hargreaves, Marilyn: Chapter 11

Hunter, Billy: Chapter 8

Joy, Karen: Chapters 4, 5, 6, 7, and 8

Kedem-Ferguson, Hila: Chapter 6

Kramer, Sophia: Chapters 2 and 9

Lysdal, Lisbeth: Chapters 1, 7, and 8

McLeod, Sylvia: Chapter 3

Noon, Angela: Chapter 5

Roepcke, Elisabeth Iwona: Chapter 10

Roser, Tianna: Chapter 1

Selinske, Joanne: Chapters 2 and 9

Starkey, Courtney: Chapter 2

Waldron, Virginia: Chapter 10

Wiley, Savarna: Chapters 3, 7, and 8

BIBLIOGRAPHY

The Newton Institute: Ann Clark, Karen Joy, Marilyn Hargreaves, and Joanne Selinske. *Llewellyn's Little Book of Life Between Lives*. Woodbury, MN: Llewellyn Publications, 2018.

Newton, Michael. *Destiny of Souls: New Case Studies of Life Between Lives*. St. Paul, MN: Llewellyn Publications, 2002.

———. *Journey of Souls: Case Studies of Life Between Lives*. 5th ed. St. Paul, MN: Llewellyn Publications, 1996.

———, ed. *Memories of The Afterlife: Life Between Lives Stories of Personal Transformation*. Woodbury, MN: Llewellyn Publications, 2009.

Parnia, Sam, ed. "AWARE—AWAreness during REsuscitation—A prospective study." *Journal of Resuscitation* 85 (2014): 1799–1805.

RESOURCES

Newton Institute Online Journal: *Stories of the Afterlife*
www.newtoninstitute.org/stories-afterlife/

Locate a practitioner: www.newtoninstitute.org/locate-a
-therapist/

Become a practitioner: www.newtoninstitute.org/become
-an-lbl-therapist/tni-training

INDEX

A

Abuse, 22–24, 26–28, 51, 61, 63, 92, 93, 117–119, 129, 141–145, 179, 183, 196–198

Abandonment, 17, 18, 53, 70, 186, 187

Acceptance, 22, 50, 54–56, 58, 59, 61, 63, 64, 67, 71, 123, 125, 127, 130, 151, 185, 186, 191, 217, 222, 225, 235

Addiction, 8, 39, 183–185, 187, 188

Advanced beings, 213

Aggressive, 105, 111, 133, 135, 139, 168, 189, 202

Alcohol, 100, 127, 139, 183–185

Alzheimer's disease, 227, 229

Amnesia, 2, 237

Angels, 2

Anger, 31, 49, 50, 54, 63, 64, 87, 88, 123, 124, 127, 138, 186, 193, 196, 228, 238

Anxiety, 7, 33–35, 37, 47, 49–51, 92, 93, 96, 185, 191, 194, 198, 213, 232

Argument, 39, 43, 73, 85, 88, 112, 117, 119, 121, 124, 127

Atlantis, 115, 116

Attachment, 74, 77, 80, 147, 169, 222

Attention deficit disorder, 47

Authentic, 81, 93

Awakening, 82, 144, 200, 201, 218, 233

B

Baby, 30, 31, 39, 47, 120, 123, 124, 146, 156, 158, 189, 191, 215

Battle, 45, 49, 85, 113, 115, 116, 190, 235

Balance—emotional, 69

Belief, 40, 44, 70, 129, 132, 180, 181, 222, 229, 234, 236

Betrayal, 111, 141, 186, 187

Blame, 107, 116, 121, 141

Brain injury, 19

Brain wave pattern, 4

Bully, 123, 160, 162

Business, 24, 81–84, 125, 163, 175

C

Cancer, 12, 13, 15, 17, 18, 55, 56

Career, 8, 10, 16, 35, 108, 132, 155–157, 160, 163, 170, 171, 178, 180, 181, 198, 204, 211, 230

Chakras, 214

Change, 9, 13, 34, 42, 45, 64, 88, 94, 95, 104, 115, 118, 123, 127, 130, 132, 137, 158, 163, 164, 178, 180, 182, 183, 205, 230

Childbirth, 156–158, 177

Children, 12, 15, 27, 28, 44–46, 55–58, 61, 62, 74, 76, 81, 99, 101, 105, 112, 113, 116–120, 139, 140, 142, 147, 149, 150, 152, 156, 157, 164, 167, 173, 175, 188, 198, 212, 223, 224, 226

Concentration camp, 48, 149, 152

Conflict, 1, 7, 35, 74, 81, 83, 84, 102, 111, 112, 116, 117, 119, 121, 198, 226–228, 230, 238

Compassion, 1, 11, 49, 57, 61, 64, 65, 88, 93, 94, 123, 126, 129, 139, 141, 144, 151, 153, 167, 186, 203, 227, 230, 231

Concentration camp, 48, 149, 152

Contentment, 75, 76, 178, 212

Council, 5, 20, 22, 38, 42, 87, 88, 109, 138, 142–144, 165, 166, 169, 170, 180, 181, 184, 204, 224, 226, 231, 232

Crystal, 114, 115, 210

D

Daughter-in-law, 112, 113, 116, 117

Death, 1–5, 7–10, 13, 15, 18, 19, 24, 25, 28, 34, 39, 40, 46, 48–50, 53–56, 58–61, 63–66, 68–70, 74, 76–79, 85–88, 95, 96, 98, 99, 102, 106, 125, 126, 133–136, 139, 140, 150, 151, 156, 157, 159, 160, 168, 171–173, 183, 186, 189, 193, 194, 197, 199–201, 203–205, 208, 211, 218, 221–224, 231–236

Dementia, 230, 236

Detachment, 47, 55, 57, 74, 107, 109, 233

Disability, 9, 19, 22, 165, 167

Disappointment, 74, 110

Disengaged, 112

Disharmony, 1, 112, 117

Drowning, 100, 234

Divorce, 53, 185, 187, 196

Duty, 108, 125, 132

E

Earth, 1–4, 6, 7, 25, 31, 33, 34, 43, 45, 47–52, 62, 65, 69, 80, 82, 84, 95, 102, 111, 114, 115, 127, 162, 165, 167, 174, 177, 180, 185, 194, 198–201, 207, 210, 213, 221, 228, 229, 237, 238

Energy, 1, 2, 5, 14, 23, 25–27, 30, 40, 45, 50, 52, 81–84, 88, 95, 107, 109, 114, 115, 120, 121, 126, 135, 152, 153, 155, 160–162, 164, 166, 167, 176, 177, 202, 209, 210, 214, 215, 223, 227, 228, 230, 233, 235, 236

Energetic restructuring, 213

Enlighten, 1

Excitement, 40, 77, 177, 191

F

Family, 3, 7, 8, 11–15, 18–20, 22, 24, 35, 39, 42, 45, 49, 57, 59, 64, 66, 68, 69, 81, 92, 94, 96, 97, 100, 105–107, 109, 111–113, 116–119, 123, 124, 127, 130, 149, 155–157, 160, 161, 167, 175, 177, 178, 183, 188, 190, 191, 195, 196, 198, 203, 222–227, 229, 230, 233

Fear (of death), 5, 18, 236

Forgiveness, 1, 7, 78, 117, 129, 141, 144, 145, 153, 197, 204, 228

Fracture, 116, 209

Free will, 1, 2, 34, 63, 82, 84, 158, 159, 177, 217, 238

Fulfillment, 7, 109, 229, 238

G

God, 54, 85, 94, 106, 150, 152, 172, 173, 225, 226

Goose bumps, 136

Grief, 49, 53–55, 59, 61, 70, 71, 78, 86, 107, 110, 111, 140, 141, 231

Guide, 2–5, 7, 8, 13–18, 20, 21, 23–26, 28, 30, 31, 35–37, 39, 40, 43–45, 51, 58, 59, 61, 62, 64–66, 68, 69, 75, 76, 80–84, 86, 87, 89, 92–96, 100, 102–105, 107, 118–120, 125–127, 129, 130, 132, 134–139, 144, 147–149, 157–159, 161–164, 168–172, 174–176, 178, 181–184, 190, 191, 201, 203, 209–212, 216, 219, 225, 227, 235, 237, 238

Guilt, 2, 30, 31, 39, 41, 43, 49, 50, 61, 63, 78, 80, 85–88, 94, 96–99, 116, 117, 119, 123, 128, 129, 134, 159, 163, 188, 190, 193, 235

H

Habits, 8, 84, 89, 99, 179, 180, 183, 185, 187, 191

Happiness, 7, 33, 37, 52, 54, 64, 70, 74, 76, 77, 104, 108, 110, 130, 158, 187

Healing, 5–8, 10, 15, 17, 18, 20, 25–27, 30, 31, 44, 45, 49, 53, 60, 61, 65, 66, 82, 115, 123, 139, 141, 145, 162, 179, 192, 194–197, 204, 209, 210, 213–219, 226, 228, 230

Health, 7, 9–11, 14, 18, 19, 22–26, 31, 51, 68, 129, 162, 165, 179, 180, 183, 198, 213, 215, 221

Heart, 9, 21, 24, 30, 58, 64–66, 71, 73, 75, 79, 84, 107–109, 119, 124, 133, 134, 136–139, 145, 148, 153, 158, 162, 166, 174, 187, 191, 194, 201, 205, 225

Helpless, 124, 130, 211, 227

Holocaust, 48

Homosexual/Gay, 96

Honesty, 89, 95, 117, 148

Hostility, 112, 148

Hurt, 5, 17, 26, 28, 78, 81, 91, 92, 100, 105, 107, 109, 113, 117, 125, 140, 143, 205, 228

I

Imprint, 135–137, 232, 234

Inadequacy, 94, 10

Incarnation, 1–3, 5, 7, 8, 25, 33, 34, 47, 51, 52, 62, 81–83, 88, 92, 100, 102, 121, 152, 156, 166, 168, 169, 177, 194, 221, 237, 238

Infatuation, 74

Intention, 44, 79, 115, 191, 215

Intimacy, 89, 101, 110

Intuition, 35, 58, 60, 93, 109, 116, 118, 122, 123, 138, 139

J

Joy, 4, 7, 22, 25–27, 33, 36–38, 48, 52, 58, 64, 66, 69–71, 73, 75, 78, 86, 94, 111, 191–193, 195, 204, 215, 217, 238, 240

Judgment, 11, 24, 30, 42, 74, 89, 97, 105, 107, 112, 119, 126, 127, 129, 153, 183, 186, 197, 236

K

Karma, 2, 125, 126, 197

L

Life challenges, 7, 34, 39, 98

Lonely, 16, 27, 67, 74, 75, 97, 98, 108, 110, 173

Loss, 7, 28, 42, 53–55, 59–61, 64–68, 70, 71, 86, 88, 91, 93, 98, 100, 110, 115, 137, 140, 156, 163, 175, 187, 211, 225, 231, 233, 234

Love, 1, 2, 4, 7, 18, 20, 21, 23, 26–29, 31, 33, 36, 42, 43, 48–52, 54, 61, 63–65, 67–71, 73–80, 84, 91, 93–96, 98–100, 102–108, 111, 112, 115, 117, 118, 121–123, 125–127, 129–135, 138–141, 145, 147–149, 152, 153, 158, 164, 172–174, 184–186, 188, 190, 191, 194–196, 198, 201, 204, 205, 207, 210, 215–217, 219, 222, 226–228, 230–235, 238

M

Marriage, 15, 17, 22, 23, 27, 36, 47, 65, 67, 74, 77, 80, 81, 84, 88, 107, 118, 142, 184, 188, 190, 195

Masters, 115, 116

Mindful, 52, 80

Meditation, 93, 107, 138, 209, 215

Money, 7, 8, 23, 59, 138, 142, 155, 159, 162, 163, 177, 178, 199

Mother, 4, 12–15, 19, 22, 28–31, 39, 40, 46, 47, 49, 51, 61, 63–66, 79, 92, 99, 100, 105, 106, 112, 117–121, 123–125, 133, 134, 139–141, 146, 147, 158, 164, 165, 167, 172, 188, 195–197, 201, 203, 204, 213, 223, 226–229

Motivation, 35, 36, 40, 91, 99, 110, 130, 141, 182

Mirror, 94, 112, 117, 129, 217

N

Near-death experience, 8, 193–195, 202, 204, 206–208, 213, 215, 218, 235

O

Obsessive, 107

Out-of-body experience, 193, 208, 209, 215, 218

P

Pain, 1, 2, 22, 24, 27–29, 31, 33, 37, 49, 51, 53, 55, 58, 59, 61, 70, 71, 91, 92, 100, 114, 124, 125, 128, 141, 143, 145, 149, 150, 156–158, 173, 175–177, 187, 211, 222, 230, 231, 233

Parents, 5, 16, 28, 31, 61, 75, 85, 105, 106, 112, 117–121, 123–125, 130, 147, 149, 175, 201–204, 212, 222, 223, 231

Partner, 43, 73, 77, 89, 91–93, 95, 104, 105, 107, 119, 177, 178, 198, 199, 226

Past-life regression, 3, 55, 231, 233

Patience, 30, 68, 93, 122, 157, 158, 181, 189, 199

Passion, 74, 77, 155, 159, 177

Perfectionism, 94

Perpetrator, 141, 145

Pregnant, 101, 124, 159, 202

Protection, 17, 22, 107, 133, 134, 136, 142, 165, 187, 202, 237

R

Rape, 195

Regret, 78, 108, 236

reincarnation, 1

Rejection, 96, 99, 104, 105, 110, 137

Religion, 132, 145, 173, 174

Resentment, 117, 127, 132, 193, 196, 228, 230

Responsibility, 7, 13, 41, 46, 62, 83, 97, 115, 165, 167, 189, 191, 201

Restructuring, 213, 214

Ritual, 77

S

Sabotage—relationships, 96, 99, 104, 110

Sabotage—self, 91, 93

Sacrifice, 69, 113, 130, 137, 139, 142, 152

Sadness, 33, 47, 54, 56, 94, 127, 139, 141, 190, 191, 232–235

Self-care, 14, 15, 27, 175, 182, 190

Self-doubt, 67, 126, 180, 184

Self-healing, 215, 219

Self-pity, 117

Self-worth, 92, 93, 96, 161

Separation, 41, 53, 70, 93, 217

Service, 81, 84, 181–183, 226, 230

Sexual, 34, 36, 83, 101, 104, 179

Silver cord, 208

Soul—agreement, 82–84, 187

Soul—contracts, 3, 24, 74, 80

Soul energy, 1, 2, 5, 25, 120

Soul—group, 4, 5, 36, 40, 41, 49, 82, 95, 121, 196, 218

Soul—growth, 50, 156

Soul—lesson(s), 134

Soul Memories, 4

Soul—path, 197

Soul—plan, 42, 68, 69, 71, 182

Soul—purpose, 81, 123, 198

Source energy, 152

Spirit world (realm), 1–5, 7, 9, 20, 24, 41, 43, 121, 155, 171, 175, 190, 203, 227, 228

Spiritual growth, 3, 6, 25, 44, 52, 64, 155, 156, 174, 192, 218

Submissive, 112, 133, 201

Suicide, 59–62, 68, 127, 129

Superconscious mind, 4

Surrender, 56, 127, 128, 130, 173

T

Tribe, 77, 101, 102, 104, 124, 127, 130, 161, 234, 235

Trust, 21, 36, 38, 43, 44, 73, 75, 87, 88, 92–95, 104, 106, 109, 116, 137, 144, 146–148, 153, 163, 164, 185, 217, 218, 224

U

Universal plan, 153

V

Victim(s), 117, 129, 177

Violence, 128, 201, 238

Vow, 88

W

War, 27, 49, 85, 108, 111, 133, 149, 152, 168, 186, 204, 205

Widowhood, 74

Will, 1–5, 7, 8, 11, 13, 15, 17–19, 21, 24–27, 29, 34, 36–40, 42, 44, 45, 50, 53–57, 60, 62, 63, 65, 68–70, 73–75, 78, 80, 82–84, 87–89, 93–95, 100, 101, 104, 109, 111, 112, 117–121, 126, 129, 130, 132, 133, 135, 138, 139, 141, 145, 148–151, 156–160, 164, 165, 167–170, 173, 174, 177, 180, 181, 183, 184, 186, 187, 189, 191, 199, 206, 212, 214, 217, 221, 222, 224–226, 229–233, 235, 238, 242

Wisdom, 3, 7, 8, 18, 50, 54, 67, 68, 71, 94, 96, 103, 111, 126, 132, 139, 149, 160, 172–174, 192, 194, 199, 204, 218, 219, 222, 235, 238

Wise elders, 2, 5

Worried, 10, 21, 39, 78, 130, 146, 160, 162

To Write to the Author

If you wish to contact the author or would like more information about this book, please write to the author in care of Llewellyn Worldwide Ltd. and we will forward your request. Both the author and the publisher appreciate hearing from you and learning of your enjoyment of this book and how it has helped you. Llewellyn Worldwide Ltd. cannot guarantee that every letter written to the author can be answered, but all will be forwarded. Please write to:

The Newton Institute
℅ Llewellyn Worldwide
2143 Wooddale Drive
Woodbury, MN 55125-2989

Please enclose a self-addressed stamped envelope for reply,
or $1.00 to cover costs. If outside the U.S.A., enclose
an international postal reply coupon.

Many of Llewellyn's authors have websites with additional information and resources. For more information, please visit our website at http://www.llewellyn.com.

GET MORE AT LLEWELLYN.COM

Visit us online to browse hundreds of our books and decks, plus sign up to receive our e-newsletters and exclusive online offers.

- Free tarot readings • Spell-a-Day • Moon phases
- Recipes, spells, and tips • Blogs • Encyclopedia
- Author interviews, articles, and upcoming events

GET SOCIAL WITH LLEWELLYN

Find us on f   🐦 @LlewellynBooks

www.Facebook.com/LlewellynBooks

GET BOOKS AT LLEWELLYN

LLEWELLYN ORDERING INFORMATION

 Order online: Visit our website at www.llewellyn.com to select your books and place an order on our secure server.

 Order by phone:
- Call toll free within the US at 1-877-NEW-WRLD (1-877-639-9753)
- We accept VISA, MasterCard, American Express, and Discover.

Order by mail:
Send the full price of your order (MN residents add 6.875% sales tax) in US funds plus postage and handling to: Llewellyn Worldwide, 2143 Wooddale Drive, Woodbury, MN 55125-2989

POSTAGE AND HANDLING

STANDARD (US):(Please allow 12 business days)
$30.00 and under, add $6.00.
$30.01 and over, FREE SHIPPING.

CANADA:
We cannot ship to Canada. Please shop your local bookstore or Amazon Canada.

INTERNATIONAL:
Customers pay the actual shipping cost to the final destination, which includes tracking information.

Visit us online for more shipping options. Prices subject to change.

FREE CATALOG!

To order, call
1-877-
NEW-WRLD
ext. 8236
or visit our
website